SIDE *by* SIDE

TEACHER'S GUIDE

Second Edition

1

Steven J. Molinsky
Bill Bliss

Contributing Authors

Mary Ann Perry / John Kopec / Christine Harvey / with Elizabeth Handley

PRENTICE HALL REGENTS Englewood Cliffs, New Jersey 07632

Editorial/production supervision: Janet Johnston
Art supervision: Karen Salzbach
Manufacturing buyers: Laura Crossland, Peter Havens
Cover illustration: Richard E. Hill
Cover design: Kenny Beck

© 1989 by Prentice-Hall, Inc.
A Division of Simon & Schuster
Englewood Cliffs, New Jersey 07632

Printed in the United States of America

10 9 8 7 6 5 4 3 2 1

ISBN 0-13-811167-7

Prentice-Hall International (UK) Limited, *London*
Prentice-Hall of Australia Pty. Limited, *Sydney*
Prentice-Hall Canada Inc., *Toronto*
Prentice-Hall Hispanoamericana, S.A., *Mexico*
Prentice-Hall of India Private Limited, *New Delhi*
Prentice-Hall of Japan, Inc., *Tokyo*
Simon & Schuster Asia Pte. Ltd., *Singapore*
Editora Prentice-Hall do Brasil, Ltda., *Rio de Janeiro*

CONTENTS

Chapter 1	*2*		**Chapter 10**	*130*
Chapter 2	*10*		**Chapter 11**	*150*
Chapter 3	*26*		**Chapter 12**	*166*
Chapter 4	*38*		**Chapter 13**	*180*
Chapter 5	*50*		**Chapter 14**	*200*
Chapter 6	*66*		**Chapter 15**	*224*
Chapter 7	*76*		**Chapter 16**	*242*
Chapter 8	*98*		**Chapter 17**	*258*
Chapter 9	*116*			

Appendix
Book 1 Final Text	*275*
Book 1 Alternative Final Test	*277*
Side by Side Picture Cards	*278*

Side by Side is an English language program for young-adult and adult learners from beginning to high-intermediate levels. The program consists of Student Books 1, 2, 3, 4 and accompanying Activity Workbooks, Teacher's Guides, an Audio Program, a Picture Program, and a Testing Program.

Side by Side offers students a dynamic, communicative approach to the language. Through the methodology of Guided Conversations, *Side by Side* engages students in meaningful conversational exchanges within carefully structured grammatical frameworks, and then encourages students to break away from the textbook and *use* these frameworks to create conversations *on their own*. All the language practice that is generated through the texts results in active communication taking place between students…practicing speaking together, "side by side."

The texts provide all-skills language practice through reading, writing, and listening activities that are totally integrated with the conversational exercises. Short reading selections offer enjoyable reading practice that simultaneously reinforces the grammatical focus of each chapter. *Check-Up* activities provide focused practice in reading comprehension and vocabulary development. *Listening* exercises enable students to develop their aural comprehension skills through a variety of listening activities. And *In Your Own Words* activities provide topics and themes for student compositions and classroom discussions in which students write about their friends, families, homes, schools, and themselves.

The goal of *Side by Side* is to engage students in active, meaningful communicative practice with the language. The aim of the *Side by Side Teacher's Guides* is to offer guidelines and strategies to help achieve that goal.

STUDENT TEXT OVERVIEW

Chapter Opening Pages

The opening page of each chapter provides an overview of the new grammatical structures treated in the chapter.

Conversation Lessons

1. GRAMMATICAL PARADIGMS

A new grammatical structure appears first in the form of a grammatical paradigm, or "grammar box"—a simple schema of the structure. (Grammar boxes are in a light blue tint.) These paradigms are meant to be a reference point for students as they proceed through a lesson's conversational activities. While these paradigms highlight the structures being taught, they are not intended to be goals in themselves. Students are not expected to memorize or parrot back these rules. Rather, we want students to take part in conversations that show they can *use* these rules correctly.

2. MODEL GUIDED CONVERSATIONS

Model Guided Conversations serve as the vehicles for introducing new grammatical structures, as well as many communicative uses of English. Since the model becomes the basis for all of the exercises that follow, it is essential that students be given sufficient practice with it before proceeding with the lesson.

3. SIDE BY SIDE EXERCISES

In the numbered exercises that follow the model, students pair up and work "side by side," placing new content into the given conversational framework. These exercises form the core learning activity of each conversation lesson.

Reading Lessons

1. READING SELECTIONS

Short reading selections offer enjoyable reading practice that simultaneously reinforces the grammatical focus of each chapter. Accompanying illustrations serve as visual cues that guide learners through the reading and help to clarify both context and new vocabulary.

2. CHECK-UP

Check-Up exercises provide focused practice in reading comprehension and vocabulary development. Also, listening exercises enable students to develop their aural comprehension skills through a variety of listening activities.

3. IN YOUR OWN WORDS

These activities provide topics and themes for student compositions and classroom discussions. Students write about their friends, families, homes, schools, jobs, and themselves.

On Your Own and *How About You?* Activities

These student-centered activities give students valuable opportunities to apply lesson content to their own lives and experiences and to share opinions in class. Through these activities, students bring to the classroom new content, based on their interests, their backgrounds, and their imaginations. Activities include role plays, questions about the students' real world, and topics for discussion and debate.

Summary Pages

Summary pages at the end of each chapter highlight functional language and grammatical structures covered in that chapter. They are useful as a review and study guide after students have completed the chapter.

ANCILLARY MATERIALS

Activity Workbooks

The Activity Workbooks offer a variety of exercises for reinforcement, fully coordinated with the student texts. A special feature of the Activity Workbooks is the inclusion of rhythm, stress, pronunciation, and intonation exercises. Periodic check-up tests are also included.

Audio Program

The Student Text tapes are especially designed to serve as a student's speaking partner, making conversation practice possible even when the student is studying alone. In addition to the guided conversation exercises, the tapes contain the listening comprehension exercises along with recordings of all of the reading selections in the text.

The Activity Workbook tapes contain the listening, pronunciation, rhythm, stress, and intonation exercises in the workbooks.

Picture Program

Side by Side Picture Cards illustrate key concepts and vocabulary items. They can be used for introduction of new material, for review, for enrichment, and for role-playing activities. Suggestions for their use are included in the Teacher's Guide. Also, the Appendix to the Teacher's Guide contains a triple listing of the Picture Cards: numerically, alphabetically, and by category.

Testing Program

The *Side by Side* Testing Program offers a placement test as well as mid-term and final examinations for each level of the program.

FORMAT OF THE TEACHER'S GUIDE

Chapter Overview

The Chapter Overview provides the following:

- Functional and grammatical highlights of the chapter
- A listing of new vocabulary and expressions
- Language and culture notes that apply to the chapter as a whole

Step-by-Step Lesson Guide

Included for each conversation lesson are the following:

- FOCUS of the lesson
- GETTING READY: suggestions for introducing the new concepts in the lesson
- INTRODUCING THE MODEL: steps for introducing the model conversation
- SIDE BY SIDE EXERCISES: suggestions for practicing the exercises, as well as a listing of new vocabulary
- LANGUAGE AND CULTURE NOTES
- WORKBOOK: page references for exercises in the Activity Workbook that correspond to the particular lesson
- EXPANSION ACTIVITIES: optional activities for review and reinforcement of the content of the lesson

Included for each reading lesson are the following:

- FOCUS of the lesson
- NEW VOCABULARY contained in the reading
- PREVIEWING THE STORY: an optional preliminary stage before students begin to read the selection
- READING THE STORY: suggestions for presenting the story as well as questions to check students' comprehension
- CHECK-UP: answer keys and listening scripts for check-up exercises
- IN YOUR OWN WORDS: suggestions for doing these writing and discussion exercises

Workbook Answer Key and Listening Scripts

Answers and listening scripts for all exercises contained in the Activity Workbooks are provided at the end of each chapter of the Teacher's Guide.

GENERAL TEACHING STRATEGIES

Introducing the Model

Since the model conversation forms the basis of each lesson, it is essential that students practice the model several times in a variety of ways before going on to the exercises. The following eight steps are recommended for introducing a model conversation. Of course, you should feel free to modify them to suit your own particular teaching style and the needs of your students.

1. Have students look at the model illustration. This helps establish the context of the conversation.
2. *Set the scene.* For every model, one or two lines are suggested in this Teacher's Guide for you to use to "set the scene" of the dialog for your students.
3. *Present the model.* With books closed, have students listen as you present the model or play the tape one or more times. To make the presentation of the model as realistic as possible, you might draw two stick figures on the board to represent the speakers in the dialog. You can also show that two people are speaking by changing your position or by shifting your weight from one foot to the other as you say each speaker's lines.
4. *Full-Class Choral Repetition.* Model each line and have the whole class repeat in unison.

5. Have students open their books and look at the dialog. Ask if there are any questions, and check understanding of new vocabulary. (All new vocabulary in the model is listed here. The illustration and the context of the dialog normally help to clarify the meaning of new words.)

6. *Group Choral Repetition.* Divide the class in half. Model line A and have Group 1 repeat; model line B and have Group 2 repeat. Continue this with all the lines of the model.

7. *Choral Conversation.* Groups 1 and 2 practice the dialog twice, without teacher model. First Group 1 is Speaker A and Group 2 is Speaker B; then reverse.

8. Call on one or two pairs of students to present the dialog.

In steps 6, 7, and 8 you should encourage students to look up from their books and *say* the lines rather than read them. (Students can of course refer to their books when necessary.) *The goal here is not memorization or complete mastery of the model.* Rather, students should become familiar with the model and feel comfortable saying it.

At this point, if you feel that additional practice is necessary before going on to the exercises, you can do Choral Conversation in small groups or by rows.

Side by Side Exercises

The numbered exercises that follow the model form the core learning activity in each conversation lesson. Here students use the pictures and word cues to create conversations based on the structure of the model. Since all language practice in these lessons is conversational, you will always call on a pair of students to do each exercise. *Your* primary role is to serve as a resource to the class: to help with the structures, new vocabulary, intonation, and pronunciation.

The following three steps are recommended in each lesson for practicing the *Side by Side* exercises. (Students should be given thorough practice with the first two exercises before going on.)

1. Exercise 1: Introduce any new vocabulary in the exercise. Call on two students to present the dialog. Then do Choral Repetition and Choral Conversation Practice.

2. Exercise 2: Same as for Exercise 1.

3. For the remaining exercises, there are two options: either Full-Class Practice or Pair Practice.

   Full-Class Practice: Call on a pair of students to do each exercise. Introduce new vocabulary one exercise at a time. (For more practice, call on other pairs of students, or do Choral Repetition or Choral Conversation.)

   Pair Practice: Introduce new vocabulary for all the exercises. Next have students practice all the exercises in pairs. Then have pairs present the exercises to the class. (For more practice, do Choral Repetition or Choral Conversation.)

   The choice of Full-Class Practice or Pair Practice should be determined by the content of the particular lesson, the size and composition of the class, and your own teaching style. You might also wish to vary your approach from lesson to lesson.

Suggestions for Pairing Up Students: Whether you use Full-Class Practice or Pair Practice, you can select students for the pairs in various ways. You might want to pair students by ability, since students of similar ability might work more efficiently together than students of dissimilar ability. On the other hand, you might wish to pair a weaker student with a stronger one. The slower student benefits from this pairing, while the more advanced student strengthens his or her abilities by helping the partner.

You should also encourage students to *look at* each other when speaking. This makes the conversational nature of the language practice more realistic. One way of ensuring this is *not* to call on two students who are sitting next to each other. Rather, call on students in different parts of the room and encourage them to look at each other when saying their lines.

Presenting New Vocabulary

Many new vocabulary words are introduced in each conversation lesson. The illustration normally helps to convey the meaning, and the new words are written for students to see and use in these conversations. In addition, you might:

1. write the new word on the board or on a word card,
2. say the new word several times and ask students to repeat chorally and individually, and

3. help clarify the meaning with *Side by Side* Picture Cards or your own visuals (pictures from magazines, newspapers, or your own drawings).

Students might also find it useful to keep a notebook in which they write each new word, its meaning, and a sentence using that word.

Open-Ended Exercises (the "Blank Box")

In many lessons, the final exercise is an open-ended one. This is indicated in the text by a blank box. Here the students are expected to create conversations based on the structure of the model, but with vocabulary that they select themselves. This provides students with an opportunity for creativity, while still focusing on the particular structure being practiced. These open-ended exercises can be done orally in class and/or assigned as homework for presentation in class the next day. Encourage students to use dictionaries to find new words they want to use.

On Your Own

On Your Own activities offer students the opportunity to contribute content of their own within the grammatical framework of the lesson. You should introduce these activities in class and assign them as homework for presentation in class the next day. In this way, students will automatically review the previous day's grammar while contributing new and inventive content of their own.

These activities are meant for simultaneous grammar reinforcement and vocabulary building. Students should be encouraged to use a dictionary when completing the *On Your Own* activities. In this way, they will not only use the words they know, but the words they would *like* to know in order to really bring their interests, backgrounds, and imaginations into the classroom.

As a result, students will teach each other new vocabulary and also share a bit of their lives with others in the class.

How About You?

How About You? activities are intended to provide students with additional opportunities to tell about themselves. Have students do these activities in pairs or as a class.

Expansion Activities

For each conversation lesson, the Teacher's Guide contains ideas for optional review and reinforcement activities. Feel free to pick and choose or vary the activities to fit the particular needs and learning styles of students in your class. The ideas are meant to serve as a springboard for developing your own learning activities.

General Guiding Principles for Working with Guided Conversations

1. When doing the exercises, students should practice *speaking* to each other, rather than *reading* to each other. Therefore, while students will need to refer to the text to be able to practice the conversations, they should not read the lines word by word. Rather, they should practice scanning a full line and then look up from the book and *speak* the line to another person.

2. Throughout, teachers should use the book to teach proper intonation and gesture. (Capitalized words are used to indicate spoken emphasis.) Students should be encouraged to truly *act out* the dialogs in a strong and confident voice.

3. Use of the texts should be as *student-centered* as possible. Modeling by the teacher should be efficient and economical, but students should have every opportunity to model for each other when they are capable of doing so.

4. Vocabulary can and should be effectively taught in the context of the conversation being practiced. Very often it will be possible to grasp the meaning from the conversation or its accompanying illustration. Teachers should spend time drilling vocabulary in isolation *only* if they feel it is absolutely essential.

5. Students need not formally study or be able to produce grammatical rules. The purpose of the texts is to engage students in active communicative practice that gets them to *use* the language according to these rules.

6. Students should be given every opportunity to apply their own lives and creative contributions to the exercises. This is directly provided for in the blank boxes at the end of many lessons as well as in the *On Your Own* and *How About You?* activities, but teachers can look to *all* exercises with an eye toward expanding them to the real world of the classroom or to the students' real lives.

Introducing Reading Selections

You may wish to preview each story either by briefly setting the scene or by having students talk about the illustrations or predict the content of the story from the title. You may also find it useful to introduce new vocabulary items before they are encountered in the story. On the other hand, you may prefer to skip the previewing step and instead have students experience the subject matter and any unfamiliar words in the context of the initial reading of the story.

There are many ways in which students can read and talk about the stories. Students may read silently to themselves or follow along as the story is read by you, by one or more students, or on the tape. You should then ask students if they have any questions and check understanding of new vocabulary. For each reading selection, the Teacher's Guide provides a list of questions based on the story. You may wish to check students' comprehension by asking these questions before going on to the Check-Up exercises.

Q & A Exercises

Q & A exercises are included as part of the Check-Up after many of the reading selections. These exercises are designed to give students conversation practice based on information contained in the stories. Italic type in the Q & A model highlights the words to be replaced by different information contained in the reading.

Call on a pair of students to present the Q & A model. Have students work in pairs to create new dialogs based on the model, and then call on pairs to present their new dialogs to the class.

In Your Own Words

These activities are designed to guide students in their creation of original stories. Students are asked to write about topics such as their homes, schools, friends, families, and themselves.

You should go over the instructions for the activities and make sure students understand what is expected. Students should do the activity as written homework, using a dictionary for any new words they wish to use. Then have students present and discuss what they have written, in pairs or as a class.

Activity Workbooks

The exercises in the Activity Workbooks are fully coordinated with the student texts. For each conversation lesson in the student text, the Teacher's Guide indicates which particular workbook exercises provide supplementary practice. This cross-referencing information can also be found at the back of the workbooks.

The workbooks provide intensive practice in grammar reinforcement, reading, writing, listening, and pronunciation. A special feature is the inclusion of exercises in rhythm, stress, and intonation of English. In these exercises, black dots are used as a kind of musical notation system to indicate the number of "beats" on each line. The dots also serve to indicate the primary word stresses and graphically show the reduced emphasis on the surrounding, unstressed words. Have students first listen to these exercises on tape, and then practice saying them. For each exercise, establish the rhythm for the students by clapping, tapping, or finger-snapping on each "beat," as indicated by the black dots. Students also enjoy doing this as they perform these exercises.

In conclusion, we have attempted to make the study of English a lively and relevant experience for our students. While we hope that we have conveyed to you the substance of our textbooks, we also hope that we have conveyed the spirit: that learning the language can be interactive...student-centered...and fun.

Steven J. Molinsky
Bill Bliss

1

GRAMMAR

To Be

am	I'm from Mexico City. (I am)
is	What's your name? (What is)
	My name is Maria.
are	Where are you from?

FUNCTIONS

Asking for and Reporting Information

What's your name?
  My name is *Maria*.
What's your address?
  My address is *235 Main Street*.
What's your phone number?
  My phone number is *741–8906*.
Where are you from?
  I'm from *Mexico City*.

I'm *American*.

My license number is *112897*.
My apartment number is *3-B*.
My Social Security number is *044-35-9862*.

NEW VOCABULARY

a
actor
actress
address
American
apartment
apartment number
are
athlete
Brooklyn
country
employment application form
famous
Florida
form
from
I'm

is
license number
Mexico City
Mr.
Mrs.
my
name
New York
number
of
phone number
president
prime minister
Social Security number
street
telephone number
the

what
where
you
your

oh (zero)
one
two
three
four
five
six
seven
eight
nine
ten

Text Page 2: *What's Your Name?*

FOCUS

> To be: Introduction

GETTING READY

1. Teach the first question and answer in the conversation before students open their books. Teach: What's your name? My name is _____.

   a. Begin by saying *your* name: "My name is _____."
   b. Then ask individual students: "What's your name?" Students answer: "My name is _____."
   c. Next, signal individual students to ask each other.

2. Teach the numbers zero to ten.

   a. Write the numbers on the board or large cards. Point to each number and have students repeat after you several times.
   b. After some practice, point to the numbers more rapidly—first in order, then out of order. Have students say the numbers as you point.
   c. Have a student go to the board and point to numbers. Have that student or the whole class say the numbers.

INTRODUCING THE MODEL

1. Have students look at the model illustration.
2. Set the scene: "A teacher and students are talking."
3. With books closed, have students listen as you present the model or play the tape one or more times.
4. **Full-Class Choral Repetition:** Model each question and answer in the dialog and have students repeat.
5. Have students open their books and look at the dialog. Ask students if they have any questions; check understanding of vocabulary.

   Language Note

   The verb *to be* is commonly contracted in speech and informal writing (*what is* → *what's*).

6. **Group Choral Repetition:** Divide the class in half. Model the 1st question of the dialog and have Group 1 repeat; model the answer and have Group 2 repeat. Continue this way with the other questions and answers in the dialog.
7. **Choral Conversation:** Groups 1 and 2 practice the dialog twice, without teacher model. First, Group 1 asks the questions and Group 2 gives the answers; then reverse.
8. Call on one or two pairs of students to present the dialog.

   (For additional practice, do Choral Conversation in small groups or by rows.)

SIDE BY SIDE EXERCISES

In the section **Answer These Questions**, students use the questions of the model to give their own names, addresses, phone numbers, and where they are from.

Call on pairs of students to present the dialog, using information about themselves in the answers. You can also use pair practice: have students practice the dialog in pairs, and then present their dialogs to the class.

Note that the numbers in the students' addresses may be higher than the ones they have learned. For this exercise you can have students read each digit in their address. For example, *232* might be read as *two, three, two*, rather than *two thirty-two*. (Higher numbers will be taught in Chapter 5.)

WORKBOOK

Pages 1–4

Exercise Note

Workbook p. 4:   In Exercise G, students practice greeting others with *Hi!* and *Hello!* In Exercise H, students practice greeting people by saying their names.

Text Page 3

ON YOUR OWN: *Interview*

This is a role play exercise that reviews the questions on text page 2. Students pretend to be famous celebrities who are being interviewed on television. One student is the interviewer and asks the questions. Another pretends to be the famous person. Talk shows are popular in the United States and usually feature a well-known host talking with famous people.

1. Have students think of famous people in the categories suggested at the bottom of text page 3. If they have difficulty, make some suggestions. You can use magazine and newspaper photographs as cues. The students can assume the role of the celebrity in the photograph.

2. Have pairs of students practice and then role play these interviews in front of the class, making up addresses and phone numbers for the famous people.

READING: *What's Your Name?*

FOCUS

To be: Introduction

NEW VOCABULARY

American	Mr.
apartment number	Mrs.
Brooklyn	nationality
Florida	Social Security number
license number	telephone number

PREVIEWING THE STORY (optional)

Have students talk about the story title and/or illustrations. Introduce new vocabulary.

READING THE STORY

1. Have students read silently or follow along silently as the story is read aloud by you, by one or more students, or on the tape.
2. Ask students if they have any questions; check understanding of vocabulary.

   Culture Note

   Social Security number: Anyone who earns money in the United States must report his or her earnings to the federal government. Individuals are given Social Security numbers. Social Security taxes are used to support a national program of life insurance and old-age pensions.

CHECK-UP

Match

1. c
2. e
3. a
4. b
5. d

Listening

Have students complete the exercises as you play the tape or read the following:

Listen and choose the best answer.

1. A. What's your name?
   B. Susan Miller. (b)

2. A. What's your address?
   B. Three ninety-four Main Street. (a)

3. A. What's your apartment number?
   B. Nine D. (a)

4. A. What's your telephone number?
   B. Seven four eight–two two six oh. (b)

5. A. What's your Social Security number?
   B. Oh six oh–eight three–eight two seven five. (b)

IN YOUR OWN WORDS

1. Make sure students understand the instructions.
2. Have students fill out the form for written homework.
3. Have students present and discuss the form, in pairs or as a class.

WORKBOOK ANSWER KEY AND LISTENING SCRIPTS

Page 1   A.   WHAT ARE THEY SAYING?

1.   name is
2.   What's your   My address
                                   is
3.   What's your   My phone
                                   number is
4.   What's your
     is Harry Ross
5.   What's your
     address is
     10 River Street
6.   What's your phone number
     is
7.   you   I'm from

Page 3   C.   WRITE

		7=seven
1=one	4=four	8=eight
2=two	5=five	9=nine
3=three	6=six	10=ten

Page 3   D.   WHAT'S THE NUMBER?

	3. 7
	4. 5
1. 4	5. 9
2. 10	6. 8

Page 3   E.   LISTEN

Listen and write the missing number.

1.   What's your phone number?
     My phone number is 231–4965.

2.   What's your phone number?
     My phone number is 743–5296.

3.   What's your phone number?
     My phone number is 492–7185.

4.   What's your phone number?
     My phone number is 637-8976.

Answers
1. 5	2. 6
3. 8	4. 7

Page 3   F.   LISTEN

Listen and put a circle around the number you hear.

1.   three
2.   eight
3.   four
4.   seven
5.   nine
6.   six

Answers
1. 3	3. 4	5. 9
2. 8	4. 7	6. 6

GRAMMAR

**Subject Pronouns
To Be + Location**

Where	am	I?	(I am)	I'm	
	is	he? she? it?	(He is) (She is) (It is)	He's She's It's	in the kitchen.
	are	we? you? they?	(We are) (You are) (They are)	We're You're They're	

FUNCTIONS

Asking for and Reporting Information

Henry is *Chinese.*
He's from *Shanghai.*

Inquiring about Location

Where are you?

Giving Location

I'm in the *kitchen.*

NEW VOCABULARY

absent
all
am
and
at
Athens
attic
bank
basement
bathroom
bed
bedroom
car
cat
Chinese
class
countries
dentist
different
dining room
dog
English
English class
even
everybody

except
French
friends
garage
Greek
he
home
hospital
I
in
interesting
it
Japanese
kitchen
Leningrad
library
living room
many
me
Mexican
monkey
movie theater
newspaper
office
our

Paris
park (n)
post office
Puerto Rican
restaurant
Russian
San Juan
Shanghai
she
Social Security office
students
supermarket
teacher
the
they
today
Tokyo
very
we
yard
yes
zoo

What a shame!

LANGUAGE NOTE

The contracted forms of the verb *to be* should be used in the chapter whenever possible. For example:

Where's Tom?
He's in the kitchen.

Text Pages 8–9: *At Home/Where Are You?*

FOCUS

The grammar box at the top of the page summarizes all the structures that are taught on text pages 9–12. The following are introduced on text page 9:

> • *Where are you?*   *I'm* ⎫
>   *We're* ⎬ *in the* _____.
> • *Where are they?*   *They're in the* _____.

GETTING READY

Teach the vocabulary on text page 8. Point to each part of the house and say the new word. Have students repeat after you—first chorally, then individually.

Or present this vocabulary using your own visuals or *Side by Side* Picture Cards 1–8. Point to one visual at a time, say the word, and have students repeat.

INTRODUCING THE MODEL

There are 3 model conversations. Introduce and practice each model before going on to the next. For each model:

1. Have students look at the model illustration.
2. Set the scene: "People are talking at home."
3. With books closed, have students listen as you present the model or play the tape one or more times.
4. **Full-Class Repetition:** Model each line and have students repeat.
5. Have students open their books and look at the dialog. Ask students if they have any questions; check understanding of new vocabulary:

    1st model: *where, are, you, I'm, in, the*
    2nd model: *we're*
    3rd model: *Mr., and, Mrs., they're*

    ### Culture Notes

    Yard: Many U.S. families relax, plant gardens, and play sports in this grassy area around the house.

    Forms of address:

    > *Mr.* refers to both married and single men.
    > *Mrs.* refers to married women.
    > *Miss* refers to single women.
    > *Ms.* has been used in recent years to refer to all women, whether they are married or single.

6. **Group Choral Repetition:** Divide the class in half. Model line A and have Group 1 repeat; model line B and have Group 2 repeat.
7. **Choral Conversation:** Groups 1 and 2 practice the dialog twice, without teacher model. First, Group 1 is Speaker A and Group 2 is Speaker B; then reverse.

8. Call on one or two pairs of students to present the dialog.
   (For additional practice, do Choral Conversation in small groups or by rows.)

9. Expand each model with further substitution practice.

   a. After students practice the model (*Where are you? I'm in the kitchen),* cue other substitutions, such as:

Teacher cue:	bedroom	Teacher cue:	living room
Teacher:	Where are you?	Teacher:	Where are you?
Student:	I'm in the bedroom.	Student:	I'm in the living room.

   This practice can be done chorally, or you can call on individual students.

   b. When practicing *we're,* you can make this more realistic by asking about two of your students. For example:

Teacher cue:	dining room
Teacher:	Where are you and (John)?
Student:	We're in the dining room.

   c. When practicing *they're,* use names of students in your class. For example:

Teacher cue:	garage
Teacher:	Where are (John) and (Bill)?
Student:	They're in the garage.

SIDE BY SIDE EXERCISES

Examples

> 1. A. Where are you?
>   B. I'm in the bedroom.
>
> 2. A. Where are you?
>   B. I'm in the dining room.
>
> 3. A. Where are you?
>   B. We're in the kitchen.

1. **Exercise 1:** Call on two students to present the dialog. Then do Choral Repetition and Choral Conversation Practice.

2. **Exercise 2:** Same as above.

3. **Exercises 3–9:**

   Culture Note

   Basement (Exercise 8): Basements are common in buildings located in colder climates. The heating system is often located in the basement.

   Either

   Full-Class Practice: Call on a pair of students to do each exercise. (For more practice, call on other pairs of students, or do Choral Repetition or Choral Conversation.)

   or

   Pair Practice: Have students in pairs practice all of the exercises. Then have pairs present the exercises to the class. (For more practice, do Choral Repetition or Choral Conversation.)

EXPANSION ACTIVITIES

1. *Practice with Visuals*

    Use your own visuals, word cards, or *Side by Side* Picture Cards 1–8 to review the structures on text page 9. Have students pretend to be in various places, and ask and answer questions. For example:

    a. To practice *I'm,* give a visual of the living room to Student A and ask: "Where are you?" Student A answers: "I'm in the living room."
    b. Practice *I'm* this way with other students, using other locations.
    c. Call on pairs of students to practice both the question and answer with *I'm* as you give a visual to one student.
    d. To practice *we're,* give a visual to Student B and ask Student A: "Where are you and Student B?" Student A answers: "We're in the _____."
    e. Practice *we're* with other students, using other locations; then call on pairs of students to practice both the question and the answer.
    f. To practice *they're,* give a visual to Student A and Student B and ask Student C: "Where are Student A and B?" Student C answers: "They're in the _____." Continue this practice with other students and locations.

2. *Pronunciation Practice*

    Practice contractions with the verb *to be*. Have students repeat after you chorally and individually. Say the full form and have students say the contracted form. For example:

    Teacher: I am
    Students: I'm

Text Page 10: *Where's Bob?*

FOCUS

Introduction of *Where's* _____ *?* $\left.\begin{array}{l}\textit{He's}\\\textit{She's}\\\textit{It's}\end{array}\right\}$ *in the* _____ .

GETTING READY

Review the vocabulary on text page 8. Use *Side by Side* Picture Cards 1–8 or the illustration in the text to practice these words. Point to a place and have students say the name. Have students respond chorally, then individually. Practice each word several times.

INTRODUCING THE MODEL

There are 3 model conversations. Introduce and practice each model before going on to the next. For each model:

1. Have students look at the model illustration.
2. Set the scene: "People are talking at home."
3. With books closed, have students listen as you present the model or play the tape one or more times.
4. **Full-Class Repetition:** Model each line and have students repeat.
5. Have students open their books and look at the dialog. Ask students if they have any questions; check understanding of new vocabulary:

1st model:	*where's, he's*
2nd model:	*she's*
3rd model:	*car, it's*

6. **Group Choral Repetition:** Divide the class in half. Model line A and have Group 1 repeat; model line B and have Group 2 repeat.
7. **Choral Conversation:** Groups 1 and 2 practice the dialog twice, without teacher model. First, Group 1 is Speaker A and Group 2 is Speaker B; then reverse.
8. Call on one or two pairs of students to present the dialog.

   (For additional practice, do Choral Conversation in small groups or by rows.)
9. Expand the first two models with further substitution practice.

   a. After students practice the first model (*Where's Bob? He's in the living room*), cue other substitutions using names of male students in the class. For example:

Teacher cue:	kitchen		Teacher cue:	basement
Teacher:	Where's (Tom)?		Teacher:	Where's (John)?
Student:	He's in the kitchen.		Student:	He's in the basement.

   b. Similarly, after presenting the second model, cue other substitutions using names of female students in the class. For example:

Teacher cue:	dining room
Teacher:	Where's (Maria)?
Student:	She's in the dining room.

SIDE BY SIDE EXERCISES

Examples

> 1. A. Where's Tom?
>   B. He's in the bedroom.
> 3. A. Where's Helen?
>   B. She's in the living room.
> 5. A. Where's the newspaper?
>   B. It's in the kitchen.

1. **Exercise 1:** Call on two students to present the dialog. Then do Choral Repetition and Choral Conversation Practice.
2. **Exercise 2:** Same as above.
3. **Exercises 3–9:**

> **New vocabulary:**   5. *newspaper*   6. *cat*   7. *dog*

Culture Note

Dog, cat (Exercises 6 and 9):   Dogs and cats are very popular in the United States. The pet often becomes a beloved family member. We may refer to pets as *he, she,* or *it. He* or *she* is used when we refer to the pet by name. For example, *Where's Rover? **He's** in the living room. It* is used when we ask, *Where's the dog (or cat)? **It's** in the living room.*

Either

Full-Class Practice: Call on a pair of students to do each exercise. Introduce the new vocabulary as you do exercises 5, 6, 7. (For more practice, call on other pairs of students, or do Choral Repetition or Choral Conversation.)

or

Pair Practice: Introduce all the new vocabulary. Next, have students in pairs practice all the exercises. Then have pairs present the exercises to the class. (For more practice, do Choral Repetition or Choral Conversation.)

WORKBOOK

Pages 6–8

Exercise Notes

Workbook p. 7:   Exercise E can be done for homework or in class as a dictation.

Workbook p. 8:   In Exercise G, students practice asking and answering questions about where people are (*Where's?, He's, She's in* _____). In Exercise H, students practice the contrast between *Where's* and *Where are.*

EXPANSION ACTIVITIES

1. Practice with Visuals

You can review the structures on text page 10 by using your own visuals or *Side by Side* Picture Cards

1–8. Use the same method you used on text page 9. Again, use visuals to show the location of students in a house. Ask questions about students in your class. For example:

"Where's Student A?"
"He's/She's in the _____."

Next, have students ask each other questions about the person holding a visual for location. Practice both *he* and *she* this way. For practicing *it*, you can use objects, such as newspapers, along with the visuals.

2. *Tell a Story*

Tell your students the following story. (This story is not found in the book.) You can use visuals if you wish. You can pause as you tell the story to ask the questions below, or you can wait until the end.

"The Wilson family is at home today. Mr. and Mrs. Wilson are in the kitchen. Mary Wilson is in the living room. Fred Wilson is in the bathroom. The cat and the dog are in the garage."

Questions: Where are Mr. and Mrs. Wilson?
Where's Mary Wilson?
Where's Fred Wilson?
Where are the cat and the dog?

3. *Listening Exercise*

Have the students open their books to text page 10. For listening practice, make a statement about a person (animal, or thing) in a certain room, and have students identify who you are talking about. For example:

Teacher: He's in the garage.
Student(s): John.

Teacher: It's in the kitchen.
Student(s): The newspaper.

Teacher: It's in the basement.
Student(s): The dog.

Teacher: She's in the dining room.
Student(s): Jane.

Teacher: He's in the bedroom.
Student(s): Tom.

READING: *The Students in My English Class*

FOCUS

- To be + location
- Subject pronouns

NEW VOCABULARY

Athens	French	Leningrad	San Juan
Chinese	friend	many	Shanghai
class	friends	Mexican	students
countries	Greek	Paris	Tokyo
different	interesting	Puerto Rican	very
English class	Japanese	Russian	yes

PREVIEWING THE STORY

Have students talk about the story title and/or illustration. Introduce new vocabulary.

READING THE STORY

1. Have students read silently, or follow along silently as the story is read aloud by you, by one or more students, or on the tape.
2. Ask students if they have any questions; check understanding of vocabulary.
3. Check students' comprehension, using some or all of the following questions:

   a. What nationality is Henry?
      Where is he from?

   b. What nationality is Natasha?
      Where is she from?

   c. What nationality are Mr. and Mrs. Ramirez?
      Where are they from?

   d. What nationality is George?
      Where is he from?

   e. What nationality is Nicole?
      Where is she from?

   f. What nationality are Mr. and Mrs. Sato?
      Where are they from?

   g. What nationality are Maria and I?
      Where are we from?

CHECK-UP

True or False?

1. False
2. True
3. False
4. True
5. False
6. True

HOW ABOUT YOU?

Have students do this activity in pairs or as a class.

Text Page 12: *Where Are They?*

FOCUS

> - Review of *Where's* _____? *Where are* _____?
> - Introduction of *Where am I?*

SIDE BY SIDE EXERCISES

Examples

> 1. A. Where's Albert?   2. A. Where's Carmen?
>   B. He's in the restaurant.   B. She's in the bank.

1. **Exercise 1:** Introduce the new word *restaurant.* Call on two students to present the dialog. Then do Choral Repetition and Choral Conversation Practice.

2. **Exercise 2:** Introduce the new word *bank.* Same as above.

3. **Exercises 3–9:**

> | **New vocabulary:** | 3. *supermarket* | 4. *library* | 5. *park* | 6. *movie theater* |
> | | 7. *post office* | 8. *monkey, zoo* | 9. *hospital* | |

Either

Full-Class Practice: Call on a pair of students to do each exercise. Introduce new vocabulary one exercise at a time. (For more practice, call on other pairs of students, or do Choral Repetition or Choral Conversation.)

or

Pair Practice: Introduce new vocabulary for all the exercises. Next have students practice all these exercises in pairs. Then have pairs present the exercises to the class. (For more practice, do Choral Repetition or Choral Conversation.)

4. **Exercises 10–12:**

In these exercises, students practice questions and answers using the patterns:

> *Where's* _____? *Where are* _____? *Where am I?*

Students can use any names and any places they wish. The object is to get students to practice the structures with vocabulary of their choice in order to talk about real-life places and people. Although only three exercises are indicated in the book, you may want your students to do more. Encourage students to use dictionaries to find new words they want to use.

This exercise can be done orally in class or for written homework. If you assign it for homework, you should do one example in class to make sure students understand what's expected. Have students present their questions and answers in class the next day.

WORKBOOK

Pages 9–11

Exercise Note

Workbook p. 11: Students practice intonation indicating surprise.

EXPANSION ACTIVITY

Practice with Visuals

Use *Side by Side* Picture Cards 9–17, or your own word visuals or word cards for the vocabulary on text page 12. Practice asking and answering questions about these locations as you did for places in the home. Use this method to practice all the subject pronouns and forms of the verb *to be*. Pay special attention to the use of contractions and pronunciation of the final *s* in *she's, he's,* and *it's*.

Text Page 13:

READING: *All the Students in My English Class Are Absent Today*

FOCUS

> • To be + location
> • Subject pronouns

NEW VOCABULARY

absent	even	our
all	everybody	Social Security office
at	except	teacher
bed	in bed	today
dentist		What a shame!

PREVIEWING THE STORY (optional)

Have students talk about the story title and/or illustration. Introduce new vocabulary.

READING THE STORY

1. Have students read silently, or follow along silently as the story is read aloud by you, by one or more students, or on the tape.
2. Ask students if they have any questions; check understanding of vocabulary.

CHECK-UP

Answer These Questions

> 1. He's in the hospital.
> 2. She's at the dentist.
> 3. They're at the Social Security office.
> 4. He's home in bed.

Listening

Have students complete the exercises as you play the tape or read the following:

Listen and choose the best answer.

1. Mr. Jones is in the park. (b)
2. Betty is in the library. (b)
3. He's in the kitchen. (a)
4. She's in the living room. (b)
5. They're in the yard. (b)
6. We're in the basement. (a)

HOW ABOUT YOU?

Have students answer the questions, in pairs or as a class.

WORKBOOK ANSWER KEY AND LISTENING SCRIPTS

Page 5 A. WHAT ARE THEY SAYING?

1. Where, I'm

2. are
living room

3. Where are
yard

4. Where are
We're
bedroom

5. are
They're, basement

6. Where, are
I'm
kitchen

Page 6 B. WHAT ARE THEY SAYING?

1. Where's
He's
kitchen

2. Where's
She's
living room

3. Where's
It's
garage

Page 6 C. WHERE ARE THEY?

1. They
2. She
3. He
4. They
5. We
6. It
7. He
8. She
9. It

Page 6 D. WHERE ARE THEY?

1. He's
2. I'm
3. We're
4. You're
5. She's
6. Where's
7. It's
8. They're

Page 7 E. THE FRANKLIN FAMILY

1. in the kitchen
2. in the yard
3. in the living room
4. is in the bedroom
5. is in the dining room
6. is in the bathroom

Page 7 F. WHERE ARE THEY?

1. He's in the kitchen.
2. She's in the yard.
3. They're in the living room.
4. She's in the bedroom.
5. It's in the dining room.
6. It's in the bathroom.

Page 9 I. WHAT'S THE SIGN?

1. LIBRARY
in the library

2. HOSPITAL
in the hospital

3. PARK
in the park

4. RESTAURANT
is in the restaurant

5. BANK
is in the bank

6. POST OFFICE
are in the post office

7. MOVIE THEATER
is in the movie
theater

8. SUPERMARKET
are in the supermarket

Page 10 J. LISTEN

Listen to each sentence. Put a check next to the
appropriate picture.

1. Where are they?
They're in the hospital.
2. Where are they?
They're in the supermarket.
3. Where's Mary?
She's in the bank.

Answers
1. _____   ✔   _____
2. _____   _____   ✔
3. ✔   _____   _____

Page 10 K. LISTEN

Listen to the following conversations.
Put a circle around the right word.

1. Where are you?
2. I'm in the car with Mrs. Jones.
3. Where's Mr. Jones?
4. He's in Mexico City.
5. Where are you?
6. I'm in the bathroom.
7. Where's the newspaper?
8. It's in the living room.

Answers

1.	you	5.	Where
2.	car, Mrs.	6.	I'm, bathroom
3.	Mr.	7.	Where's
4.	He's	8.	It's

3

GRAMMAR

Present Continuous Tense

	am	I	
What	is	he she it	doing?
	are	we you they	

(I am)	I'm	
(He is) (She is) (It is)	He's She's It's	eating.
(We are) (You are) (They are)	We're You're They're	

FUNCTIONS

Asking for and Reporting Information

What are you doing?
   I'm *reading*.

What's *Mr. Jones* doing?
   He's reading the newspaper.

Inquiring about Location

Where's *Walter*?

Giving Location

He's in the *kitchen*.

NEW VOCABULARY

a
baseball
beach
beautiful
birds
book
breakfast
cafeteria
cards
classroom
coffee
cooking
dancing
day
dinner

doing
drinking
eating
family
flowers
guitar
happy
lemonade
listening to
lunch
mathematics
Miss
night club
piano
planting

playing
radio
reading
shining
singing
sleeping
studying
sun
swimming
TV
watching TV
what
with

It's a beautiful day!

Text Pages 16–17: *What Are They Doing?*

FOCUS

> Introduction of the present continuous tense

GETTING READY

Review contractions of the verb *to be*. Say the full forms and have students tell you the correct contracted forms:

I am – I'm	we are – we're
he is – he's	you are – you're
she is – she's	they are – they're
it is – it's	

INTRODUCING THE MODEL

There are 6 model conversations. Introduce and practice each model before going on to the next. For each model:

1. Have students look at the model illustration.
2. Set the scene: "Neighbors are talking."
3. With books closed, have students listen as you present the model or play the tape one or more times.
4. **Full-Class Choral Repetition:** Model each line and have students repeat.
5. Have students open their books and look at the dialog. Ask students if they have any questions; check understanding of new vocabulary:

1st model:	*what, doing, reading*
2nd model:	*cooking*
3rd model:	*studying*
4th model:	*eating*
5th model:	*watching* TV
6th model:	*sleeping*

   Culture Note

   > *Breakfast, lunch, and dinner:* In general, people in the United States like to eat three meals a day: breakfast (before work or school), lunch (around noon), and dinner (in the early evening).

6. **Group Choral Repetition:** Divide the class in half. Model line A and have Group 1 repeat; model line B and have Group 2 repeat.
7. **Choral Conversation:** Groups 1 and 2 practice the dialog twice, without teacher model. First, Group 1 is Speaker A and Group 2 is Speaker B; then reverse.
8. Call on one or two pairs of students to present the dialog.

   (For additional practice, do Choral Conversation in small groups or by rows.)
9. After all of the models have been introduced, go back to the first and practice it again by cuing the substitution of other verbs. For example:

Teacher cue:	cooking		Teacher cue:	eating
Teacher:	What are you doing?		Teacher:	What are you doing?
Student:	I'm cooking.		Student:	I'm eating.

   Continue this with the next four models to practice *we're, they're, he's, she's.*

Examples

---

1. A. What are you doing?
   B. I'm reading the newspaper.

2. A. What are Mr. and Mrs. Jones doing?
   B. They're eating dinner.

---

1. **Exercise 1:** Call on two students to present the dialog. Then do Choral Repetition and Choral Conversation Practice.

2. **Exercise 2:** Introduce the new word *dinner.* Same as above.

3. **Exercises 3–7:**

New vocabulary: 7. *playing the piano*

Either

Full-Class Practice: Call on a pair of students to do each exercise. Introduce the new vocabulary before doing exercise 7. (For more practice, call on other pairs of students, or do Choral Repetition or Choral Conversation.)

   or

Pair Practice: Introduce the new vocabulary. Next have students practice all of the exercises in pairs. Then have pairs present the exercises to the class. (For more practice, do Choral Repetition or Choral Conversation.)

4. **Exercise 8:** In this exercise, the window is *blank.* Ask students to imagine they are living in the building, and have them answer using any vocabulary they wish. Call on several pairs of students to practice this exercise.

WORKBOOK

(Page 12)

EXPANSION ACTIVITIES

1. *Practice with Real Objects*

   Use real objects to represent on-going activities that students can talk about. Some suggested objects are:

   - a pot and spoon for *cooking*
   - a newspaper for *reading*
   - a textbook for *studying*
   - an eating utensil (such as a fork or chopsticks) for *eating*

   Use one object at a time to practice *What _____ doing?,* using all the pronouns. For example:

   a. Hold a pot and spoon and say: "I'm cooking." Have students repeat.
   b. Give the objects to Student A and ask: "What are you doing?" Student A answers: "I'm cooking."
   c. Ask another student: "What's *(Student A)* doing?" ("He's/She's cooking.") Ask several other students. Give the objects to different students in order to practice *he's* and *she's.*
   d. Practice *we're.* Give objects to 2 students. Ask each one: "What are you and _____ doing?" ("We're cooking.") Practice *we're* with several pairs of students.

e. Practice *they're*. Give the objects to two students. Ask another student: "What are they doing?" Give the visual to several pairs of students; call on other pairs of students to ask and answer "What are they doing?"

f. Practice *you're*. Hold an object and ask: "What am I doing?"

Practice this way using other objects. Be sure to have students practice asking as well as answering.

2. *Practice with Visuals*

Use your own visuals, word cards, or *Side by Side* Picture Cards 18–24 to practice the present continuous tense. Use the same method as in 1 above, but use visuals in place of objects.

Text Pages 18–19: *What's Everybody Doing?"*

FOCUS

Review and contrast *Where* _____? and *What* _____ doing?

GETTING READY

Review vocabulary for places in the home and community. Use *Side by Side* Picture Cards or your own visuals, or the illustrations on text pages 8 and 12. Indicate a place and have students say the name.

INTRODUCING THE MODEL

1. Have students look at the model illustration.
2. Set the scene: "Two people are talking about Walter."
3. Present the model.
4. Full-Class Choral Repetition.
5. Ask students if they have any questions; check understanding of new vocabulary: *breakfast.*
6. Group Choral Repetition.
7. Choral Conversation.
8. Call on one or two pairs of students to present the dialog.
   (For additional practice, do Choral Conversation in small groups or by rows.)

SIDE BY SIDE EXERCISES

Examples

> 1. A. Where's Betty?
>   B. She's in the park.
>   A. What's she doing?
>   B. She's eating lunch.
>
> 2. A. Where are Mr. and Mrs. Smith?
>   B. They're in the dining room.
>   A. What are they doing?
>   B. They're eating dinner.

1. **Exercise 1:** Introduce the new word *lunch.* Call on two students to present the dialog. Then do Choral Repetition and Choral Conversation Practice.
2. **Exercise 2:** Introduce the new word *dinner.* Same as above.
3. **Exercises 3–13:**

> **New vocabulary:**   3. *guitar*   4. *cards*   5. *baseball*   6. *Miss, drinking, coffee*
>   7. *cafeteria, lemonade*   9. *classroom, mathematics*   10. *night club, dancing*
>   11. *singing*   13. *listening to, radio*

Culture Note

Baseball (Exercise 5):   Along with football, baseball is a very popular spectator sport in the United States.

Either

Full-Class Practice: Call on a pair of students to do each exercise. Introduce the new vocabulary one exercise at a time. (For more practice, call on other pairs of students, or do Choral Repetition or Choral Conversation.)

or

Pair Practice: Introduce all the new vocabulary. Next have students practice all of the exercises in pairs. Then have pairs present the exercises to the class. (For more practice, do Choral Repetition or Choral Conversation.)

4. **Exercise 14:** Have students use the model as a guide to create their own conversations, using vocabulary of their choice. (They can use any names, places, and activities they wish.) Encourage students to use dictionaries to find new words they want to use. This exercise can be done orally in class or for written homework. If you assign it for homework, you should do one example in class to make sure students understand what's expected. Have students present their conversations in class the next day.

WORKBOOK
Pages 13–18

Exercise Notes

Workbook p. 14: Students review WH-questions, *to be,* and the present continuous tense. They practice the reduction of *Where are → Where're, What are → What're,* and the dropping of the *h* in *What's he.*

Workbook p. 18: Students practice the present continuous tense and intonation indicating surprise.

EXPANSION ACTIVITIES

1. *Practice with Visuals or Real Objects*

   Review *Where* _____? and *What* _____ *doing?* by using a combination of visuals and objects as cues for oral practice. Use two cues at a time: one represents a **location,** such as *park, kitchen,* or *library;* the other represents an **on-going activity,** such as *eating* or *studying English.* For locations, use your own visuals, word cards, or *Side by Side* Picture Cards 1–17. For activities, use your own visuals, word cards, *Side by Side* Picture Cards 18–30, or objects such as:

   > a few cards—for *playing cards*
   > an eating implement, such as a knife or chopsticks—for *eating lunch*
   > a cup—for *drinking coffee*
   > a book—for *studying English*
   > a ball—for *playing baseball*

   a. Hold up a cue for *park* and *eating;* say: "I'm in the park. I'm eating lunch." Give these cues to a student; ask: "Where are you?" and "What are you doing?"

   b. Use these two cues (either visuals or a combination of visuals and objects) to practice all the other pronouns:

   > Where am I? What am I doing?
   > Where is _____? What is he/she doing?
   > Where are _____ and _____? What are they doing?
   > Where are you and _____? What are you doing?

   c. As you practice each pronoun, call on pairs of students to ask and answer whenever possible.

2. **Picture Card Game**

Use *Side by Side* Picture Cards for *locations* and *on-going activities* that the students know. Place the cards in two separate piles, face down. Have a student take the top card from each pile; that student must use the location and activity shown on the cards to answer the questions "Where are you?" and "What are you doing?" Have students take turns asking the questions. Give each student a turn at drawing cards. You can play this game in teams, keeping score for correct or incorrect answers.

3. **Listening Exercise: Guess Who!**

Have students open their books to text pages 18–19. For listening practice, make a statement about a person in a certain place or doing a certain activity, and have students identify the person. For example:

Teacher: I'm in the hospital.   Teacher: We're eating dinner.
Student(s): Barbara.   Student(s): Mr. and Mrs. Smith.

Teacher: I'm in the restaurant.   Teacher: I'm singing.
Student(s): Miss Jackson.   Student(s): Harry.

Teacher: I'm dancing.   Teacher: I'm in the bathroom
Student(s): Gloria.   Student(s): Harry.

READING: *In the Park*
At Home in the Yard

FOCUS

Present continuous tense

NEW VOCABULARY

Story 1		Story 2
a	happy	book
beautiful	shining	flowers
birds	sun	planting
day		with
family	It's a beautiful day!	

PREVIEWING THE STORIES (optional)

Have students talk about the story titles and/or illustrations. Introduce the new vocabulary.

READING THE STORIES

1. Have students read silently, or follow along silently as the stories are read aloud by you, or by one or more students, or on the tape.
2. Ask students if they have any questions; check understanding of vocabulary.
3. Check students' comprehension, using some of the following questions:

Story 1
a. Where's the Jones family today?
b. What's Mr. Jones doing?
c. What's Mrs. Jones doing?
d. What are Sally and Patty Jones doing?
e. What's Tommy Jones doing?

Story 2
a. Where's the Smith family today?
b. What's Mr. Smith doing?
c. What's Mrs. Smith doing?
d. What are Mary and Billy Smith doing?
e. What's Sam Smith doing?

CHECK-UP

True or False

1. False
2. True
3. True
4. False
5. False
6. True

Q & A

1. Call on a pair of students to present the model.
2. Have students work in pairs to create new dialogs.
3. Call on pairs to present their new dialogs to the class.

Listening

Have students complete the exercises as you play the tape or read the following:

Listen and choose the best answer.

1. What are you doing? (b)
2. What's Mr. Smith doing? (a)
3. What's Mrs. Larson doing? (b)
4. What are Bill and Mary doing? (b)
5. What are you and Henry doing? (a)
6. What am I drinking? (a)

IN YOUR OWN WORDS

1. Make sure students understand the instructions.
2. Have students do the activity as written homework, using a dictionary for any new words they wish to use.
3. Have students present and discuss what they have written, in pairs or as a class.

WORKBOOK

Check-Up Test: Page 19

WORKBOOK ANSWER KEY AND LISTENING SCRIPTS

Page 12 A. WHAT ARE THEY SAYING?

1. What
   I'm
2. are you
   cooking
3. are
   doing
   They're
   studying

4. doing
   He's
5. What's
   doing
   She's
   watching
6. your dog
   doing
   It's
   sleeping

Page 13 B. WHAT ARE THEY DOING?

1. reading
2. singing
3. dancing
4. sleeping
5. listening
6. playing
7. eating
8. drinking
   9. watching

Page 16 D. LISTEN

Listen to each sentence. Put a check next to the appropriate picture.

1. The cat is in the garage.
2. What's she doing?
3. They're reading.
4. I'm playing the guitar.
5. He's listening.
6. You're in the cafeteria.
7. What are they doing?
8. He's in the classroom.

Answers
1. ✔ ___   ___
2. ___   ✔
3. ___   ✔
4. ___   ✔   5. ✔ ___   ___
6. ___   ✔   7. ___   ___   ✔
8. ✔ ___   ___

Page 17 E. WHAT'S THE QUESTION?

1. Where are you?
2. What's she doing?

3. Where is he?
4. What are you doing?
5. What's he doing?
6. Where are they?
7. Where are you?
8. Where is it?
9. Where is she?
10. What's it doing?
11. What are they doing?
12. What are you doing?

CHECK-UP TEST: *CHAPTERS 1–3*

Page 19 B.

1. breakfast
2. He's
3. zoo
4. We're
5. reading
6. coffee
7. cards

Page 19 C.

1. Where
2. doing
3. in
4. She's
5. It's
6. and
7. watching
8. listening
9. What
10. We're

Page 19 D.

Listen and write the number you hear.

1. 695–3352
2. 496–8577
3. 724–0681
4. 358–9677
5. 582–4196

Answers
1. 5
2. 6
3. 2
4. 7
5. 9

TEACHER'S NOTES

CHAPTER 4 OVERVIEW: *Text Pages 23—30*

4

GRAMMAR

To Be: Short Answers

Yes,	I	am.
	he she it	is.
	we you they	are.

Possessive Adjectives

I'm He's She's It's We're You're They're	cleaning	my his her its our your their	room.

FUNCTIONS

Greeting People

Hi!

Asking for and Reporting Information

What are you doing?
  I'm *fixing my sink.*

Are you busy?
  Yes, I am. I'm *washing my hair.*

Inquiring about Location

Where's *Miss Johnson?*

Giving Location

She's in the *parking lot.*

NEW VOCABULARY

apartment
bicycle
brushing *their* teeth
busy
children
cleaning
clothes
doing *his* exercises
doing *their* homework
exercises
feeding
fixing

hair
her
his
homework
kitchen sink
laudromat
my
neighbor
of course
our
painting

parking lot
room
sink
teeth
their
too
washing
watching
windows

Hi!

LANGUAGE NOTES

1. Some students have difficulty distinguishing *his* from *he's* and *watching* from *washing*.
2. The homonyms *it's* and *its* are easily confused in writing.
3. *Yes* can be pronounced *yuh* and *yeah* in informal speech.

CULTURE NOTE

Traditional U.S. culture assigns household chores to women and repairs or outdoor jobs to men. The illustrations in this chapter reflect the fact that many people in the United States are breaking from these traditional patterns.

FOCUS

> • Possessive adjectives
> • Practice with the present continuous tense

GETTING READY

1. Read the forms in the grammar box at the top of the page. Have students repeat after you.

2. Demonstrate the idea of possession: Point to your book and say ***my*** *book*. Point to a male student's book and say ***his*** *book*. Point to a female student's book and say ***her*** *book*.

INTRODUCING THE MODEL

There are 5 model conversations. Introduce and practice each model before going on to the next. For each model:

1. Have students look at the model illustration.
2. Set the scene: "People are talking on the telephone."
3. Present the model.
4. Full-Class Repetition.
5. Ask students if they have any questions; check understanding of new vocabulary:

    1st model: *Hi!, fixing, my, sink*
    2nd model: *his*
    3rd model: *cleaning, her, room*
    4th model: *our, apartment*
    5th model: *children, doing, their, homework*

6. Group Choral Repetition.
7. Choral Conversation.
8. Call on one or two pairs of students to present the dialog.

    (For additional practice, do Choral Conversation in small groups or by rows.)

WORKBOOK

Page 20

EXPANSION ACTIVITIES

1. ***Practice with Students' Names***

    Have pairs of students practice the model conversations again. This time have students pretend to call other students on the telephone and use names of people in the class in place of those in the book.

2. ***Practice with Visuals***

    Use visuals to practice *What _____ doing?* and answers with possessive adjectives. Use your own visuals or *Side by Side* Picture Cards 31–33 to represent a broken sink, car, or TV. Hold up a visual and say: "I'm fixing my (*sink/car/TV*)." Give the visual to a student and ask: "What are you doing?" Ask another student: "What's he/she doing?" Call on a pair of students to talk about the student holding the visual. Expand this activity so that students ask and answer many questions about broken objects, using the possessive adjectives. For added realism you can bring a wrench or other tool to class and give it to students along with the visual.

3. ***Practice with Students' Belongings***

a. Collect personal items from students (for example, a pen, a pencil, a book, a notebook, homework). If necessary, teach new vocabulary. Hold up the item for the class to see and have students identify their particular belongings.

Teacher:	(holding up student's pen)	Student:	*my* pen
	(holding up student's book)	Student:	*my* book

b. Have students identify the items again, this time using *his, her, our, their.*

Teacher:	(holding up Student A's pen)	Student B:	(*his/her*) pen
	(holding up Student A's book)	Student B:	(*his/her*) book
	(holding up several books)	Student:	(*their/our*) books

Text Pages 25–26: *Are You Busy?*

FOCUS

> - Yes/No questions: *Is Nancy busy?*
> - Short answers: *Yes, she is.*
> - Present continuous tense: *She's washing her car.*

GETTING READY

1. Have students listen and repeat as you read the short answers in the grammar box at the top of the page.

2. Review contractions with the verb *to be*. Say the full form and have students give the contracted form.

INTRODUCING THE MODEL

1. Have students look at the model illustration.
2. Set the scene: "Two friends are talking on the telephone."
3. Present the model.
4. Full-Class Repetition.
5. Ask students if they have any questions; check understanding of new vocabulary: *busy, washing, hair.*
6. Group Choral Repetition.
7. Choral Conversation.
8. Call on one or two pairs of students to present the dialog.
   (For additional practice, do Choral Conversation in small groups or by rows.)

SIDE BY SIDE EXERCISES

Examples

> 1. A. Is Nancy busy?
>   B. Yes, she is.
>   She's washing her car.
>
> 2. A. Is Ted busy?
>   B. Yes, he is.
>   He's feeding his dog.
>
> 3. A. Are you busy?
>   B. Yes, we are.
>   We're cleaning our yard.
>
> 4. A. Are Mr. and Mrs. Jones busy?
>   B. Yes, they are.
>   They're painting their kitchen.

1. **Exercise 1:** Call on two students to present the dialog. Then do Choral Repetition and Choral Conversation Practice.
2. **Exercise 2:** Introduce the new word *feeding*. Same as above.
3. **Exercises 3–14:**

> **New vocabulary:** 4. *painting* 6. *exercises* 7. *bicycle* 9. *windows*
> 11. *clothes* 14. *brushing, teeth*

Either Full-Class Practice or Pair Practice.

Many of these exercises can be a springboard for a discussion of men's and women's responsibilities in the home (see **Chapter Overview**).

WORKBOOK

Pages 21–24

Exercise Note

Workbook p. 23: Students practice the present continuous tense and the dropping of the *h* in *Is he, Yes he,* and *What's he.*

EXPANSION ACTIVITIES

1. *Practice with Word Cards*

   a. Make word cards for the following:

car	apartment	exercises	TV
dog	bicycle	teeth	garage
yard	clothes	windows	hair
kitchen	homework	cat	

   b. Create a conversation according to the model:

      A. Are you busy?
      B. Yes, I am.
      A. What are you doing?
      B. I'm _____.

   Each student must answer using an appropriate verb (such as *cleaning* or *fixing*) and the object on the card. For example, for the card *bicycle* a student can answer: "I'm washing my bicycle" or "I'm fixing my bicycle."

   c. You can also practice other pronouns. For example:

      A. Is _____ busy?
      B. Yes, (he/she) is.
      A. What's (he/she) doing?
      B. (He's/She's) _____.

2. *Practice with Visuals*

   Use your own visuals or *Side by Side* Picture Cards 31–41 to review the conversations on text pages 25–26.

3. *Vocabulary Review: Finish the Sentence*

   Review vocabulary by saying a verb and having students repeat the verb and adding an appropriate ending to the sentence. For example:

Teacher	Student
I'm washing . . .	I'm washing my car / my windows / my clothes.
He's feeding . . .	He's feeding his dog / his cat.
We're cleaning . . .	We're cleaning our yard / our apartment / our garage.
She's doing . . .	She's doing her homework / her exercises.
They're painting . . .	They're painting their kitchen / their bedroom / their apartment.

ON YOUR OWN: *Where Are They and What Are They Doing?*

FOCUS

Review of the present continuous tense and possessive adjectives

The illustration for this exercise shows people involved in different activities in various places around town. Students use the model conversation at the bottom of the page to talk about the illustration.

INTRODUCING THE MODEL

1. Have students look at the model illustration.
2. Introduce the new words *parking lot, laundromat.*
3. Present the model.
4. Full-Class Choral Repetition.
5. Ask students if they have any questions; check understanding of new vocabulary.

    Culture Note

    Laundromat: In the United States many people take their laundry to a *laundromat*—a place where they pay to use machines to wash and dry their clothes.

6. Group Choral Repetition.
7. Choral Conversation.
8. Call on one or two pairs of students to present the dialog.

SIDE BY SIDE EXERCISES

Examples

A. Where's Mr. Nathan?	A. Where's Bobby Davis?
B. He's in the park.	B. He's in the library.
A. What's he doing?	A. What's he doing?
B. He's reading the newspaper.	B. He's studying.
	or
	He's reading.
	or
	He's doing his homework.

Call on pairs of students to ask and answer questions about the people in the illustration.

For the ? location, next to the night club, students can choose any vocabulary to answer the question.

This exercise can be done as either Full-Class Practice or Pair Practice. You can also assign it as written homework.

WORKBOOK

Pages 25-26

Exercise Notes

Workbook p. 25: Exercise H is a fill-in drill that reviews the vocabulary and structures of Chapter 4. Students can do this for homework, or you can do this exercise as a dictation in class.

Workbook p. 26: Students review prepositional phrases of location and the dropping of the *h* in *What's ̸he* and *Where's ̸he.*

READING: *A Busy Day*

FOCUS

> Possessive adjectives

NEW VOCABULARY

> kitchen sink   of course   too
> neighbor   watching

PREVIEWING THE STORY (optional)

Have students talk about the story title and/or illustration. Introduce new vocabulary.

READING THE STORY

1. Have students read silently, or follow along silently as the story is read aloud by you, by one or more students, or on the tape.
2. Ask students if they have any questions; check understanding of vocabulary.
3. Check students' comprehension, using some of the following questions:

    a. What's Mr. Anderson doing?

    b. What's Mrs. Wilson doing?

    c. What are Mr. and Mrs. Thomas doing?

    d. What's Mrs. Black doing?

    e. What's Tommy Lee doing?

    f. What are Mr. and Mrs. Lane doing?

    g. What am I doing?

CHECK-UP

True or False?

> 1. True
> 2. False
> 3. False
> 4. True
> 5. False

Q & A

1. Call on a pair of students to present the model.
2. Have students work in pairs to create new dialogs.
3. Call on pairs to present their new dialogs to the class.

Listening

Have students complete the exercises as you play the tape or read the following:

Listen and choose the best answer.
1. What are you painting? (a)
2. What are you playing? (a)
3. What are they reading? (a)
4. What is she eating? (b)
5. What is he washing? (b)
6. What are you watching? (b)

IN YOUR OWN WORDS

1. Make sure students understand the instructions.
2. Have students do the activity as written homework, using a dictionary for any new words they wish to use.
3. Have students present and discuss what they have written, in pairs or as a class.

Page 20   A.   ON THE PHONE

1. What
   my sink
2. doing
   fixing his
3. What's
   her
4. What are
   cleaning our
5. children
   their homework

Page 21   B.   WHAT'S THE WORD?

1. my
2. our
3. her
4. their
5. his
6. its
7. your

Page 21   C.   PUZZLE

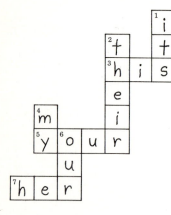

Page 22   D.   SHORT ANSWERS

1. Yes, she is.
2. Yes, I am.
3. Yes, they are.
4. Yes, we are.

5. Yes, he is.
6. Yes, you are.
7. Yes, they are.
8. Yes, she is.

Page 24   F.   WHAT ARE THEY DOING?

1. feeding
   dog
2. washing
   windows
3. fixing
   sink
4. painting
   living room
5. brushing
   teeth
6. cleaning
   garage

Page 24   G.   WHAT'S THE WORD?

1. Where
2. We're, our
3. watching
4. Is
5. He's, his
6. Are
7. They're, their
8. It's, It's, its

Page 25   H.   A BUSY DAY IN ROCKVILLE

2. restaurant
3. They're
4. night club
5. playing
6. Mrs., laundromat
7. clothes
8. Mr., newspaper, his
9. Miss, are
10. fixing, bicycle
11. Miss, her
12. Where's
13. library
14. What's
15. studying

TEACHER'S NOTES

5

GRAMMAR

To Be: Yes/No Questions

Am	I	
Is	he she it	tall?
Are	we you they	

To Be: Short Answers

Yes,	I	am.
	he she it	is.
	we you they	are.

No,	I'm	not.
	he she it	isn't.
	we you they	aren't.

Adjectives

tall	short
young	old
new	old
heavy/fat	thin
beautiful/pretty/ handsome	ugly
rich	poor
large	small
big	little
loud/noisy	quiet
expensive	cheap
married	single
easy	difficult

Possessive Nouns

Is Albert's house large or small?
Are Mary's neighbors noisy or quiet?

FUNCTIONS

Asking for and Reporting Information

Is *Bob tall* or *short?*
　He's tall.

Tell me about *your new car.*

I'm calling from *Miami.*

What are you doing *in Miami?*

How's the weather *in Miami?*
　It's *raining.*

Is it *hot?*
　No, it isn't. It's *cold.*

Describing

He's *tall.*

Greeting People

Hi, *Jack.* This is *Jim.*

Expressing Dissatisfaction

I'm having a terrible time.

Sympathizing

I'm sorry to hear that.

NEW VOCABULARY

about
a few
aren't
big
bored
boss
brother
but
calling
champagne
chapter
cheap
city
cloudy
cold
cool
difficult
doctor's office
easy
expensive
fat
food
good
handsome
having
heavy
here
Honolulu
hot
hotel
house
how

isn't
large
little
loud
married
Miami
mother
new
noisy
not
old
or
other
out
poor
pretty
question
quiet
raining
repairman
rich
right now
Santa Claus
short
single
sister
sitting
small
snowing
soon
stomach

sunny
Switzerland
tall
tea
terrible
thin
this
to be
together
toilet
ugly
warm
weather
writing (to)
young

as you can see
Dear *Mother,*
for a few days
having a good time
having problems (with)
Hi, *Jack.*
I'm sorry to hear that.
in fact
looking out the window
Love, *Ethel.*
on vacation
"raining cats and dogs"
See you soon.
tell me about
to tell the truth

Text Pages 32–33: *Tall or Short?*

FOCUS

> - Yes/No questions with the verb *to be*
> - Questions with *or*
> - Possessive nouns: *Albert's*

GETTING READY

1. Introduce possessive nouns.

   a. Point to a few students and name some of their possessions. Have students repeat after you. For example:

   > "Jane"   "Bob"
   > "Jane's pencil"   "Bob's pen"

   b. Write the possessive forms on the board. For example:

   > Jane<u>'s</u> pencil   Joe<u>'s</u> book

2. Demonstrate the idea of opposites.

   a. Draw and label 2 stick figures on the board:

   Say: "Bob is **tall**."
   "Bill is **short**."

   Have students repeat.

   b. Draw 2 more stick figures on the board:

   Say: "Herman is **heavy**."
   "David is **thin**."

   Have students repeat.

INTRODUCING THE MODEL

1. Have students look at the model illustration.
2. Set the scene: "Two people are talking about Bob and Bill."
3. Present the model.
4. Full-Class Choral Repetition.
5. Ask students if they have any questions; check understanding of new vocabulary: *tall, short, or.*
6. Group Choral Repetition.
7. Choral Conversation.
8. Call on one or two pairs of students to present the dialog.
   (For additional practice, do Choral Conversation in small groups or by rows.)

SIDE BY SIDE EXERCISES

Examples

1.	A. Is Alice young or old?		2.	A. Is Margaret young or old?
	B. She's young.			B. She's old.
5.	A. Is Herman's car new or old?		6.	A. Is David's car new or old?
	B. It's new.			B. It's old.

1. **Exercises 1 and 2:** Introduce the new words *young, old.* Call on two students to present each dialog. Then do Choral Repetition and Choral Conversation Practice.

2. **Exercises 3 and 4:** Introduce the new words *heavy, fat, thin.* Same as above.

3. **Exercises 5–22:**

> **New vocabulary:**   5–6. *new, old*   7–8. *beautiful, pretty, ugly*
> 9–10. *handsome, ugly*   11–12. *rich, poor*   13–14. *large, big, little, house, apartment*
> 15–16. *noisy, quiet*   17–18. *expensive, cheap, champagne, tea*
> 19–20. *married, single*   21–22. *easy, difficult, questions*

Language Note

   Beautiful and *pretty* (Exercises 7 and 8) are commonly used to refer to women and things; *handsome* (Exercises 9 and 10) is commonly used for men.

Either Full-Class or Pair Practice.

4. Have students use the model as a guide to create their own conversations using vocabulary of their choice. (They can use any names, adjectives, and objects they wish.) Encourage students to use dictionaries to find new words they want to use. This exercise can be done orally in class or for written homework. If you assign it for homework, you should do one example in class to make sure students understand what's expected. Have students present their conversations in class the next day.

WORKBOOK

Page 27

EXPANSION ACTIVITIES

1. Practice with Visuals

You can review the structures and vocabulary on text pages 32–33 using visuals of opposite adjectives. Use your own visuals, stick figures on the board, or *Side by Side* Picture Cards 42–50.

  a. Point to visuals of a tall person and a short person. Ask: "Is he/she tall or short?" Students answer: "He's/She's tall" or "He's/She's short."

  b. Practice other adjectives this way.

  c. Give visuals to students or have students point to visuals: have them ask each other questions.

2. Picture Story

Review the structures and vocabulary by telling a story using the board.

  a. Draw a fat man.
      Say: "Herman is heavy."
             "He's young."

  b. Draw a house.
      Say: "His house is old."
             "It's large."

  c. Draw a car.
      Say: "His car is new."
             "It's expensive."

  d. Have students tell you about Herman, using the pictures as cues. You can also ask students *or* questions, such as "Is Herman thin or heavy?" Students can ask each other questions about Herman.

Another Picture Story

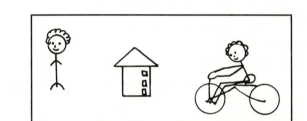

  a. "Helen is tall."
      "She's beautiful."

  b. "Her apartment building is big."
      "Her neighbors are noisy."

  c. "Her bicycle is old."

3. Practice with Visuals from Newspapers and Magazines

Use photographs from the media to have students review adjectives. Advertisements are particularly useful. For example:

(Picture of a dress in an advertisement): It's expensive.
                                               She's beautiful.
                                             He's handsome.
                                            They're thin.

(Picture from a newspaper): He's rich.
                                   They're married.

(Picture of food): It's cheap.
                      It's expensive.
                      It's big.

Text Pages 34–35: *Tell Me About . . .*

FOCUS

Yes/No questions with *to be* and negative short answers:
    Are you married?   *Is he tall?*
    No, I'm not.   *No, he isn't.*

GETTING READY

Say the sentences in the grammar boxes at the top of the page and have students repeat after you. (Read from left to right.)

Am I tall?	Yes, I am.	No, I'm not.
Is he tall?	Yes, he is.	No, he isn't.
Is she tall?	Yes, she is.	No, she isn't.
It it tall?	Yes, it is.	No, it isn't.
Are we tall?	Yes, we are.	No, we aren't.
Are you tall?	Yes, you are.	No, you aren't.
Are they tall?	Yes, they are.	No, they aren't.

INTRODUCING THE MODEL

There are 3 model conversations. Introduce and practice each model before going on to the next. For each model:

1. Have students look at the model illustration.
2. Set the scene: "Two people are talking."
3. Present the model.
4. Full-Class Choral Repetition.
5. Ask students if they have any questions; check understanding of new vocabulary: *tell me about.*
6. Choral Choral Repetition.
7. Choral Conversation.
8. Call on one or two pairs of students to present the dialog.
   (For additional practice, do Choral Conversations in small groups or by rows.)

SIDE BY SIDE EXERCISES

Examples

1. A. Tell me about your brother.
     Is he tall?
  B. No, he isn't. He's short.
	2. A. Tell me about your sister.
	     Is she single?
	  B. No, she isn't. She's married.

1. Introduce the new word *brother.* Call on two students to present the dialog. Then do Choral Repetition and Choral Conversation Practice.
2. **Exercise 2:** Introduce the new word *sister.* Same as above.

3. **Exercises 3–10:**

> **New vocabulary:**   4. *boss*   10.   *Santa Claus*

Culture Note

Santa Claus (Exercise 10)—a legendary man who is traditionally associated with Christmas celebrations (December 25th) in the United States. Children believe he lives at the North Pole and brings Christmas gifts to their homes every year.

Either Full-Class Practice or Pair Practice.

WORKBOOK

Pages 28–31

Exercise Note

Workbook p. 29: Students practice yes/no questions with adjectives.

EXPANSION ACTIVITIES

1. **Practice with Visuals**

   Use visuals of opposite adjectives for people and things.

   a. Point to a visual and say: "Tell me about _____." For example:

   > "Tell me about Bill."   "Tell me about your house."
   > ("He's thin.")   ("It's large.")

   Suggestion: when you refer to a visual of a person, give that person a name.

   b. Have students ask each other Yes/No questions about visuals. For example:

   > "Is he tall?"   "Is he short?"
   > ("No, he isn't. He's short.")   ("Yes, he is.")

2. **Students Talk about Themselves**

   Write these words on the board:

brother	boss	cat	young	cheap	quiet	single
sister	apartment	dog	new	fat	noisy	married
neighbors	house	car	rich	thin	beautiful	big
			old	expensive	handsome	
			poor	loud	ugly	

   Practice according to the pattern:

   > A. Tell me about your (*car*). Is (*it old*)?
   > B. Yes, (*it is*).
   >   or
   >   No, (*it isn't. It's new*).

This can be done as Full–Class Practice or Pair Practice. If Pair Practice, have students report back to the class. For example:

"Bill's car is new."
"His house is old."
"His dog is little."

3. **Opposites**

a. Write the following sentences on the board and have students repeat after you. (Read from left to right.)

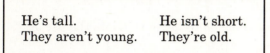

> He's tall.   He isn't short.
> They aren't young.   They're old.

b. Say a sentence with an adjective and have students give you a sentence with an opposite adjective. For example:

Teacher	Student
He isn't short.	He's tall.
She's single.	She isn't married.
My neighbors aren't noisy.	They're quiet.
My sister is young.	She isn't old.
My car is old.	It isn't new.
Henry isn't thin.	He's heavy.
The questions are easy.	They aren't difficult.

Text Page 36: *The Weather*

FOCUS

> Weather expressions

INTRODUCING THE MODEL

There are 8 weather expressions. Practice each one before going on to the next. (Note the use of thermometers to indicate *hot, warm, cool,* and *cold.*)

1. Have students listen as you read from the book or play the tape.
2. Have students repeat after you chorally and individually.
3. Practice conversationally by asking students: "How's the weather?" Students answer "It's sunny" chorally and individually.
4. Call on pairs of students to ask each other.
5. Practice the other weather expressions this way.
6. When students have learned and practiced all the vocabulary, ask "How's the weather today?"

WORKBOOK

Pages 32–34

EXPANSION ACTIVITIES

1. *Practice with Visuals*

   Use your own visuals or *Side by Side* Picture Cards 51–58 to review weather vocabulary.

   a. Point to visuals one by one and ask: "How's the weather?" Have students answer chorally and/or individually: "It's _____."
   b. Have students point to visuals and ask each other: "How's the weather?"

2. *Talk about the Weather*

   a. Teach the numbers 10–100. See the suggestions for teaching numbers on page 4 of this *Teacher's Guide.* These numbers are given on page 151 of the Student Text.
   b. Contrast difficult numbers. Put this list on the board:

A	B
13	30
14	40
15	50
16	60
17	70
18	80
19	90

Listening Practice: Say a number from column A or column B. Have students indicate the correct column by saying or writing *A* or *B*.

Pronunciation Practice: Have students say a number from column A or B. Other students indicate which is the correct column.

c. Ask students about the weather in different regions of your country or nearby countries: "How's the weather in _____ today?" "Is it sunny?"

d. Say the following temperatures in Fahrenheit and Centigrade/Celsius. Have students tell you if they are *hot, cold, warm,* or *cool.*

0°F	40°F	50°F
90°F	20°C	0°C

ON YOUR OWN: *A Long Distance Telephone Call*

FOCUS

- Review of weather expressions
- Review of yes/no questions and short answers

INTRODUCING THE MODEL

1. Have students look at the model illustration.
2. Set the scene: "Jim is on vacation in Miami, Florida. He's calling his friend Jack on the telephone. Jim is very upset."
3. With books closed, have students listen as you present the model or play the tape one or more times.
4. Full-Class Choral Repetition.
5. Have students open their books and look at the dialog. Ask students if they have any questions and check understanding of new vocabulary: *Hi, _____, This is _____ calling, Miami, on vacation, having a good time, having a terrible time, here, I'm sorry to hear that.*
6. Group Choral Repetition.
7. Choral Conversation.
8. Call on one or two pairs of students to present the dialog.
9. Pair Practice: Have students practice the model in pairs as you walk around the room listening and helping.

SIDE BY SIDE EXERCISES

The skeletal dialog on text page 37 is the same as the one on text page 36 with key words left out. Students use the dialog as a guide for the exercises that follow. In these exercises Student A pretends to be on vacation and is calling Student B. You can add realism to the dialog by bringing a telephone to class or by having each student pretend to hold a telephone receiver to his or her ear.

Example

> A. Hi, *(name)*. This is *(name)*. I'm calling from Switzerland.
> B. From Switzerland? What are you doing in Switzerland?
> A. I'm on vacation.
> B. How's the weather in Switzerland? Is it cool?
> A. No, it isn't. It's warm.
> B. Is it snowing?
> A. No, it isn't. It's raining.
> B. Are you having a good time?
> A. No, I'm not. I'm having a TERRIBLE time. The weather is TERRIBLE here.
> B. I'm sorry to hear that.

1. Do exercises 1 and 2 in class, either as Full-Class Practice or as Pair Practice.
2. Assign the third exercise for homework. Have students write a dialog using *weather* vocabulary about any vacation place they know. Allow students, if they wish, to expand the dialog with their own words and ideas. Have students present their dialogs in the next class.

READING: *Dear Mother*

FOCUS

Adjectives

NEW VOCABULARY

a few	for a few days	mother	sitting
as you can see	good	other	stomach
bored	having	problems	to be
but	hotel	raining cats and dogs	together
Dear _____,	in fact	repairman	toilet
doctor's office	looking out the window	right now	to tell the truth
food	Love _____,	See you soon	writing (to)

PREVIEWING THE STORY (optional)

Have students talk about the story title and/or illustrations. Introduce new vocabulary.

READING THE STORY

1. Have students read silently, or follow along silently as the story is read aloud by you, by one or more students, or on the tape.
2. Ask students if they have any questions; check understanding of vocabulary.
3. Check students' comprehension, using some or all of the following questions:

   a. Where are Ethel and Ralph?
   b. How's the weather at Sludge Beach?
   c. Is it raining?
   d. Are the children happy?
   e. What are they doing?
   f. Tell about the restaurants at Sludge Beach.
   g. Where's Ralph?
   h. Why?
   i. Tell about the other hotels at Sludge Beach.
   j. Is Ethel and Ralph's hotel beautiful and new?
   k. Ethel and Ralph are having a few problems on their vacation, but they're happy. Why?

CHECK-UP

True or False?

1. False
2. False
3. True
4. False
5. True
6. False

Listening

Have students complete the exercises as you play the tape or read the following:

Listen and choose the best answer.

1. How's the weather? (b)
2. Tell me about your hotel. (a)
3. How are the children? (a)
4. Tell me about your boyfriend. (b)
5. Tell me about your new apartment. (a)
6. How's your new car? (b)

WORKBOOK ANSWER KEY AND LISTENING SCRIPTS

Page 27   A.   MATCHING OPPOSITES

1. f
2. a
3. b
4. e
5. c
6. i
7. d
8. g
9. j
10. h

Page 27   B.   WHAT ARE THEY SAYING?

1. poor
2. short
3. thin
4. old
5. ugly
6. married

7. small
8. quiet
9. cheap

Page 28   C.   WHAT'S WRONG?

1. He isn't quiet.
   He's noisy.
2. It isn't cheap.
   It's expensive.
3. He isn't thin.
   He's heavy (fat).
4. She isn't ugly.
   She's pretty (beautiful).
5. He isn't short.
   He's tall.
6. They aren't young.
   They're old.

Page 28   D.   SCRAMBLED QUESTIONS

1. Is English difficult?
2. Are you tall?
3. Are they rich?
4. Is your apartment large?

5. Am I beautiful?
6. Is she rich or poor?/Is she poor or rich?
7. Are your neighbors noisy?
8. Are John and Mary married?/Are Mary and John married?

Page 30   F.   MARGARET'S PHOTOGRAPHS

1. Helen's car
2. Judy's bicycle
3. Mr. and Mrs. Pepper's cat
4. Patty's dog
5. Michael's boss
6. John's house
7. Mr. Sharp's piano
8. Peter's sink
9. Jim's guitar

Page 31   G.   WHAT'S THE WORD?

1. His
2. Her
3. Their
4. Her
5. Their
6. His
7. Her
8. His
9. Its

Page 31   H.   MEET FRED McQUEEN

1. Yes, he is.
2. No, he isn't.
3. No, he isn't.
4. No, he isn't.
5. Yes, he is.
6. No, he isn't.
7. Yes, it is.
8. No, it isn't.
9. No, it isn't.
10. No, it isn't.
11. Yes, they are.
12. No, they aren't.
13. Yes, he is.

Page 32   I.   LISTEN

Listen to the addresses of the buildings. Fill in the correct numbers on the buildings.

1. The movie theater is at 14 Main Street.
2. The cafeteria is at 19 Main Street.
3. The hospital is at 22 Main Street.
4. The library is at 27 Main Street.

5. The post office is at 28 Main Street.
6. The laundromat is at 31 Main Street.
7. The zoo is at 54 Central Street.
8. The supermarket is at 59 Central Street.

9. The restaurant is at 62 Central Street.
10. The bank is at 65 Central Street.
11. The night club is at 73 Central Street.

Answers

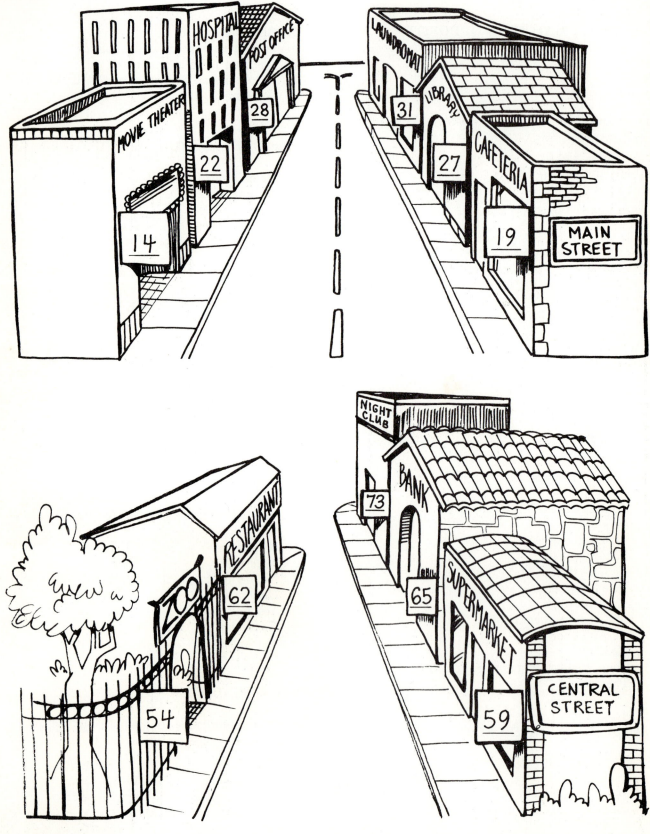

Page 33 J. THE WEATHER

1. It's sunny.
2. It's raining.
3. It's warm.
4. It's cold.
5. It's cool.
6. It's cloudy.
7. It's hot.
8. It's snowing.

Page 33 K. LISTEN

Listen to the temperature in Fahrenheit and Celsius.
Write the numbers you hear.

1. In Moscow, it's 34°F/1°C.
2. In Cairo, it's 86°F/30°C.
3. In Caracas, it's 93°F/34°C.
4. In San Francisco, it's 72°F/22°C.
5. In Paris, it's 41°F/5°C.
6. In Athens, it's 68°F/20°C.
7. In Tokyo, it's 57°F/14°C.
8. In Rio de Janeiro, it's 98°F/37°C.

Answers

1. 34°/1°   5. 41°/5°
2. 86°/30°   6. 68°/20°
3. 93°/34°   7. 57°/14°
4. 72°/22°   8. 98°/37°

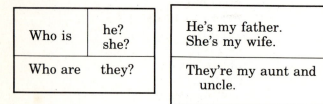
GRAMMAR

To Be

Who is	he? she?
Who are	they?

He's my father. She's my wife.
They're my aunt and uncle.

Present Continuous Tense

What's	he she	doing?
What are	they	doing?

He's She's	playing soccer.
They're	having dinner.

Prepositions of Location

in	He's in Paris. She's in her bedroom.
at	He's at the beach. They're at my wedding.
on	She's sitting on the sofa.
in front of	He's in front of his house.

FUNCTIONS

Asking for and Reporting Information

Who is he?
  He's *my father*.
What's his name?
  His name is *Paul*.
What's he doing?
  He's *standing in front of the Eiffel Tower*.

Inquiring about Location

Where is *he*?

Giving Location

He's in *Paris*.

NEW VOCABULARY

a lot of
angry
apartment building
argument
aunt
band
barking
bench
birthday party
brother-in-law
carpet
clock
corner
cousin
crying
daughter
Eiffel Tower
father
favorite
fireplace
grandfather
grandmother
grandparents
having dinner

husband
in front of
late
laughing
making noise
man
music
night
people
photograph
picture
politics
popular music
practicing
rock music
sentimental
sister-in-law
soccer
sofa
son
special
standing
Statue of Liberty
taking *her* photograph

talking (about)
teenagers
tired
uncle
vacuuming
violin
Washington
Washington Monument
wearing
wedding
wedding cake
wedding day
wedding gown
white
who
wife
woman
wonderful

getting to know each other
having a big argument
having a wonderful time
"the good old days"
What a *terrible night!*

Text Pages 42–44: *My Favorite Photographs*

FOCUS

- To be:
Who is he?	*Who are they?*
He's my father.	*They're my aunt and uncle.*

- Present continuous tense:
  What's she doing?
  She's sleeping.

- Prepositions of location:
in	*She's in her bedroom.*
at	*He's at the beach.*
on	*She's sitting on the sofa.*
in front of	*He's in front of his house.*

GETTING READY

Introduce the vocabulary for family members. Write on the board and have students repeat after you:

father	husband	son	brother	grandfather
mother	wife	daughter	sister	grandmother

INTRODUCING THE MODEL

1. Have students look at the model illustration.
2. Set the scene: "Two friends are talking."
3. Present the model.
4. Full-Class Choral Repetition.
5. Ask students if they have any questions; check understanding of new vocabulary: *who, father, photograph, Paris, standing, in front of, Eiffel Tower.*

   ### Culture Note

   The Eiffel Tower is a well-known landmark in Paris, France.

6. Group Choral Repetition.
7. Choral Conversation.
8. Call on one or two pairs of students to present the dialog.

   (For additional practice, do Choral Conversation in small groups or by rows.)

SIDE BY SIDE EXERCISES

Examples

> 1. A. Who is she?
>   B. She's my wife.
>   A. What's her name?
>   B. Her name is _____.*
>   A. Where is she?
>   B. She's in New York.
>   A. What's she doing?
>   B. She's standing in front of the Statue of Liberty.
>
> 2. A. Who is he?
>   B. He's my son.
>   A. What's his name?
>   B. His name is _____.*
>   A. Where is he?
>   B. He's in the park.
>   A. What's he doing?
>   B. He's playing soccer.
>
> *Students may use any name they wish.

1. **Exercise 1:** Introduce the new words *wife, Statue of Liberty*. Call on two students to present the dialog. Then do Choral Repetition and Choral Conversation Practice.

2. **Exercise 2:** Introduce the new words *son, soccer*. Same as above.

3. **Exercises 3–14:**

> **New vocabulary:** 3. *daughter* 4. *husband* 5. *sister, brother, fireplace*
> 6. *sofa* 7. *aunt, uncle, having dinner* 8. *cousin*
> 9. *grandmother, grandfather, wedding, crying* 10. *sitting, bench, birds*
> 11. *friend, bed* 12. *brother-in-law, Washington Monument*
> 13. *sister-in-law* 14. *birthday party*

Culture Notes

The Statue of Liberty (Exercise 1): This well-known statue is located in New York City's harbor. It is a symbol of welcome to immigrants to the United States.

The Washington Monument (Exercise 2): This famous landmark is in Washington, D.C., the U.S. capital. It is dedicated to the first president of the United States, George Washington.

Language Note

Exercise 7: The word *aunt* has two accepted pronunciations: [ænt] and [ant].

Either Full-Class Practice or Pair Practice.

ON YOUR OWN: *Your Favorite Photographs*

Have students bring in photographs from home. Bring several of your own. (Note that large photographs with a limited number of people in them work best.)

1. Introduce the example in the text. Call on a few students to read about the photograph of Carlos and his brother.

2. Tell about one of your photographs in a similar way.

3. Have students tell about photographs they have brought in.

WORKBOOK

Pages 35–38

Exercise Note

Workbook p. 38: Students practice word stress to indicate contrast.

EXPANSION ACTIVITIES

1. Practice with Visuals

Use newspaper or magazine photos of famous local, national, and international personalities. Have students follow the model on text page 42 to talk about the pictures. You may have to introduce some new vocabulary, especially for the answers to the question *What is he/she doing?*

a picture of a national politician

A. Who is she?
B. She's the (prime minister, queen, vice-president . . .).
A. What's her name?
B. Her name is _____.
A. Where is she?
B. She's in _____.
A. What's she doing?
B. She's _____ing.

2. Listening: Finish the Sentence

Make a statement about an activity using the vocabulary from text pages 42–44 and have students add any location they wish to the sentence. For example:

Teacher: She's washing her car . . .
Student: She's washing her car in front of her apartment building/in front of the garage.

Teacher: They're singing and dancing . . .
Student: They're singing and dancing at my birthday party/in the park.

Teacher: She's sleeping . . .
Student: She's sleeping in the bedroom/in the living room.

READING: *Arthur Is Very Angry*

FOCUS

To be: Review

NEW VOCABULARY

a lot of	having a big argument	night	tired
angry	late	people	vacuuming
barking	making noise	practicing	violin
carpet	man	rock music	What a terrible night!
clock	music	teenagers	woman

PREVIEWING THE STORY (optional)

Have students talk about the story title and/or illustration. Introduce new vocabulary.

READING THE STORY

1. Have students read silently, or follow along silently as the story is read aloud by you, by one or more students, or on the tape.
2. Ask students if they have any questions; check understanding of vocabulary.
3. Check students' comprehension, using some or all of the following questions:

   a. What's Arthur doing?
   b. Is he happy?
   c. Why not?
   d. What are the people in Apartment 2 doing?
   e. What's the man in Apartment 3 doing?
   f. What's the woman in Apartment 4 doing?
   g. What are the teenagers in Apartment 5 doing?
   h. What's the dog in Apartment 6 doing?
   i. What are the people in Apartment 7 doing?

CHECK-UP

Q & A

1. Call on a pair of students to present the model.
2. Have students work in pairs to create new dialogs.
3. Call on pairs to present their new dialogs to the class.

Choose

1. a	4. a
2. b	5. b
3. a	6. a

READING: *Tom's Wedding Day*

FOCUS

> To be: Review

NEW VOCABULARY

band	politics	wearing
corner	popular music	wedding cake
favorite	sentimental	wedding day
getting to know each other	special	wedding gown
grandparents	taking her photograph	white
laughing	talking (about)	wonderful
	"the good old days"	

PREVIEWING THE STORY (optional)

Have students talk about the story title and/or illustrations. Introduce new vocabulary.

READING THE STORY

1. Have students read silently, or follow along silently as the story is read aloud by you, by one or more students, or on the tape.
2. Ask students if they have any questions; check understanding of vocabulary.

CHECK-UP

Answer These Questions

1. She's standing in front of the fireplace.
2. She's wearing a beautiful white wedding gown.
3. He's taking her photograph.
4. She's crying.
5. They're standing in the yard, eating wedding cake and talking about politics.
6. They're sitting in the corner, drinking champagne and talking about "the good old days."

Listening

Have students complete the exercises as you play the tape or read the following:

Listen to the sentence. Are the people quiet or noisy?

1. They're listening to loud music. (b)
2. I'm reading. (a)
3. She's sleeping. (a)
4. The band is playing. (b)
5. Everybody is singing and dancing. (b)
6. He's studying. (a)

IN YOUR OWN WORDS

1. Make sure students understand the instructions.
2. Have students do the activity as written homework, using a dictionary for any new words they wish to use.
3. Have students present and discuss what they have written, in pairs or as a class.

WORKBOOK

Check-Up Test: Page 39

WORKBOOK ANSWER KEY AND LISTENING SCRIPTS

Page 35   A.   OUR FAMILY

1. husband
2. wife
3. son
4. daughter
5. mother
6. father
7. brother
8. sister
9. grandmother
10. grandfather
11. grandson
12. granddaughter

Page 36   B.   WHERE ARE THEY? WHAT ARE THEY DOING?

1. sitting
2. beach
3. swimming
4. standing
5. in front of
6. bench

Page 36   C.   OUT OF PLACE

1. cooking
2. sink
3. bank
4. sink
5. sleeping
6. neighbor
7. classroom
8. short
9. newspaper
10. birds
11. car
12. pretty
13. fat
14. cloudy

Page 37   D.   A LETTER FROM NEW YORK CITY

1. It's hot and sunny.
2. It's 80°F.
3. They're at the Statue of Liberty.
4. She's Michael's sister.
5. She's at the beach.
6. She's swimming.
7. He's Michael's brother.
8. He's in the park.
9. He's playing soccer.
10. He's in Aunt Martha and Uncle Charlie's apartment.
11. She's cooking a big dinner.

12. He's Michael's uncle.
13. He's singing and playing the guitar.
14. They're in front of the TV.
15. They're doing their homework.
16. He's Michael's cousin.

CHECK-UP TEST: *CHAPTERS 4–6*

Page 39   A.

1. in
2. beach
3. brushing
4. homework
5. sink
6. sofa
7. am
8. they
9. its
10. His
11. Her
12. Their
13. Who
14. grandmother
15. our

Page 39   B.

1. They're noisy.
2. He's handsome.
3. We're thin.
4. She's old.
5. It's easy.

Page 39   C.

1. Is it cold?
2. Is he tall?
3. Are you rich?
4. Are they cheap?
5. Are you married?

Page 39   DICTATION

Read or play the tape three times. Students listen the first time, write what they hear the second time, and correct their work the third time. Have students write this dictation on a separate piece of paper.

John isn't in his apartment. He's doing his homework in the library. John's sister and brother are busy. They're washing their car in the yard.

GRAMMAR

Prepositions

next to	It's next to the bank.
across from	It's across from the movie theater.
between	It's between the library and the park.
around the corner from	It's around the corner from the hospital.

There Is/There Are

Is there a laundromat in this neighborhood?
There's one window in the bedroom.
Yes, **there is.**   No, **there isn't.**

Are there any pets in the building?
There are two windows in the bedroom.
Yes, **there are.**   No, **there aren't.**

Singular/Plural

There's one bedroom in the apartment.

There are two bedrooms in the apartment.

Is there	**a** superintendent **an** elevator	in the building?

There are two	superintendents elevators	in the building.

FUNCTIONS

Inquiring about Location

Where's the *restaurant*?
Where is it?

Giving Location

It's next to *the bank.*
It's across from *the movie theater.*
It's between *the library* and *the park.*
It's around the corner from *the hospital.*

There's a *laundromat* on *Main Street,* next to *the supermarket.*

Attracting Attention

Excuse me.

Checking Understanding

Two bedrooms?
　Yes. That's right.

Asking for and Reporting Information

Is there *a laundromat* in *this neighborhood?*
Is there a *laundromat* nearby?
　Yes. There's a *laundromat* on *Main Street.*

Is there a *stove* in *the kitchen?*
　Yes, there is.
　No, there isn't.
Are there any *mice* in *the basement?*
　Yes, there are.
　No, there aren't.

How many *bedrooms* are there in *the apartment?*
　There are *two bedrooms* in *the apartment.*

Tell me, _____?

NEW VOCABULARY

across from
airport
all day
all night
almost
any
around the corner from
avenue
bakery
barber shop
beauty parlor
because
between
broken
building
bus station
bus stop
center
church
city
clinic
closet
clothing store
cockroach
convenient
department store
drug store
elevator
every

fire escape
fire station
floor
gas station
hole
how many
jacuzzi
landlord
mailbox
mall
men
mice
more than
near
nearby
neighborhood
next to
nice
now
open (adj.)
outside
owner
pet
place
police station
radiator
refrigerator
school
shoe store

shopping
shopping mall
sidewalk
some
store
stove
superintendent
tenant
there
there are
there's (there is)
though
town
toy store
train station
TV antenna
upset
walking
wall
washing machine
women

Excuse me.
in this neighborhood
Oh, good.
Oh, I see.
Tell me, . . .
That's right.

Text Page 50: *Where's the Restaurant?*

FOCUS

Prepositions: *next to, across from, between, around the corner from*

GETTING READY

1. Use your own visuals, *Side by Side* Picture Cards 9–17, 59, or refer to the illustrations on text pages 12 and 27 to practice locations in the community.

   Review: *restaurant, bank, post office, supermarket, movie theater, park, library, hospital*
   Introduce: *school*

2. Introduce the prepositions *next to, across from* and *between*. Use your students' names and locations in the classroom and say:

   (Bill) is *next to* (Mary).
   (Mary) is *across from* (Joe).
   (Jane) is *between* (Ted) and (Bob).

INTRODUCING THE MODEL

There are 4 model conversations. Introduce and practice each model before going on to the next. For each model:

1. Have students look at the model illustration.
2. Set the scene: "Two people are talking."
3. Present the model.
4. Full-Class Choral Repetition.
5. Ask students if they have any questions; check understanding of new vocabulary: *next to, across from, between, around the corner from.*
6. Group Choral Repetition.
7. Choral Conversation.
8. Call on one or two pairs of students to present the dialog.
   (For more practice, do Choral Conversation in small groups or by rows.)
9. Give students extra pronunciation practice with the final [z] sound in *where's*.
   a. Have students repeat: "Where's the restaurant?" Then cue substitutions, such as:
      park: "Where's the park?"
      church: "Where's the church?"
   b. Practice the final [s] sound in *it's*. Have students repeat "It's next to the bank." Cue substitutions as above.

SIDE BY SIDE EXERCISES

Examples

1. A. Where's the park?	2. A. Where's the bank?
B. It's next to the hospital.	B. It's across from the supermarket.

1. **Exercise 1:** Call on two students to present the dialog. Then do Choral Repetition and Choral Conversation Practice.

2. **Exercise 2:** Same as above.

3. **Exercises 3–8:**

> **New vocabulary:**   3. *church*   6. *police station, fire station*   7. *bus station*
> 8. *train station*

Use your own visuals, *Side by Side* Picture Cards 60–64, or the illustrations in the book to introduce these new words.

Either Full-Class Practice or Pair Practice.

WORKBOOK

Page 40

Exercise Note

Workbook p. 40: Students practice prepositions of place and locations in the community. For oral practice, have students ask and answer *where* questions about locations on the map. For example, "Where's the church?" "It's next to the hospital." "It's across from the park."

EXPANSION ACTIVITIES

1. Create a Street Scene with Your Students

Give visuals of the places in the community to 10 students. Use your own visuals, word cards, or *Side by Side* Picture Cards. Have students hold these visuals and stand in front of the class in 2 lines, to form 2 intersecting streets. For example:

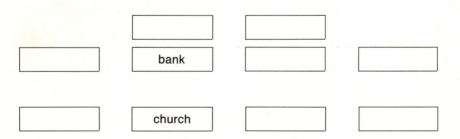

Call on pairs of students to ask and answer *where* questions about the locations in this *street scene*. For example:

"Where's the bank?"
"It's across from the church."

2. *Create a Street Scene on the Board*

On the board, create a simple street map showing 2 intersecting streets. You can tape visuals of locations to the board or you can write place names. For example:

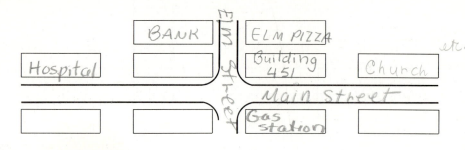

Call on pairs of students to ask and answer *where* questions about these locations as in Expansion Exercise 1 above.

3. *Game: What's the Building?*

Use the illustrations for exercises 1–8 on text page 50. (Students should ignore the questions and just look at the illustrations.) Have students look at these illustrations as you describe the location of different buildings. For example, "It's across from the library." Students then tell which building fits the location you described. Students can compete individually or in teams.

Teacher	Student
It's around the corner from the bus station.	the fire station
It's across from the restaurant.	the library
It's between the library and the bank.	the church
It's next to the post office.	the train station/the bus station
It's next to the park.	the hospital
It's around the corner from the bank.	the movie theater
It's across from the bank.	the supermarket
It's next to the police station.	the fire station

Text Page 51: *Is There a Laundromat in This Neighborhood?*

FOCUS

> There is/There's:
>
> *There's a bank on Main Street.*
> *Is there a bank on Main Street?*

GETTING READY

Teach these abbreviations:

> *St.* for Street, as in *Main St.* and *State St.*
> *Ave.* for Avenue, as in *Central Ave.*

INTRODUCING THE MODEL

1. Have students look at the model illustration.
2. Set the scene: "A man and a woman are talking. The man is in a new neighborhood. He's looking for a laundromat."
3. Present the model.
4. Full-Class Choral Repetition.
5. Ask students if they have any questions; check understanding of new vocabulary: *Excuse me, there's, in this neighborhood.*

   ### Language Note

   Many students have difficulty with the final *s* sound in the contraction *there's*, as in *There's a laundromat on Main Street.*

6. Group Choral Repetition.
7. Choral Conversation.
8. Call on one or two pairs of students to present the dialog.
   (For additional practice, do Choral Conversation in small groups or by rows.)
9. Point out the alternative expression *nearby*, given below the model. Have students practice the model with *nearby*.

SIDE BY SIDE EXERCISES

Examples

> 1. A. Excuse me. Is there a post office in this neighborhood?*
>   B. Yes. There's a post office on Main Street, across from the laundromat.
>
> 2. A. Excuse me. Is there a bank in this neighborhood?*
>   B. Yes. There's a bank on Central Avenue, around the corner from the post office.
>
> *Or: Is there a post office *nearby*?/Is there a bank *nearby*?

1. **Exercise 1:** Call on two students to present the dialog. Then do Choral Repetition and Choral Conversation Practice.
2. **Exercise 2:** Same as above.
3. **Exercises 3–8:**

> **New vocabulary:** 4. *gas station* 7. *drug store*
>
> Use your own visuals, *Side by Side* Picture Cards 66–67, or the illustrations in the book to introduce these words.

Either Full-Class Practice or Pair Practice.

WORKBOOK

Page 41

EXPANSION ACTIVITIES

1. *Create a Street Scene*

   Create a simple street map on the board (as in the Expansion Activities for text page 50). Tape visuals or write names on the board to show various locations on two intersecting streets. Have pairs of students role play the model conversation. Student A pretends to be looking for an unfamiliar location; Student B tells where it is.

2. *Pronunciation Practice*

   Have students practice saying these words with [s] sounds. The [s] sound may be at the beginning, middle, or end of the word.

snowing	statue	small	sister
sleeping	store	sofa	Albert's
supermarket	Stanley's	sunny	Alice
address	swimming	its	what's
station	school	Paris	listening
state	studying	fireplace	singing
street	standing	yes	baseball

3. *Game: Building a Town*

   a. Create a street map on the board showing 2 intersecting streets. You can tape visuals of locations to the board or you can write place names. Do NOT write all of the place names. For example:

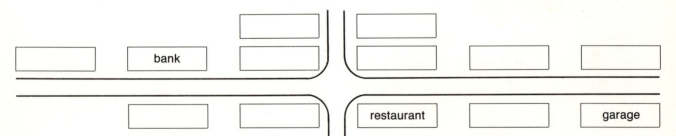

b. Give students cards with place names on them, tell students where the place is located on the board, and have students either tape the card on the board or write the place in the appropriate spot. For example:

(The teacher gives a card that says . . .)   (and tells students the directions . . .)

church	between the restaurant and the garage
post office	across from the bank
park	across from the church
fire station	next to the post office

The student places the card or writes the name in the appropriate spot.

Text Page 52

ON YOUR OWN: *What's in Your Neighborhood?*

In this exercise, students ask and answer questions about their own neighborhoods using the model conversation as a guide.

FOCUS

> Short answers with *there is*:
> *Yes, there is.*
> *No, there isn't.*

INTRODUCING THE MODEL

1. Have students look at the model illustration.
2. Set the scene: "A man and a woman are talking. The man is asking the woman about her neighborhood."
3. Present the model.
4. Ask students if they have any questions; check understanding of vocabulary.
5. Group Choral Repetition.
6. Choral Conversation.
7. Call on one or two pairs of students to present the dialog.

   (For additional practice, do Choral Conversation in small groups or by rows.)

SIDE BY SIDE EXERCISES

> **New vocabulary:**   *bakery, barber shop, beauty parlor, clinic, department store*
>
> Use your own visuals or *Side by Side* Picture Cards 69–74 to introduce these new words.

Have students work independently in pairs, asking and answering questions about each other's neighborhoods. (They can draw simple maps of their neighborhoods if they wish.)

WORKBOOK

Pages 42–44

Exercise Notes

Workbook p. 42:   You can practice Exercise D orally in the following ways: (a) Have students ask and answer additional yes/no questions about locations on the map. (For example, "Is there a gas station next to the school?") (b) Have students ask and answer *where* questions about locations on the map. (For example, "Where's the hospital?" "It's next to the church.")

Workbook p. 43:   In Exercise E, students practice prepositions of location. In Exercise F, students practice *there's* and *Is there?*

Text Page 53: *Is There a Stove in the Kitchen?*

FOCUS

> Review of: *Is there _____?*
>   *Yes, there is.*
>   *No, there isn't.*

GETTING READY

1. For an object that is in the classroom, say:

    "Is there a (window) in the room?"
    "Yes, there is."

    For an object that is not in the classroom, say:

    "Is there a (TV) in the room?"
    "No, there isn't."

    Do Choral Repetition and Choral Conversation Practice.

2. Ask about other objects.

INTRODUCING THE MODEL

There are 2 model conversations. Introduce and practice each separately. For each model:

1. Have students look at the model illustration.
2. Set the scene: "Someone is talking to a real estate agent about an apartment."
3. Present the model.
4. Full-Class Choral Repetition.
5. Ask students if they have any questions; check understanding of new vocabulary: *stove, nice, refrigerator, Oh, good., Oh, I see.*

    ### Culture Note

    Many people in the United States rent their apartments or houses. A person who rents an apartment is called a *tenant*. A person who helps someone to rent an apartment is called a *real estate agent* and works in a *rental office*. A person who owns the apartment building is called the *landlord*. A person who the landlord hires to live in the building and take care of it is called the *superintendent*.

6. Group Choral Repetition.
7. Choral Conversation.
8. Call on one or two pairs of students to present the dialog.

    (For additional practice, do Choral Conversation in small groups or by rows.)

SIDE BY SIDE EXERCISES

Examples

1. A. Is there a closet in the bedroom?
   B. Yes, there is. There's a very nice closet in the bedroom.
   A. Oh, good.

2. A. Is there an elevator in the building?
   B. No, there isn't.
   A. Oh, I see.

1. **Exercise 1:** Introduce the new word *closet*. Call on two students to present the dialog. Then do Choral Repetition and Choral Conversation Practice.

2. **Exercise 2:** Introduce the new words *elevator, building*. Same as above.

3. **Exercises 3–6:**

New vocabulary: 3. *window*   4. *fire escape*   5. *superintendent*
6. *jacuzzi*

Either Full-Class or Pair Practice.

EXPANSION ACTIVITIES

1. *Review House and Room Vocabulary with Visuals*

   Use your own visuals from magazines, *Side by Side* Picture Cards 1–8, or the illustrations on text page 8 to review house and room vocabulary.

   a. Hold up a visual and ask a question such as:

   > "Is there a window in the kitchen?"
   > "Is there a closet in this room?"

   Have students answer: "Yes, there is" or "No, there isn't."

   b. Have pairs of students practice asking and answering questions about the visuals.

   c. This is an excellent activity for introducing new household vocabulary. For example:

   > "Is there a *bed* in the bedroom?"
   > "Is there a *sink* in the bathroom?"
   > "Is there a *bathtub* in the bathroom?"

2. *My Ideal House*

   a. Have students work in pairs or in small groups to design their *ideal* house. They should draw a simple sketch and label the rooms and objects in the rooms.

   Introduce new vocabulary when necessary. For example: *patio, balcony, swimming pool, porch, study/den.*

   b. Have students ask about each other's ideal houses:

   A. Is there a _____ in the _____?
   B. Yes, there is.
   No, there isn't.

Text Page 54: *How Many Bedrooms Are There in the Apartment?*

FOCUS

Introduction of: *How many _____s are there?*
There are _____ _____s.

GETTING READY

1. Briefly introduce the final **s** for plural nouns. (Plural nouns are taught more fully in Chapter 8.) Have students listen and repeat after you:

   "one student–two students"
   "one window–two windows"
   "one book–two books"

2. Introduce: How many _____s are there?
   There are _____ _____s.

   a. Present this model and then do Choral Repetition and Choral Conversation Practice.

      "How many (windows) are there in this room?"
      "There are (4) windows."

   b. Ask other questions with *how many,* using people and objects in the room. Then have students ask each other questions.

INTRODUCING THE MODEL

1. Have students look at the model illustration.
2. Set the scene: "Someone is talking to a real estate agent about an apartment."
3. Present the model.
4. Full-Class Choral Repetition.
5. Ask students if they have any questions; check understanding of new vocabulary: *tell me, how many, there are, that's right.*

   ### Language Note

   In line 3 of the dialog, Speaker A repeats: "Two bedrooms?" In English it is common to repeat information with rising intonation to confirm what the other person has said.

6. Group Choral Repetition.
7. Choral Conversation.
8. Call on one or two pairs of students to present the dialog.

   (For additional practice, do Choral Conversation in small groups or by rows.)

SIDE BY SIDE EXERCISES

Examples

> 1. A. Tell me, how many windows are there in the living room?
>   B. There are three windows in the living room.
>   A. Three windows?
>   B. Yes. That's right.
>
> 2. A. Tell me, how many floors are there in the building?
>   B. There are five floors in the building.
>   A. Five floors?
>   B. Yes. That's right.

1. **Exercise 1:**   Call on two students to present the dialog. Then do Choral Repetition and Choral Conversation Practice.

2. **Exercise 2:**   Introduce the new word *floor*. Same as above.

3. **Exercises 3–6:**

> **New vocabulary:**   6. *washing machine*

Culture Note

Two and a half bathrooms: In the United States, many homes have full bathrooms (a toilet, a sink, a shower and/or bathtub) and half bathrooms (just a toilet and sink).

Either Full-Class Practice or Pair-Practice.

WORKBOOK

Page 45

EXPANSION ACTIVITIES

1. *How Many?*

   a. Write key words on the board or on word cards. For example:

books	students	chairs	rooms	shoes	people

   b. Have students use these as cues to ask questions with "how many." For example:

   > A. How many students are there in this room?
   > B. There are (18) students in this room.
   >
   > A. How many rooms are there in this building?
   > B. There are (25) rooms in this building.

   c. Have students think of other questions to ask people in the class.

2. *Geography Game*

a. Divide the class into two teams.

b. Ask questions about world geography using "how many." Give one point for each correct answer. The team with the most points wins the game. Possible questions include:

> How many continents are there?
> How many oceans are there?
> How many countries are there in Europe?
> How many countries are there in Asia/in North America/in South America . . . ?
> How many rivers are there in (country)?

ON YOUR OWN: *Looking for an Apartment*

FOCUS

- Review of: *Is there a _____ ?*
  Yes, there is.
  No, there isn't.

- Introduction of: *Are there any _____ s?*
  Yes, there are.
  No, there aren't.

- Review of: *How many _____ s are there?*
  There are _____ .

GETTING READY

1. Introduce:

   Are there any _____ ?
   Yes, there are.
   No, there aren't.

   a. Present these models, and then do Choral Repetition and Choral Conversation Practice:

      "Are there any (*students*) in the room?"
      "Yes, there are."

      "Are there any (*dogs*) in the room?"
      "No, there aren't."

   b. Ask about other objects.

2. Introduce these new words. Use your own visuals, or have students look at the illustration.

TV antenna	mailbox	landlord	cockroaches
roof	bus stop	tenant	broken windows
radiator	pets	mice	holes in the walls

ON YOUR OWN ACTIVITY

One student pretends to be looking for an apartment. Another pretends to be the landlord of the apartment building on text page 55. (In the United States it's very common for a prospective tenant to ask for information about the apartment and the building.)

1. **Questions 1–15:** Call on a pair of students to ask and answer each question. The student who asks the question is the prospective *tenant*. The one who answers is the *landlord*; that student answers by looking at the illustration on text page 55.

2. **Ask the Landlord Some Other Questions**

Now you pretend to be the landlord and have the class think of additional questions to ask you about the building and the neighborhood. For example, students can ask:

> "Is there a laundromat in the neighborhood?"
> "Is there a school nearby?"
> "How many supermarkets are there?"
> "Are there any parks nearby?"

3. **Are There Any Problems in the Apartment?**

The *prospective tenant* is looking for more information and asks various tenants in the building. Call on pairs of students to ask and answer questions 16–19. Encourage students to think of additional questions to ask the tenant.

WORKBOOK

Pages 46–49

> *Exercise Notes*
>
> Workbook p. 47:   You can give students additional oral practice with this exercise by having them look at the illustration and ask and answer questions about *Barbara's Living Room.*
>
> Workbook p. 49:   Students practice *there's, there are* and surprise intonation *(The bedroom has a sliding glass door?!).*

Text Page 57:

READING: *The New Shopping Mall*

FOCUS

There is/There are

NEW VOCABULARY

airport	men	owner	store
almost	more than	shoe store	town
because	now	shopping	toy store
center	open	shopping mall	upset
city	outside	some	women
clothing store			

PREVIEWING THE STORY (optional)

Have students talk about the story title and/or illustration. Introduce new vocabulary.

READING THE STORY

1. Have students read silently, or follow along silently as the story is read aloud by you, by one or more students, or on the tape.
2. Ask students if they have any questions; check understanding of vocabulary.

   Culture Note

   Shopping malls typically have large parking areas around a main building in which many stores are located. They are often located on the outskirts of cities and towns. In many places, the opening of these malls has reduced the business of older stores located in downtown areas.

3. Check students' comprehension, using some or all of the following questions:

   a. What's everybody talking about?
   b. Where's the mall?
   c. What's in the mall?
   d. Who isn't happy about the new mall?
   e. Why?

CHECK-UP

Choose

1.	c	3.	b
2.	b	4.	a

HOW ABOUT YOU?

Have students answer the questions, in pairs or as a class.

READING: *Jane's Apartment Building*

FOCUS

> Prepositions
> There is/There are

NEW VOCABULARY

all day	convenient	place	there
all night	live	sidewalk	though
because			walking

PREVIEWING THE STORY (optional)

Have students talk about the story title and/or illustration. Introduce new vocabulary.

READING THE STORY

1. Have students read silently, or follow along silently as the story is read aloud by you, by one or more students, or on the tape.
2. Ask students if they have any questions; check understanding of vocabulary.
3. Check students' comprehension, using some or all of the following questions:

   a. Where is Jane's apartment building?
   b. Why is Jane very happy there?
   c. What's across from the building?
   d. What's next to the building?
   e. What's around the corner from the building?
   f. Is Jane's neighborhood quiet? Why not?
   g. Is Jane upset about the noise? Why not?

CHECK-UP

Answer These Questions

1. It's in the center of town.
2. Across from her building, there's a laundromat, a bank, and a post office.
3. Yes, there is.
4. There's a lot of noise near Jane's apartment building because there are a lot of cars on the street and there are a lot of people walking on the sidewalk all day and all night.
5. She's happy there because it's a very convenient place to live.

True or False?

1. True
2. False
3. True
4. False
5. True

Listening

Have students complete the exercises as you play the tape or read the following:

What words do you hear?

Ex.   My neighborhood is very nice. There's a park nearby, and there's a drug store around the corner.   (a, c)

1. My neighborhood is very convenient. There's a bank around the corner and a restaurant across the street.   (b, c)
2. My neighborhood is very noisy. There's a gas station next to my building, and there's a police station across the street.   (a, b)
3. The sidewalks in my neighborhood are very busy. There's a school across the street and a department store around the corner.   (b, c)
4. There's a big shopping mall outside my city. There's a toy store and a movie theater in the mall.   (a, c)
5. There are many small stores in the center of my town. There's a bakery, a shoe store, and a clothing store.   (b, c)

IN YOUR OWN WORDS

1. Make sure students understand the instructions.
2. Have students do the activity as written homework, using a dictionary for any new words they wish to use.
3. Have students present and discuss what they have written, in pairs or as a class.

HOW ABOUT YOU?

Have students answer the questions, in pairs or as a class.

Page 40 A. WHERE IS IT?

1. next to
2. next to
3. across from
4. between
5. around the corner from
6. next to
7. between
8. across from
9. next to
10. around the corner from

Page 41 B. WHAT ARE THEY SAYING?

1. There's
   across from
2. Is there
   There's
   next to
3. there is, There's
   around the corner from
4. Is there
   There's
   between
   bank
5. Is there
   there is, There's
   Main, across from

Page 42 C. LISTEN

Listen to these sentences about the buildings on the map. After each sentence write the name on the correct building.

1. There's a fire station between the hospital and the bank.
2. There's a police station next to the bank.
3. There's a gas station across from the fire station.
4. There's a train station around the corner from the gas station.
5. There's a school next to the gas station.
6. There's a drug store next to the school.
7. There's a church across from the drug store.
8. There's a cafeteria around the corner from the church.
9. There's a restaurant across from the cafeteria.
10. There's a movie theater across from the train station.
11. There's a clinic across from the bank.
12. There's a post office next to the clinic.
13. There's a supermarket around the corner from the drug store.
14. There's a library across from the supermarket.

Page 42 D. YES OR NO

1. Yes, there is.
2. Yes, there is.
3. Yes, there is.
4. No, there isn't.
5. No, there isn't.
6. No, there isn't.
8. Yes, there is.
9. Yes, there is.
10. No, there isn't.

Page 45 G. WHAT ARE THEY SAYING?

1. Is there
2. there is
3. are there
4. There's
   there are
5. Are there
6. there aren't
   there's

Page 46 H. OUR APARTMENT BUILDING

1. roof
2. stove
3. radiators
4. fire escape
5. pets
6. closet
7. mailbox
8. mice
9. superintendent
10. broken

Page 47 I. BARBARA'S LIVING ROOM

1. Yes, there is.
2. Yes, there is.
3. Yes, there are.
4. No, there aren't.
5. Yes, there are.
6. Yes, there is.
7. No, there isn't.
8. Yes, there are.
9. No, there aren't.
10. Yes, there are.
11. Yes, there is.
12. No, there isn't.
13. Yes, there is.
14. There are three books on the sofa.
15. There are four photographs on the piano.
16. There are four pets in the room.
17. There are six cards on the piano.
18. There are two windows in the room.

Page 48 J. LOOKING FOR AN APARTMENT

1. Detroit
2. sunny
3. bedroom, bathroom
4. fireplaces
5. children

6. Boston
7. large
8. bedrooms

9. There's
10. school
11. aren't

12. Los Angeles
13. beautiful
14. There are bedrooms
15. building

8

GRAMMAR

Singular/Plural

[s]
> I'm looking for **a** jacket.
> Purple jacket**s** are very popular this year.

[z]
> I'm looking for **an** umbrella.
> Purple umbrella**s** are very popular this year.

[ɪz]
> I'm looking for **a** dress.
> Pink dress**es** are very popular this year.

I'm looking for	a	jacket. hat. blouse.
	a pair of	gloves. pants. shoes.

This/That/These/Those

> Is this your umbrella?
> That umbrella is brown.

> Are these your boots?
> Those boots are dirty.

Adjectives

> This is a purple jacket.
> These are green gloves.

FUNCTIONS

Offering to Help

May I help you?
Can I help you?
 Yes, please.

Expressing Want-Desire

I'm looking for *a jacket.*

I'm looking for *a brown briefcase* for *my husband.*

Describing

Here's a nice *jacket.*

But this is a *PURPLE jacket!*
But these are *GREEN gloves!*

That *umbrella* is *brown.*
Those *boots* are *dirty.*

Expressing Agreement

You're right.

Expressing Disagreement

I don't think so.

Asking for and Reporting Information

Is this your *umbrella?*
 No, it isn't.
Are these your *boots?*
 No, they aren't.

Inquiring about Certainty

Are you sure?

Expressing Certainty

I think *that's my jacket.*

Apologizing

I'm sorry.

Admitting an Error

I guess I made a mistake.

Attracting Attention

Excuse me.

Expressing Surprise-Disbelief

But this is a PURPLE jacket!

NEW VOCABULARY

belt
blouse
boot
boy
bracelet
briefcase
child
Christmas
clean (adj)
clothesline
coat
color
cotton
dirty
dress
dry cleaner's
earring
empty
exercise (n)
father-in-law
frustrated
getting dressed
gift
glasses
glove
hat
inexpensive

island
jacket
leather
looking for
lost and found
mitten
morning
mother-in-law
mouse
necklace
nothing
pair (of)
pajamas
pants
pen
pencil
person
plain
please
polka dot
polyester
popular
purse
raincoat
ripped
shirt
shoe

shop (n)
skirt
sock
something
sports jacket
stocking
striped
suit
sure
sweater
that
these
think
this
this morning
this year
those
tie
tooth
trouble
umbrella
vinyl
watch
work (n)
year

black

blue
brown
gray
green
gold
orange
pink
purple
red
silver
white
yellow

Can I help you?
good luck
having a difficult time
having a lot of trouble
I don't think so.
I guess I made a mistake.
May I help you?
Merry Christmas!
Oh.
That's okay.
You're right.

LANGUAGE NOTES

1. **Pronunciation of the plural ending:**

   a. When a noun ends in a voiceless consonant sound, the plural ending is pronounced [s]:

      [p] shops
      [t] students
      [k] books

   b. When a noun ends in a voiced consonant or a vowel sound, the plural ending is pronounced [z]:

      [b] jobs   [g] dogs   [l] girls   [n] pens
      [d] yards   [v] gloves   [r] mothers   [m] rooms

   c. When a noun ends in any of the following sounds, the plural ending is pronounced [ɪz], which forms an additional syllable on the end of the noun:

      [s] glasses   [š] dishes   [č] benches
      [z] exercises   [ž] garages   [ǰ] judges

2. **Indefinite articles *a/an*:**

   a. *a* before words beginning with consonant sounds: a book, a car

   b. *an* before words beginning with vowel sounds: an airport, an elevator

   c. *a* before *h,* when *h* is pronounced: a hole
       an before *h,* when *h* is silent: an honest man

Text Pages 62–63: *Clothing*

FOCUS

- Articles of clothing
- Plural of regular nouns: *a book–books, a car–cars, a class–classes*
- Irregular plurals: *a man–men, a woman–women*
- Indefinite articles: *a/an*

GETTING READY

Introduce the vocabulary on text page 62. Use the illustration in the book, your own visuals, or real articles of clothing.

1. Point to an article of clothing and say the new word several times. Whenever possible, also point to a student who is wearing that article of clothing.

2. Have students repeat the new word chorally and individually.

SINGULAR/PLURAL (text page 63)

This exercise gives students practice saying and writing the regular plural nouns that are introduced on text page 62.

1. Give examples of singular and plural nouns by pointing out objects in the classroom. For example: *a book–books, a window–windows.*

2. Introduce the 3 different pronunciations of the plural as they are shown on text page 63. Practice each final sound separately.

    a. Begin with the final [s] sound. Say the singular and plural form of each noun; then say the words again and have students repeat after you chorally and individually. Point out the articles *a* and *an*.

    b. Practice the words in the [z] column this way; then the words in the [ɪz] column.

3. Listening practice with books closed:

    a. Write on the board:

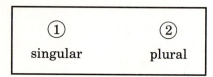

    Have your students listen as you read the nouns below. For each word, have students say "1" if they think the noun is singular, or "2" if they think the noun is plural:

    car, schools, bank, sock, class, classes, office, belts, book, umbrellas

b. Write on the board:

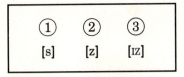

Have students listen as you read the plural nouns at the top of text page 63 in mixed-up order. For each noun have students say

"1" if they hear a final [s] sound;
"2" if they hear a final [z] sound;
"3" is they hear a final [ɪz] sound.

4. Practice forming plurals using the vocabulary on text page 62.

a. Make 3 columns on the board: [s] [z] [ɪz]

b. Say each noun on text page 62 and call on a student to give the plural form.

c. Then have the class tell you which of the 3 final sounds they hear. You write the singular and plural forms under the appropriate column on the board. Have students write these forms in the correct column on text page 63 or in their notebooks.

Answer key for text page 63

[s]	[z]	[ɪz]
hats	ties	watches
shirts	shoes	necklaces
jackets	earrings	blouses
belts	stockings	purses
pants	gloves	dresses
socks	umbrellas	glasses
bracelets	sweaters	briefcases
skirts	mittens	
coats		
suits		
raincoats		
boots		

5. Introduce irregular plurals. Point out the irregular plural nouns at the bottom of text page 63. Say the singular and plural forms and have students repeat after you. Practice by saying the singular form and have students tell you the plural form and vice versa.

WORKBOOK

Pages 50–52 (Exercises A, B, C, D)

EXPANSION ACTIVITY

Practice Singular/Plural

Point to articles of clothing that people in the class are wearing. Have one student tell you the name of that article of clothing. Have another student tell you the plural form of that word.

Text Page 64: *I'm Looking for a Jacket*

FOCUS

> • Singular and plural nouns (articles of clothing)
> • Colors

GETTING READY

Teach the colors at the top of the page. Use visuals or real objects and clothing in the classroom. As you say each new word, have students listen and repeat chorally and individually.

INTRODUCING THE MODEL

1. Have students look at the model illustration.
2. Set the scene: "A salesperson and a customer are talking in a department store."
3. Present the model.
4. Full-Class Choral Repetition.
5. Ask students if they have any questions; check understanding of new vocabulary: *May I help you? please, looking for, here's, this, That's okay, popular, this year.*
6. Group Choral Repetition.
7. Choral Conversation.
8. Call on one or two pairs of students to present the dialog.

   (For additional practice, do Choral Conversation in small groups or by rows.)

SIDE BY SIDE EXERCISES

Examples

> 1. A. May I help you?
>   B. Yes, please. I'm looking for a hat.
>   A. Here's a nice hat.
>   B. But this is a GREEN hat!
>   A. That's okay. Green hats are very POPULAR this year.
>
> 2. A. May I help you?
>   B. Yes, please. I'm looking for a blouse.
>   A. Here's a nice blouse.
>   B. But this is an ORANGE blouse!
>   A. That's okay. Orange blouses are very POPULAR this year.

1. **Exercise 1:** Call on two students to present the dialog. Then do Choral Repetition and Choral Conversation Practice.
2. **Exercise 2:** Same as above.
3. **Exercises 3–8:**

   > **New vocabulary:** 7. *polka dot* 8. *striped*

   Either Full-Class Practice or Pair Practice.

WORKBOOK

Page 52 (Exercise E)

EXPANSION ACTIVITIES

1. *Practice Colors*

   Point to articles of clothing or any item in the classroom. Have students tell you the color.

2. *Role Play: In the Department Store*

   With books closed, have students role play a dialog based on the model conversation on text page 64. Put these words on the board as a guide for students:

   A. May I . . . ?
   B. Yes, please . . .
   A. Here's . . .
   B. But . . .
   A. That's okay . . .

   Speaker A is the *salesperson* and Speaker B is the *customer*. Make word cards or visuals of articles of clothing with unusual colors or patterns. Call on pairs of students to role play the dialog using one of these visuals or word cards.

Text Page 65: *I'm Looking for a Pair of Gloves*

FOCUS

> *A pair of* with articles of clothing

GETTING READY

Introduce *a pair of* by pointing out examples in the classroom. For example:

> *a pair of pants*
> *a pair of shoes*
> *a pair of socks*

Have students repeat after you chorally and individually.

INTRODUCING THE MODEL

1. Have students look at the model illustration.
2. Set the scene: "A salesperson and a customer are talking in a department store."
3. Present the model.
4. Full-Class Repetition.
5. Ask students if they have any questions; check understanding of new vocabulary: *Can I help you? a pair of, these.*
6. Group Choral Repetition.
7. Choral Conversation.
8. Call on one or two pairs of students to present the dialog.

   (For additional practice, do Choral Conversation in small groups or by rows.)

SIDE BY SIDE EXERCISES

Examples

1. A. Can I help you?
   B. Yes, please. I'm looking
      for a pair of pants.
   A. Here's a nice pair of pants.
   B. But these are PINK pants!
   A. That's okay. Pink pants are
      very POPULAR this year
	2. A. Can I help you?
	   B. Yes, please. I'm looking
	      for a pair of earrings.
	   A. Here's a nice pair of earrings.
	   B. But these are BLACK earrings!
	   A. That's okay. Black earrings are
	      very POPULAR this year.

1. **Exercise 1:** Call on two students to present the dialog. Then do Choral Repetition and Choral Conversation Practice.
2. **Exercise 2:** Same as above.

3. **Exercises 3–8:**

> **New vocabulary:**   5. *pajamas*

Either Full-Class Practice or Pair Practice.

HOW ABOUT YOU?

Have students answer the questions, in pairs or as a class.

WORKBOOK

Page 53

EXPANSION ACTIVITIES

1. *Practice Clothing with Magazine Pictures*

   Bring magazine pictures of people to class. Give the pictures to students and have them describe what the person or people are wearing. This exercise can be done orally or in writing. You can also call on pairs of students to ask and answer questions about a picture.

2. *Guessing Game*

   a. Describe the clothing of someone else in the class. Have students listen and guess who you are describing. For example:

   > "She's wearing a green dress and a gold watch."
   > "He's wearing yellow socks."

   b. Call on students to describe the clothing of someone in the class. Have the other students guess who it is.

3. *Chain Game*

   In this game, students practice all the vocabulary for clothing.

   a. You begin the game by saying:

   > "I'm in the department store and I'm looking for a *(shirt)*."
   > (You can name any article of clothing you wish.)

   b. Have each student take a turn in which he or she repeats what the person before has said *and* adds an article of clothing. For example:

   > "I'm in the department store and I'm looking for a *(shirt)* and a *(pair of pants)*."
   > "I'm in the department store and I'm looking for a *(shirt), (a pair of pants),* and *(a watch)*."

READING: *Nothing to Wear*

FOCUS

Singular/Plural

NEW VOCABULARY

clean	empty	something
clothesline	getting dressed	sports jacket
dirty	morning	this morning
dry cleaner's	nothing	work
	ripped	

PREVIEWING THE STORY (optional)

Have students talk about the story title and/or illustration. Introduce new vocabulary.

READING THE STORY

1. Have students read silently, or follow along silently as the story is read aloud by you, by one or more students, or on tape.
2. Ask students if they have any questions; check understanding of vocabulary.
3. Check students' comprehension, using some or all of the following questions:

   a. Why is Fred upset?
   b. Is there a clean shirt in Fred's closet?
   c. Why not?
   d. Is there a sports jacket?
   e. Why not?
   f. Is there a pair of pants for Fred to wear?
   g. Why not?
   h. Is there a pair of socks?
   i. Why not?

CHECK-UP

Choose

1.	b	4.	b
2.	a	5.	a
3.	a	6.	b

Choose

1. c
2. c
3. a
4. d
5. b

Text Page 67: *Excuse Me. I Think That's My Jacket.*

FOCUS

> *This – That – These – Those*

GETTING READY

1. Introduce the word *this.*

   a. Hold up a book (or a pen or other object) and say: "*this* book."

   b. Give the book to several students; have each student repeat "*this* book" while holding the book.

2. Introduce the word *that.*

   a. Put the same book (used for *this*) some distance away from you and the students. Point to the book and say: "*that* book" chorally and individually.

   b. Have students point to the book and repeat: "*that* book" chorally and individually.

3. Introduce the words *these* and *those* the same way, using **several** books (or pens or other objects).

4. Put the following stick figures on the board to summarize the meanings of *this, that, these,* and *those.*

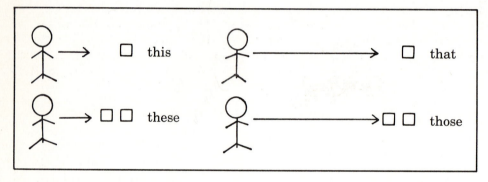

INTRODUCING THE MODEL

There are 2 model conversations. Introduce and practice each model before going on to the next. For each model:

1. Have students look at the model illustration.
2. Set the scene: "Two people are talking."
3. Present the model.
4. Full-Class Choral Repetition.
5. Ask students if they have any questions; check understanding of new vocabulary: *this, that, think, Hmm, I don't think so, Oh, You're right, I guess I made a mistake.*
6. Group Choral Repetition.
7. Choral Conversation.
8. Call on one or two pairs of students to present the dialog.

   (For additional practice, do Choral Conversation in small groups or by rows.)

SIDE BY SIDE EXERCISES

Examples

> 1. A. Excuse me. I think that's my pen.
>   B. Hmm. I don't think so. I think this is my pen.
>   A. Oh. You're right. I guess I made a mistake.
>
> 2. A. Excuse me. I think those are my pencils.
>   B. Hmm. I don't think so. I think these are my pencils.
>   A. Oh. You're right. I guess I made a mistake.

1. **Exercise 1:** Introduce the new word *pen.* Call on two students to present the dialog. Then do Choral Repetition and Choral Conversation Practice.

2. **Exercise 2:** Introduce the new word *book.* Same as above.

3. **Exercises 3–7:**

> **New vocabulary:** 2. *pencil*

Either Full-Class or Pair Practice.

4. **Exercise 8:** Have students use the model as a guide to create their own conversations, using vocabulary of their choice. (They can use any objects or articles of clothing they wish. Encourage students to use dictionaries to find new words they want to use.) This exercise can be done orally in class or for written homework. If you assign it for homework, you should do one example in class to make sure students understand what's expected. Have students present their conversations in class the next day.

WORKBOOK

Pages 54–56   *W 5 4 – 6*

Exercise Note

> Workbook p. 54: In Exercise G, students listen for the difference between *this* and *these* and for the final *s* in plural nouns. Have students do Exercise G orally for pronunciation practice. For additional oral practice with Exercise H, students can create their own sentences with *this* and *these.* For example, 1: *This book* is red. 2: *These questions* are easy.

EXPANSION ACTIVITY

Role Play: I Guess I Made a Mistake

Review the model conversations; then close the book and act out the conversations using real objects taken from the students in class, such as gloves, books, a handbag, or a wallet. Call on pairs of students to come to the front of the class. Give one student the object or objects; have the students act out the conversation.

Text Page 68: *Lost and Found*

FOCUS

> Review of *this, that, these, those*

INTRODUCING THE MODEL

There are 2 model conversations. Introduce and practice each model before going on to the next. For each model:

1. Have students look at the model illustration.
2. Set the scene: "People are at the lost and found department."
3. Present the model.
4. Full-Class Choral Repetition.
5. Ask students if they have any questions; check understanding of new vocabulary: *sure.*

   ### Culture Note

   Lost and Found: Many restaurants, large stores, and other public buildings in the United States have *lost and found* departments where people may turn in and pick up lost items.

6. Group Choral Repetition.
7. Choral Conversation.
8. Call on one or two pairs of students to present the dialog.
   (For additional practice, do Choral Conversation in small groups or by rows.)

SIDE BY SIDE EXERCISES

In these exercises, students use colors or adjectives of their own choice.

Examples

> 1. A. Is this your watch?
>   B. No, it isn't.
>   A. Are you sure?
>   B. Yes. THAT watch is
>   *(old)* and MY watch is *(new).*
>
> 2. A. Are these your glasses?
>   B. No, they aren't.
>   A. Are you sure?
>   B. Yes. THOSE glasses are
>   *(black)* and MY glasses
>   are *(brown).*

1. **Exercise 1:** Call on two students to present the dialog. Then do Choral Repetition and Choral Conversation Practice.
2. **Exercise 2:** Same as above.
3. **Exercises 3–5:**

   > **New vocabulary:**   5. *little boy*

   Either Full-Class Practice or Pair Practice.

4. **Exercise 6:** Have students create two dialogs, using the models as a guide and using vocabulary of their choice, one dialog using *this* and *that,* the other using *these* and *those.* Encourage students to use dictionaries to find new words they want to use. This exercise can be done orally in class or for written homework. If you assign it for homework, you should do one example in class to make sure students understand what's expected. Have students present their conversations in class the next day.

WORKBOOK

Pages 57–58

Exercise Note

Workbook p. 57: In Exercise L, students practice colors and the contrast of *this/that* and *these/those.* In Exercise M, students practice color adjective + noun.

EXPANSION ACTIVITIES

1. ***Pronunciation Practice:***   **[ɪ] [i]**
   The following groups of words have the sound [ɪ] as in *this* and [i] as in *these.* Write some or all of these words on the board and have students practice saying these sounds.

[ɪ] – "th<u>i</u>s"		[i] – "th<u>e</u>se"
s<u>i</u>ngle	s<u>i</u>nk	sh<u>e</u>
s<u>i</u>t	l<u>i</u>ving room	h<u>e</u>
m<u>i</u>stake	m<u>i</u>ss	sl<u>ee</u>ping
sw<u>i</u>mming	b<u>u</u>sy	r<u>ea</u>ding
b<u>i</u>g	s<u>i</u>ster	<u>ea</u>ting
<u>i</u>n	hosp<u>i</u>tal	f<u>ee</u>ding
th<u>i</u>n	<u>i</u>t's	<u>ea</u>sy
k<u>i</u>tchen	Sm<u>i</u>th	cl<u>ea</u>ning
		t<u>ee</u>th
		ch<u>ea</u>p
		b<u>ea</u>ch
		b<u>e</u>tw<u>ee</u>n

2. ***Listening Practice:***   **[ɪ] [i]**

   Write on the board:

   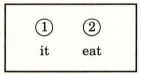

   ① it   ② eat

   Have students listen as you read the following words. For each word, have students say "1" if the word has the same sound as in *it,* or "2" if the word has the same sound as in *eat.*

   big, miss, he, cheap, sister, beach, she, thin, sink, teeth, swimming, easy

3. ***Role Play:*** **Lost and Found** *P. 68*

   Review the model conversations; then have students close the books and in pairs act out the conversations using real objects belonging to students, such as gloves, books, or a wallet.

READING: *Christmas Shopping*

FOCUS

Singular/Plural

NEW VOCABULARY

Christmas	good luck	plain
cotton	inexpensive	plastic
father-in-law	leather	polyester
frustrated	Merry Christmas!	trouble
gift	mother-in-law	vinyl

PREVIEWING THE STORY (optional)

Have students talk about the story title and/or illustration. Introduce new vocabulary.

READING THE STORY

1. Have students read silently, or follow along silently as the story is read aloud by you, by one or more students, or on the tape.
2. Ask students if they have any questions; check understanding of vocabulary.

CHECK-UP

Q & A

1. Call on a pair of students to present the model.
2. Have students work in pairs to create new dialogs.
3. Call on pairs to present their new dialogs to the class.

Listening   T69

Have students complete the exercises as you play the tape or read the following:

Listen and choose the word you hear.

1. These ties are fancy. (b)
2. This jacket is dirty. (a)
3. Excuse me. I'm looking for a cotton blouse. (a)
4. I'm wearing my new socks. (b)
5. Is this your boot? (a)
6. Purple umbrellas are very popular. (b)

WORKBOOK

Check-Up Test: Pages 59–60

WORKBOOK ANSWER KEY AND LISTENING SCRIPTS

Page 50   A.   WHAT ARE THEY WEARING?

1. hat	11. earring
2. glasses	12. necklace
3. shirt	13. blouse
4. tie	14. bracelet
5. jacket	15. skirt
6. watch	16. stocking
7. belt	
8. pants	
9. sock	
10. shoe	

17. coat	21. suit
18. glove	22. raincoat
19. purse	23. umbrella
20. dress	24. briefcase

25. sweater
26. mitten
27. boot

Page 51   B.   A/AN

1. a	7. a	13. an	19. an
2. a	8. an	14. a	20. a
3. an	9. an	15. an	21. a
4. a	10. a	16. a	22. an
5. an	11. a	17. a	23. a
6. a	12. an	18. an	24. an

Page 51   C.   SINGULAR/PLURAL

1. hats	10. benches
2. a glove	11. churches
3. a sweater	12. exercises
4. necklaces	13. a man
5. ties	14. women
6. dresses	15. a child
7. a class	16. mice
8. watches	17. a tooth
9. a beach	18. a person

Page 52   D.   LISTEN.

Listen to each word. Put a circle around the word you hear.

1. coats	9. necklaces
2. cars	10. earrings
3. umbrella	11. belt
4. exercise	12. watch
5. dogs	13. banks
6. shoe	14. houses
7. dress	15. jackets
8. restaurants	16. glove

Page 53   F.   WHAT'S IN MR. AND MRS. JACKSON'S CLOSET?

hat	pajamas	blouses
raincoat	pants	dresses
briefcase	mittens	purses
umbrella	gloves	belts
	socks	sweaters
	shoes	
	boots	

Page 54   G.   LISTEN

Listen to each sentence. Put a check next to the appropriate picture.

1. I'm washing these dresses.
2. She's reading these books.
3. I'm looking for this man.
4. He's cleaning this room.
5. He's fixing these refrigerators.

Answers

Listen and circle the correct word to complete the sentence.

1. This bicycle . . .
2. These exercises . . .
3. These apartments . . .
4. This car . . .
5. These women . . .
6. This necklace . . .
7. This house . . .
8. These shirts . . .

Answers

1.	is	5.	are
2.	are	6.	is
3.	are	7.	is
4.	is	8.	are

Page 55   I.   THIS/THAT/THESE/THOSE

1. This book is blue.
2. That book is red.
3. These earrings are gold.
4. Those earrings are silver.
5. This bicycle is green.
6. That bicycle is purple.
7. These pants are small.
8. Those pants are big.
9. This watch is cheap.
10. That watch is expensive.

Page 56   J.   SINGULAR → PLURAL

1. These hats are red.
2. Those skirts are short.
3. These watches are gold.
4. These necklaces aren't expensive.
5. Those dresses are beautiful.
6. These women are rich.
7. These are my children.
8. Those aren't your pencils.
9. Are those your gloves?
10. These aren't my socks.

Page 56   K.   PLURAL → SINGULAR

1. This bracelet is silver.
2. That exercise is easy.
3. Is this your friend?

4. Is that your book?
5. This is Sally's blouse.
6. This man is my neighbor.
7. This isn't my mitten.
8. That isn't my shoe.
9. That church is nearby.
10. That is George's pet.

Page 58   N.   ALICE'S PHOTOGRAPH

This	That
This	that
these	
this	those
these	those
These	That
this	

CHECK-UP TEST: *CHAPTERS 7–8*

Page 59   A.

1. pants
2. homework
3. There's
4. there isn't
5. How
6. woman
7. children

Page 59   B.

1. glove
2. briefcase
3. fire escape
4. house

Page 59   C.

1. It's next to the bank.
2. It's between the library and the park.
3. It's across from the movie theater.

Page 60 D.

1. This book is blue.
2. Those shoes are brown.
3. That car is expensive.

Page 60 E.

1. These dresses are beautiful.
2. Those aren't my pens.
3. Are those your briefcases?
4. These watches aren't gold.

Page 60 F. W 60

Listen to the beginning of each sentence. Circle the correct word to complete the sentence.

Ex. My teeth . . .

1. These gloves . . .
2. This house . . .
3. This bicycle . . .
4. These stockings . . .

Answers
1. are
2. is
3. is
4. are

GRAMMAR

Simple Present Tense

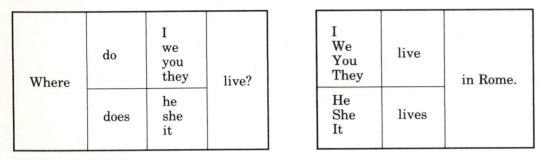

Where	do	I we you they	live?
	does	he she it	

I We You They	live	in Rome.
He She It	lives	

FUNCTIONS

Asking for and Reporting Information

What's your name?
  My name is *Antonio.*
Where do you live?
  I live in *Rome.*
What language do you speak?
  I speak *Italian.*
What do you do every day?
  I *eat Italian food.*

Tell me, _____ ?

NEW VOCABULARY

a little
afraid
beer
Berlin
Canadian
Chicago
culture
do
does
every day
forget
German
grocery store
Hong Kong
Italian

language
live (v)
London
Madrid
Moscow
New York City
only
Polish
program
Rome
sad
so
song
Spanish
speak

Stockholm
suburb
suburban
Swedish
telephone
time
Toronto
usually
visit
weekend
when
wine

life back in "the old country"

LANGUAGE NOTE

The third person singular of verbs in the simple present tense has an *s* ending; the other persons do not. Students typically need extra practice hearing and saying this *s* ending. (This ending has three pronunciations. These are treated in Chapter 12.)

CULTURE NOTE

Many cities and nationalities are introduced in this chapter. You can bring in a world map to show where these places are. You can also bring in pictures of different countries, people, and customs. If students have visited any of the cities mentioned in this chapter, they can tell about them.

Text Page 72: *Interviews Around the World*

FOCUS

- Simple present tense with the pronouns *I, we, you, they*

  To express a generally known fact:
  I live in Rome.
  I speak Italian.

  To express a habitual activity:
  Every day I eat Italian food.

- Questions with *where* and *what*

GETTING READY

1. Introduce yourself this way. Say:

   "My name is *(your name)*."
   "I live in *(city)*."
   "I speak *(native language)*."

2. Write the following categories on the board; under each one write the correct information about yourself:

Name	City	Language
(your name)	(your city)	(native language)
   ---

3. Repeat your introduction as in 1 above, then call on students to introduce themselves the same way. Add their information to the chart. (Leave the chart on the board—you will use it again for the Side by Side Exercises.)

INTRODUCING THE MODEL

1. Have students look at the model illustration.
2. Set the scene: "A TV reporter is interviewing somebody in Rome." (Use a world map to show where Rome, Italy, is.)
3. Present the model.
4. Full-Class Choral Repetition.
5. Write the information about Antonio on the board, under the same 3 categories: *Name, City,* and *Language*.
6. Ask students if they have any questions; check understanding of new vocabulary: *live, Rome, speak, Italian, language, tell me, every day, food, wine, songs.*
7. Group Choral Repetition.
8. Choral Conversation.
9. Call on one or two pairs of students to present the dialog.
   (For additional practice, do Choral Conversation in small groups or by rows.)
10. Practice the questions in the box; write them on the board. Say each question and have students repeat after you chorally and individually.

SIDE BY SIDE EXERCISES

In these exercises students pretend to be the people in the illustrations living in various countries around the world. Other students *interview* them using the questions in the box. You can add realism by having students pretend to hold a microphone as in a radio or TV interview.

Before doing each exercise, use the chart on the board to write in the new information for that exercise. Use a world map to show where the cities are. Your chart should look like this:

Name	City	Language
(your name)	(your city)	(your native language)
Antonio	Rome	Italian
1. Marie	Paris	French
2. Carlos	Madrid	Spanish
.	.	.
.	.	.
.	.	.

Introduce the vocabulary under the model: *coffee, tea,* and *beer.* Encourage students to use these words in place of *wine* when appropriate. For example:

3. "I drink German beer."
4. "I drink Japanese tea."

Examples

1. A. What's your name?
   B. My name is Marie.
   A. Where do you live?
   B. I live in Paris.
   A. What language do you speak?
   B. I speak French.
   A. Tell me, what do you do every day?
   B. I eat French food, I drink French wine (or tea/coffee/ beer), and I sing French songs!

5. A. What are your names?
   B. Our names are Sara and Mark.
   A. Where do you live?
   B. We live in London.
   A. What language do you speak?
   B. We speak English.
   A. Tell me, what do you do every day?
   B. We eat English food, we drink English tea (or wine/coffee/ beer), and we sing English songs!

1. **Exercise 1:** Introduce *Paris, French.* Call on two students to present the interview. Then do Choral Repetition and Choral Conversation Practice.

2. **Exercise 2:** Introduce *Madrid, Spanish.* Call on two students to present the interview. Then do Choral Repetition and Choral Conversation Practice.

3. **Exercises 3–6:**

> **New vocabulary:**   3. *Berlin, German*   4. *Tokyo, Japanese*   5. *London, English*
> 6. *Moscow, Russian*

Either Full-Class Practice or Pair Practice.

Exercise Note

Workbook p. 61:   In Exercise B, students practice asking and answering questions in the simple present tense with *he* and *she*. For oral practice, have students read their answers and practice the final *s* of each verb clearly.

EXPANSION ACTIVITIES

1. ***Practice* I *and* We *with Word Cards***

    Make up word cards with information about new people. On each card write a new name, city, and language. Have some students draw cards and pretend to be those people. Have other students interview them using the questions on page 72. You can do this as Full-Class Practice or Pair Practice.

    Some suggestions for word cards:

Mr. Tonetti Venice Italian	Juanita Bueno Aires Spanish	Mr. and Mrs. Schultz Bonn German

2. ***Practice* They *with Word Cards***

    Make word cards that show two or more people. Include their names, a city, and a language. Have students ask and answer about the people on the cards:

    > What are their names?
    > Where do they live?
    > What language do they speak?
    > What do they do every day?

    You can do this as Full-Class Practice or Pair Practice.

    Some suggestions for word cards:

Sara and Mark London English	Boris and Natasha Moscow Russian
Mr. and Mrs. Ono Tokyo Japanese	Carlos and Maria Madrid Spanish

3. ***Practicing* I: *Amnesia***

    Call on two students. Have Student A pretend to be in the hospital with amnesia, a condition that causes a person to forget things. Have Student B pretend to be a friend, relative, or a doctor. Have Student A ask the questions on text page 72 with *I*. For example:

    > "What's my name?"
    > "Where do I live?"

    Have Student B answer, using any information he or she wishes.

Text Page 73: *People Around the World*

FOCUS

> Simple present tense with *he* and *she*

INTRODUCING THE MODEL

1. Have students look at the model illustration.
2. Set the scene: "Two people are talking about Miguel."
3. With books closed, have students listen as you present the model or play the tape one or more times.
4. Full-Class Choral Repetition.
5. Put the following chart on the board and write the information about Miguel (note that language and nationality are different):

Name	City	Language	Nationality
Miguel	Mexico City	Spanish	Mexican

6. Ask students if they have any questions; check understanding of new vocabulary: *Mexico City, Spanish, Mexican, music.*
7. Group Choral Repetition.
8. Choral Conversation.
9. Call on one or two pairs of students to present the dialog.

   (For additional practice, do Choral Conversation in small groups or by rows.)

SIDE BY SIDE EXERCISES

Before doing each exercise, use the chart on the board to write in the new information for that exercise. Use a world map to show where the cities are. Your chart should look like this:

	Name	City	Language	Nationality
	Miguel	Mexico	Spanish	Mexican
1.	Anna	Athens	Greek	Greek
2.	Lee	Hong Kong	Chinese	Chinese
3.	Margarita	San Juan	Spanish	Puerto Rican
	·	·	·	·
	·	·	·	·
	·	·	·	·

Examples

1. A. What's her name?	3. A. What's her name?
B. Her name is Anna.	B. Her name is Margarita.
A. Where does she live?	A. Where does she live?
B. She lives in Athens.	B. She lives in San Juan.
A. What language does she speak?	A. What language does she speak?
B. She speaks Greek.	B. She speaks Spanish.
A. What does she do every day?	A. What does she do every day?
B. She eats Greek food, she reads Greek newspapers, and she listens to Greek music.	B. She eats Puerto Rican food, she reads Puerto Rican newspapers, and she listens to Puerto Rican music.

1. Model the questions in the box and have students repeat chorally and individually.

2. **Exercise 1:** Introduce *Athens, Greek.* Call on two students to present the dialog. Then do Choral Repetition and Choral Conversation Practice.

3. **Exercise 2:** Introduce *Hong Kong.* Same as above.

4. **Exercises 3–6:**

New vocabulary:	4. *Toronto, Canadian* 6. *Stockholm, Swedish*

Either Full-Class Practice or Pair Practice.

WORKBOOK

Pages 62–64 (Exercises B, C, D)

Exercise Notes

Workbook p. 63:   In Exercise C, students answer questions about themselves. Encourage them to use different verbs when answering question 4.

Workbook p. 64:   Students practice the 3rd person singular of the simple present tense.

EXPANSION ACTIVITIES

1. Pronunciation Practice

Practice the final *s* sound. Write on the board and have students repeat chorally and individually (read from left to right):

I live	he lives	she lives	I drink	he drinks	she drinks
I speak	he speaks	she speaks	I read	he reads	she reads
I eat	he eats	she eats			

2. Practice with Word Cards

Make up word cards with information about new men and women from different countries. Include the person's name, city, language, and nationality. Have students draw cards; then ask and answer questions about the person. Suggestions for word cards:

Olaf Stockholm Swedish Swedish	Raquel Rome Italian Italian	Rosa Cancun Spanish Mexican	Mrs. Yen Hong Kong Chinese Chinese

3. *Listening Practice:* **I or He?**

Have students listen as you read each of the words below. Have students say "he" (for 3rd person) if they hear a final *s* sound. Have students say "I" (for non-3rd person) if they do not hear a final *s* sound.

1.	eat	6.	read
2.	lives	7.	does
3.	drinks	8.	do
4.	listen	9.	thinks
5.	listens	10.	eats

4. *Dictation*

Read these sentences slowly and have students write them on a separate piece of paper. When you have finished you can collect them and correct them later; or write the sentences on the board and have students correct their own papers.

1.	He speaks English.	4.	She lives in Rome.
2.	She eats Italian food.	5.	He listens to music.
3.	He drinks coffee.	6.	~~She~~ sings songs.

They

5. *Talk about Students in the Class*

Use the questions in the box on text page 73 to answer questions about students in the class. You can begin by asking about one student; then call on pairs of students to ask and answer questions about someone in the class. Encourage students to use any vocabulary they wish to answer the last question, *"What does he/she do every day?"*

Text Page 74

ON YOUR OWN: *A Famous Person*

FOCUS

Review of the simple present tense

GETTING READY

Read the forms in the grammar boxes at the top of the page. Form sentences by reading from left to right. Have students repeat after you. For example:

(1)	(2)	(3)
I live.	Where do I live?	What do I do?
We live.	Where do we live?	What do we do?
.	.	.
.	.	.
.	.	.

ON YOUR OWN ACTIVITY

In this role play exercise, students pretend to be famous celebrities who are being interviewed on television. One student is the interviewer and asks the questions; another pretends to be the famous person and answers using any information he or she wishes.

1. For homework, have students choose a famous person and make up information about that person. Encourage students to use dictionaries to find new vocabulary. For example:

   1. Pélé
      Brazil
      Portuguese
      play soccer

   2. Princess Anne
      England
      English
      ride horses

2. In class the next day, call pairs of students to the front of the class; have one role play the famous person (using the information prepared at home) and another ask the questions. For example:

   A. What's your name?
   B. My name is Princess Anne.
   A. Where do you live?
   B. I live in England.
   A. What language do you speak?
   B. I speak English.
   A. What do you do every day?
   B. I ride horses.

3. After each interview, ask someone who watched it to *report* or tell about the famous person. For example:

   "Her name is Princess Anne.
   She lives in England.
   She speaks English.
   Every day she rides horses."

WORKBOOK

Pages 65–67

Exercise Notes

Workbook p. 65:   Students practice the simple present tense with all pronouns. For oral practice, have students read the story aloud, pronouncing the final s clearly when it is used.

Workbook p. 67:   These pronunciation exercises should be done as an oral activity. Students practice saying the sounds č as in children and š as in shirt. Make sure that they hear the difference between the č sound and the š sound. Have many students read the sentences in Exercise I aloud. For additional oral practice, students can ask and answer questions about the pictures. (For example, 1: "What's Charlie doing?" "Charlie is eating Chinese food.")

READING: *Mr. and Mrs. DiCarlo*

FOCUS

Simple present tense

NEW VOCABULARY

afraid	New York City	telephone
a little	only	time
culture	program	usually
forget	sad	visit
grocery store	suburb	weekend
life back "in the old country"	suburban	when

PREVIEWING THE STORY (optional)

Have students talk about the story title and/or illustrations. Introduce new vocabulary.

READING THE STORY

1. Have students read silently, or follow along silently as the story is read aloud by you, by one or more students, or on the tape.
2. Ask students if they have any questions; check understanding of vocabulary.

   Culture Note

   Many large, American cities have ethnic neighborhoods where many people of one nationality live (Chinese, Italian, Polish, Cuban, etc.). These neighborhoods often have grocery stores that sell ethnic food, as well as other businesses that provide services in the customers' native language. These communities often resemble neighborhoods back in the native country.

3. Check students' comprehension, using some or all of the following questions:

   a. Where do Mr. and Mrs. DiCarlo live?
   b. How much English do they speak?
   c. What language do they usually speak?
   d. What do they read?
   e. What do they listen to?
   f. Where do they shop?
   g. Who do they visit every day?
   h. What do they talk about?
   i. Who are Mr. and Mrs. DiCarlo upset about?
   j. Why?
   k. What does Joe read?
   l. What does he listen to?
   m. Where does he shop?

n. Who does he visit? What language does he speak?
o. When does Joe speak Italian?
p. Why are Mr. and Mrs. DiCarlo sad?

CHECK-UP

Answer These Questions

1. They live in an old Italian neighborhood in New York City.
2. He lives in a small suburb outside the city.
3. They speak a little English.
4. He speaks a little Italian.
5. They read the Italian newspaper.
6. He reads American newspapers.
7. They listen to Italian radio programs.
8. He listens to American radio programs.
9. They shop at the Italian grocery store around the corner from their apartment building.
10. He shops at big suburban supermarkets and shopping malls.

What's the Word?

1.	speaks	6.	speak
2.	shops	7.	visits
3.	read	8.	talks
4.	lives	9.	live
5.	listens to	10.	call

Choose

1. b
2. c
3. d
4. c
5. a
6. d

Listening

Have students complete the exercises as you play the tape or read the following:

Listen and choose the best answer.

1. What does she read?   (a)
2. What does she eat?   (b)
3. What do they watch?   (b)
4. What do they wash?   (a)
5. What do you sing?   (a)
6. What do you drink?   (b)

IN YOUR OWN WORDS

1. Make sure students understand the instructions.
2. Have students do the activity as written homework using a dictionary for any new words they wish to use.
3. Have students present and discuss what they have written, in pairs or as a class.

HOW ABOUT YOU?

Have students answer the questions, in pairs or as a class.

WORKBOOK ANSWER KEY AND LISTENING SCRIPT

Page 61   A.   INTERVIEWS AROUND THE WORLD

1. What's
2. name is
3. do you
4. live
5. What language
6. speak
7. do you
8. eat, sing

9. are
10. Our names
11. you live
12. We live
13. What, do you
14. speak
15. do, do
16. we drink, read

17. What are
18. Their names are
19. Where do
19. They live
21. What language do they
22. speak
23. do, do
24. they eat they drink

Page 62   B.   PEOPLE AROUND THE WORLD

1. His name is Frank.
2. He lives in Montreal.
3. Every day he plays the guitar and he sings songs.

4. What's his name
5. Where does he live
6. He speaks French.
7. does he do, reads and he listens to French music

8. Her name is Inga.
9. Where does, She lives in Stockholm.
10. does she speak, speaks Swedish
11. What does she do does exercises and she plays soccer.

Page 65   E.   MARIA'S FAMILY

2. live
3. speak
5. speaks
6. speak
7. sing
8. live

9. cook, clean
10. cooks, cleans
11. eat
12. read
13. drink, listen
14. read, reads
15. do
16. do

Page 66   F.   WRITE ABOUT MARIA'S FAMILY

1. She lives in London.
2. She speaks English and Spanish.
3. He speaks English.
4. They speak English and Spanish.
5. They sing English and Spanish songs.
6. She cooks lunch and dinner, and she cleans the house.
7. He cooks breakfast, and he cleans the yard.

Page 66   G.   LISTEN

Listen to the story. Write the missing words.

Every day I sit in the park. I read the newspaper, I play cards, I eat my lunch, and I listen to the radio. I'm not a busy person.

My friend Harry lives around the corner from my house. Every day Harry cleans his apartment, he plays the piano, he reads books, he does exercises, and he cooks. My friend Harry is a very busy person.

Answers
1. read
2. play
3. eat
4. listen
5. I'm
6. lives
7. cleans
8. plays
9. reads
10. does
11. cooks
12. is

Page 67   I.   LOUD AND CLEAR

1. Charlie, Chinese, beach
2. Natasha, station, Washington
3. children, watching, kitchen
4. Sharp, washing, shirt
5. teacher, bench, church
6. She's, English, shoes

GRAMMAR

Simple Present Tense: Yes/No Questions

Do	I we you they	go to Stanley's Restaurant?
Does	he she it	

Short Answers

Yes,	I we you they	do.
	he she it	does.

No,	I we you they	don't.
	he she it	doesn't.

Simple Present Tense: Negatives

I We You They	don't	like American food.
He She It	doesn't	

FUNCTIONS

Asking for and Reporting Information

What *do you do there?*
What kind of *food does Stanley cook on Monday?*
When *does he cook Japanese food?*

Do you *go to Stanley's Restaurant?*
   Yes, I do.
   No, I don't.
Does *Stanley cook Greek food on Tuesday?*
   Yes, *he* does.
   No, *he* doesn't.

Inquiring about Likes/Dislikes

What kind of *food* do you like?
Which *sports* do you like?

Do you like *comedies?*

Who is your favorite *actor?*
What's your favorite *food?*

Expressing Likes

I like *Chinese food.*

Expressing Dislikes

I don't like *American food.*

Complimenting

You *speak English* very well.

NEW VOCABULARY

active
adventure movie
afternoon
alone
ask
athletic
author
basketball
cartoon
city hospital
classical music
comedy
doesn't
don't
downtown
drama
during
elementary school
Ethiopian
evening
football
game show
garden
golf

hockey
Hungarian
important
international
kind(n)
like
movie
much
musical instrument
news program
novel
often
on
outgoing
poetry
science fiction movie
short story
shy
singer
sports
stay home
tennis

Thai
TV star
Vietnamese
volleyball
week
well (adv)
western
what kind of
why
why not
work (v)

Sunday
Monday
Tuesday
Wednesday
Thursday
Friday
Saturday

have time together
spend time

CULTURE NOTE

This chapter, like Chapter 9, has an international theme. Talk with your students about ethnic foods, customs, and clothing they know. They might also sing songs they know from different countries.

Text Page 80: *Stanley's International Restaurant*

FOCUS

- Simple present tense with *he*
- Days of the week: *on Monday*
- Yes/No questions with *does* and short answers: *Yes, he does. No, he doesn't.*
- Questions with *when* and *what kind of*

GETTING READY

1. Introduce the days of the week. Write them on the board or use word cards or a calendar. Say each word and have students repeat after you chorally and individually.
2. Review the nationalities: *Italian, Greek, Chinese, Puerto Rican, Japanese, Mexican, American.*

STANLEY'S INTERNATIONAL RESTAURANT

Text pages 80–82 are about a chef named Stanley and his restaurant, called Stanley's International Restaurant. For the Side by Side Exercises on these pages, students will need to look at the picture of Stanley's *menu,* which shows each day of the week with the type of food served on that day. You can have students look at the illustration on text page 80, or you can draw a simple version of Stanley's menu on the board.

There are 3 model conversations on text page 80, each followed by Side by Side Exercises.

INTRODUCING THE 1st MODEL

1. Have students look at Stanley's *menu.*
2. Set the scene: "Stanley's International Restaurant is a very special place. Every day Stanley cooks a different kind of food. On Monday he cooks Italian food. On Tuesday he cooks Greek food. On Wednesday he cooks Chinese food. On Thursday he cooks Puerto Rican food. On Friday he cooks Japanese food. On Saturday he cooks Mexican food. And on Sunday he cooks American food."
3. Present the model.

A. What kind of food does Stanley cook on Monday?
B. On Monday he cooks Italian food.
---

4. Full-Class Choral Repetition.
5. Have students open their books; check understanding of new vocabulary: *international, special, place, cook, kind, what kind of, does, on.*
6. Group Choral Repetition.
7. Choral Conversation.
8. Call on one or two pairs of students to present the model.

   (For additional practice, do Choral Conversation in small groups or by rows.)

SIDE BY SIDE EXERCISES

Examples

> A. What kind of food does Stanley cook on Tuesday?
> B. On Tuesday he cooks Greek food.
>
> A. What kind of food does Stanley cook on Wednesday?
> B. On Wednesday he cooks Chinese food.

1. **Tuesday:** Call on two students to ask and answer about Tuesday. Then do Choral Repetition and Choral Conversation Practice.
2. **Wednesday:** Same as above.
3. **Thursday–Sunday:** Either Full-Class Practice or Pair Practice.

INTRODUCING THE 2nd MODEL

1. Have students look at Stanley's menu.
2. Set the scene: "Somebody is calling Stanley's International Restaurant."
3. Present the model.

> A. Does Stanley cook Greek food on Tuesday?
> B. Yes, he does.

4. Full-Class Choral Repetition.
5. Have students open their books and look at the dialog. Ask if there are any questions.
6. Group Choral Repetition.
7. Choral Conversation.
8. Call on one or two pairs of students to present the dialog.
   (For additional practice, do Choral Conversation in small groups or by rows.)

SIDE BY SIDE EXERCISES

Examples

> A. Does Stanley cook Chinese food on Wednesday?
> B. Yes, he does.
>
> A. Does Stanley cook Puerto Rican food on Thursday?
> B. Yes, he does.

1. **Wednesday:** Call on two students to ask and answer about Wednesday. Then do Choral Repetition and Choral Conversation Practice.
2. **Thursday:** Same as above.
3. **Friday–Monday:** Either Full-Class Practice or Pair Practice.

INTRODUCING THE 3rd MODEL

1. Have students look at Stanley's menu.
2. Set the scene: "A customer is talking to a waiter at Stanley's International Restaurant."
3. Present the model.
4. Full-Class Choral Repetition.
5. Have students open their books and look at the dialog. Check understanding of *doesn't, when.*
6. Group Choral Repetition.
7. Choral Conversation.
8. Call on one or two pairs of students to present the dialog.
   (For additional practice, do Choral Conversation in small groups or by rows.)

SIDE BY SIDE EXERCISES

Students can ask about any food and any day. For example:

A. Does Stanley cook Mexican food on Tuesday? Sunday
B. No, he doesn't.
A. When does he cook Mexican food?
B. He cooks Mexican food on Saturday.

A. Does Stanley cook Puerto Rican food on Sunday?
B. No, he doesn't.
A. When does he cook Puerto Rican food?
B. He cooks Puerto Rican food on Thursday.

1. Call on two students to create a dialog. Then do Choral Repetition and Choral Conversation Practice.
2. Call on two other students to create a dialog. Then do Choral Repetition and Choral Conversation Practice.
3. Have pairs of students create 4 more dialogs. This can be Full-Class Practice or Pair Practice.

WORKBOOK

Pages 68–69

Exercise Note

Workbook p. 68: You can give students additional oral practice with this exercise by covering up the questions and having students ask and answer questions about *Franklin's International Night Club* based on the illustration.

EXPANSION ACTIVITY

Role Play: Calling Stanley's International Restaurant on the Telephone

The questions and answers on text page 80 can be reviewed through a *telephone conversation* in which students pretend to call the restaurant for information about Stanley's menu. Use the illustration of Stanley's menu on text page 80 or a simplified version on the board. Have one student pretend to work at the restaurant; have another student *call* for information.

Write this skeletal dialog on the board for students to use as a guide:

(ring, ring)
A. Hello, Stanley's International Restaurant.
    May I help you?
B. Yes, please. _____?
A. _____.
B. Thank you very much.
A. You're welcome.

In the blank lines, students can ask and answer questions such as:

"What kind of food does Stanley cook on *(Monday)*?"
"Does Stanley cook *(Greek)* food on *(Tuesday)*?"

FOCUS

- Simple present tense with *I, you,* and *we* (non-3rd person singular)
- Yes/No questions with *do* and short answers: *Yes, I do. No, I don't.*
- Questions with *when* and *what kind of*

GETTING READY

Briefly review Stanley's menu.

INTRODUCING THE 1st MODEL

1. Have students look at Stanley's menu.
2. Set the scene: "A TV reporter is interviewing somebody."
3. Present the model.
4. Full-Class Choral Repetition.
5. Ask students if they have any questions; check understanding of new vocabulary: *do, go, to, why, because, like.*
6. Group Choral Repetition.
7. Choral Conversation.
8. Call on one or two pairs of students to present the dialog.

   (For additional practice, do Choral Conversation in small groups or by rows.)

SIDE BY SIDE EXERCISES

Examples

---

1. A. Do you go to Stanley's Restaurant on Friday?
   B. Yes, I do.
   A. Why?
   B. Because I like Japanese food.

2. A. Do you go to Stanley's Restaurant on Saturday?
   B. Yes, we do.
   A. Why?
   B. Because we like Mexican food.

---

1. **Exercise 1:** Call on two students to present the dialog. Then do Choral Repetition and Choral Conversation Practice.
2. **Exercise 2:** Same as above.
3. **Exercises 3–4:** Either Full-Class Practice or Pair Practice.

INTRODUCING THE 2nd MODEL

Same as above. Check understanding of *don't, why not.*

SIDE BY SIDE EXERCISES

Examples

5. A. Do you go to Stanley's Restaurant on Monday?
   B. No, I don't.
   A. Why not?
   B. Because I don't like Italian food.

7. A. Do you go to Stanley's Restaurant on Wednesday?
   B. No, we don't.
   A. Why not?
   B. Because we don't like Chinese food.

1. **Exercise 5:** Call on two students to present the dialog. Then do Choral Repetition and Choral Conversation Practice.
2. **Exercise 6:** Same as above.
3. **Exercises 7–8:** Either Full-Class Practice or Pair Practice.

INTRODUCING THE 3rd MODEL

Same as above. Check understanding of *there.*

SIDE BY SIDE EXERCISES

Examples

9. A. What kind of food do you like?
   B. I like Vietnamese food.
   A. When do you go to Stanley's Restaurant?
   B. I don't go there.
   A. Why not?
   B. Because Stanley doesn't cook Vietnamese food.

10. A. What kind of food do you like?
    B. We like Ethiopian food.
    A. When do you go to Stanley's Restaurant?
    B. We don't go there.
    A. Why not?
    B. Because Stanley doesn't cook Ethiopian food.

1. **Exercise 9:** Call on two students to present the dialog. Then do Choral Repetition and Choral Conversation Practice.
2. **Exercise 10:** Same as above.

3. **Exercises 11–12:**

> **New vocabulary:** 9. *Vietnamese* 10. *Ethiopian* 11. *Thai* 12. *Hungarian*

Either Full-Class Practice or Pair Practice.

WORKBOOK

Page 70

EXPANSION ACTIVITIES

1. ***Students Talk about Themselves***

   Have students create conversations about themselves. Write the conversation cues below on the board as a guide. Call on pairs of students to ask and answer questions according to their own likes and dislikes.

   Conversation cues:

   > A. Do you go to Stanley's Restaurant on _____?
   > B. _____.
   > A. Why/Why not?
   > B. Because _____.
   >
   > A. What kind of food do you like?
   > B. _____.
   > A. When do you go _____?
   > B. I go _____/I don't go because _____.

   You can do this as Full-Class Practice or Pair Practice.

2. ***International Foods***

   If you feel it is appropriate for your class, name different kinds of *international foods* and have students tell you what kind of food each one is. For example:

Teacher	Student
tacos	Mexican
lasagna	Italian
chop suey	Chinese
sushi	Japanese
hot dogs	American
moussaka	Greek

   Have students tell the names of popular foods from their countries.

Text Page 82: *Stanley's International Restaurant (continued)*

FOCUS

> Simple present tense:
> • Practice with all pronouns
> • Questions with *what, when, why*

GETTING READY

Write the following verb forms on the board:

speak	speaks
eat	eats
drink	drinks
listen	listens

Make sentences with the *non-s* and *s* forms of each verb and have students repeat. For example:

"They speak."   "He speaks."
"I eat."   "She eats."

INTRODUCING THE MODEL

1. Have students look at the model illustration.
2. Set the scene: "People are talking about Stanley's International Restaurant."
3. Present the model.

> A. What do people do at Stanley's International Restaurant?
> B. On Monday they speak Italian, eat Italian food, drink Italian wine, and listen to Italian music.

4. Full-Class Choral Repetition.
5. Ask students if they have any questions.
6. Group Choral Repetition.
7. Choral Conversation.
8. Call on one or two pairs of students to present the model.
9. Give further practice with the model by calling on pairs of students to ask and answer about Friday and Sunday.

SIDE BY SIDE EXERCISES

Examples

> 1. A. Henry likes Greek food.
>   When does he go to Stanley's International Restaurant?
>   B. He goes there on Tuesday.
>   A. What does he do there?
>   B. He speaks Greek, eats Greek food, drinks Greek wine,
>   and listens to Greek music.
>
> 3. A. Mr. and Mrs. Wilson go to Stanley's International Restaurant
>   on Wednesday.
>   What kind of food do they like?
>   B. They like Chinese food.
>   A. What do they do there?
>   B. They speak Chinese, eat Chinese food, drink Chinese wine,
>   and listen to Chinese music.

1. **Exercise 1:** Call on two students to present the dialog. Then do Choral Repetition and Choral Conversation Practice.

2. **Exercise 2:** Same as above.

3. **Exercises 3–4:** Either Full-Class Practice or Pair Practice.

WORKBOOK

Pages 71–72

Exercise Notes

Workbook p. 71: For oral practice with Exercise D, have students read their answers, pronouncing the final *s* clearly when it is used.

Workbook p. 72: Students practice yes/no questions in the simple present tense with a contrast of 3rd person singular and 3rd person plural.

EXPANSION ACTIVITY

Talk about Local Restaurants

Have students ask each other about restaurants they go to. Write these question cues on the board as a guide:

> (Do/Does) _____ go to _____ Restaurant?
> When (do/does) _____ go there?
> What (do/does) _____ do there?

CLASSROOM DRAMA: *You Speak English Very Well*

FOCUS

Simple present tense: Short answers

In this exercise, students practice short answers in a playful context—one in which a teacher and two students are disagreeing.

1. Review the short answers in the boxes at the top of the page. Have students repeat after you. For example: "Yes, I do," "Yes, we do," "Yes, you do."

2. Have students listen and follow along in the text as you read the dialog or play the tape one or more times.

3. Check understanding of the new words *very well.*

4. Act out the drama with two of your most outgoing and playful students. You take the part of the teacher.

5. Have several groups of students act it out.

   You can *activate* this dialog at any future time by complimenting a student with, "You speak English very well!"

READING: *Every Weekend Is Important to the Franklin Family*

FOCUS

> Simple present tense

NEW VOCABULARY

afternoon	elementary school	important	spend time
alone	evening	much	stay home
downtown	garden	musical instrument	week
during			work

PREVIEWING THE STORY (optional)

Have students talk about the story title and/or illustrations. Introduce new vocabulary.

READING THE STORY

1. Have students read silently, or follow along silently as the story is read aloud by you, by one or more students, or on the tape.
2. Ask students if they have any questions; check understanding of vocabulary.
3. Check students' comprehension, using some or all of the following questions:

    a. Do the Franklins spend a lot of time together during the week?
    b. When do they spend a lot of time together?
    c. Where does Mr. Franklin work?
    d. Does he work on the weekend?
    e. When does he work?
    f. Where does Mrs. Franklin work?
    g. Does she work on the weekend?
    h. When does she work?
    i. Where do Bobby and Sally Franklin go to school?
    j. Do they go to school on the weekend?
    k. When do they go to school?
    l. Where does the Franklins' dog Rover stay?
    m. Does he stay home alone on the weekend?
    n. When does he stay home alone?
    o. What do the Franklins do on Saturday morning? on Saturday afternoon? on Saturday evening?
    p. What do the Franklins do on Sunday morning? on Sunday afternoon? on Sunday evening?
    q. Why is every weekend important to the Franklins?

CHECK-UP

Q & A

1. Call on a pair of students to present each model.
2. Have students work in pairs to create new dialogs.
3. Call on pairs to present their new dialogs to the class.

Answer These Questions

1. Yes, he does.
2. Yes, they do.
3. No, she doesn't.
4. No, they don't.
5. Yes, she does.
6. Yes, they do.
7. No, he doesn't.

Do or *Does*?

1. do
2. Does
3. Do
4. does
5. Does
6. do

Don't or *Doesn't*?

1. doesn't
2. don't
3. don't
4. doesn't
5. don't
6. doesn't

Listening

Have students complete the exercises as you play the tape or read the following:

Choose the best answer to finish the sentence.

1. A. Do I speak English very well?
   B. Yes, . . .   (a)

2. A. Does Mr. Miller live in Toronto?
   B. No, . . .   (b)

3. A. Does your brother work in New York?
   B. Yes, . . .   (b)

4. A. Do you and your wife clean the house together?
   B. Yes, . . .   (b)

5. A. Do your neighbors work in their garden?
   B. No, . . .   (a)

6. A. Does your grandmother talk about life back in "the old country"?
   B. Yes, . . .   (a)

7. A. Do you go to school on the weekend?
   B. No, . . .   (b)

8. A. Does she live in this neighborhood?
   B. No, . . .   (b)

READING: *A Very Outgoing Person*

FOCUS

Simple present tense

NEW VOCABULARY

active	often
athletic	outgoing
basketball	sports
movie	volleyball

PREVIEWING THE STORY (optional)

Have students talk about the title and/or illustration. Introduce new vocabulary.

READING THE STORY

1. Have students read silently, or follow along silently as the story is read aloud by you, by one or more students, or on the tape.
2. Ask students if they have any questions; check understanding of vocabulary.
3. Check students' comprehension, using some or all of the following questions:

   a. Is Alice an outgoing person?
   b. Where does she go with her friends?
   c. Is she popular?
   d. Does she like sports?
   e. Which sports does she play?
   f. Is she athletic?
   g. Does Alice stay home alone very often?
   h. Does she read many books?
   i. Does she watch much TV?
   j. Does she listen to music?
   k. Is she active?

IN YOUR OWN WORDS

1. Make sure students understand the instructions.
2. Have students do the activity as written homework, using a dictionary for any new words they wish to use.
3. Have students present and discuss what they have written, in pairs or as a class.

HOW ABOUT YOU?

Have students answer the questions, in pairs or as a class.

ON YOUR OWN: *Who Is Your Favorite . . . ?*

FOCUS

Use of the simple present tense to talk about personal likes and dislikes:

Do you like _____?
Yes, I do.
No, I don't.

Who ⎫
What ⎭ *is your favorite _____?*

My favorite _____ is _____.

What kind of _____ do you like?
Which _____ do you like?

I like _____.
I don't like _____.

ON YOUR OWN ACTIVITY

1. Go over the questions. Introduce new vocabulary:

   a. *movies, comedies (comedy), dramas, westerns, adventure movies, science fiction movies, cartoons*
   b. *novels, poetry, short stories (story), author*
   c. *TV programs, TV star, game shows, news programs*
   d. *classical music, popular music, jazz, rock music, singer*
   e. *sports, football, golf, hockey, tennis*

2. For homework, have students write answers to these questions. In the next class, have students ask and answer the questions. (They should not refer to their written homework when practicing.)

   This can be Full-Class Practice or Pair Practice.

WORKBOOK

Page 73
Check-up Test: Page 74

Exercise Note

Workbook p. 73: In Exercise H, encourage students to look up new words in the dictionary when writing about themselves.

WORKBOOK ANSWER KEY AND LISTENING SCRIPTS

Page 68 A. FRANKLIN'S INTERNATIONAL NIGHT CLUB

1. On Tuesday he plays Japanese music.
2. On Tuesday she sings Japanese songs.
3. On Wednesday he plays Mexican music.
4. On Thursday she sings Italian songs.
5. What kind of songs does Mary Franklin sing on Friday?
6. What kind of music does John Franklin play on Saturday?
7. Yes, she does.
8. No, he doesn't.
9. Does John Franklin play German music
10. Does Mary Franklin sing (anything but Greek) songs
11. Does Mary Franklin sing Russian songs
12. He plays Mexican music on Wednesday.
13. She sings French songs on Friday.
14. She sings Japanese songs on Tuesday.
15. does John Franklin play
    He plays Italian music on Thursday.
16. does John Franklin play
    He plays Greek music on Saturday.
17. does Mary Franklin sing
    She sings Mexican songs on Wednesday.

Page 70 B. WHAT'S THE WORD?

1. do
2. Does
3. does
4. do
5. does
6. does
7. Do
   do
8. does
9. do
10. do
11. do
12. Does
    does

Page 70 C. LISTEN

Listen to each question. Put a circle around the correct answer.

1. What kind of music does Mrs. Harris like?
2. Where do Gloria and Barbara study English?
3. Do Frank and Martha go to school?
4. Why do you go to Wilson's Department Store?
5. What does Mr. Larson do in the park?
6. Why do your aunt and uncle eat at Lee's Chinese Restaurant?
7. When does Mrs. Williams go to the bank?
8. What do the children do at the beach?
9. Does your sister do her homework?
10. When do you and your husband go to the supermarket?

Answers

1. a
2. b
3. c
4. c
5. a
6. c
7. a
8. b
9. a
10. b

Page 71 D. YES AND NO

1. doesn't drink
2. don't play
3. doesn't play
4. don't drink
5. doesn't clean
6. go
7. read
8. like
9. doesn't sleep
10. likes
11. don't wear
12. wears
13. doesn't feed
14. goes
15. doesn't speak
16. lives

CHECK-UP TEST: *CHAPTERS 9–10*

Page 74 A.

1. feeds
2. don't
3. does
4. play
5. drink
6. does

Page 74 B.

1. Where
2. What
3. When
4. Why
5. Does
   does
6. What

Page 74   C.

1. lives
2. does
3. cleans
4. plays
5. listens
6. reads
7. go

Page 74   D.

Listen to each question. Put a circle around the correct answer.

Ex.   What kind of songs does Carmen Jones sing?

1. Do Bob and Judy go to school?
2. When does Mr. Johnson go to the park?
3. What do you do at school?
4. Where do John's cousins live?
5. Why do you go to Mario's Italian Restaurant?

Answers

1. b
2. c
3. a
4. c
5. b

TEACHER'S NOTES

GRAMMAR

Object Pronouns

He calls	me him her it us you them	every night.

Have/Has

I We You They	have	brown eyes.
He She It	has	

Simple Present Tense: s vs. non-s Endings

I We You They	eat. read. wash.

Adverbs of Frequency

I	always usually sometimes rarely never	wash my car.

He She It	eats. reads. washes.	[s] [z] [ɪz]

FUNCTIONS

Asking for and Reporting Information

How often *does your boyfriend call you?*
  He calls me every night.

Does *Carmen* usually *study in her room?*
  No. *She* rarely *studies in her room.*
  She usually *studies in the library.*

Do you have *quiet neighbors?*

I'm a *teacher.*
I live in *Chicago.*
I have *a small house.*
I'm *married.*
I play *golf.*
I play *the piano.*
I usually *watch* TV and rarely *go out.*

Describing

We have noisy neighbors.
They have an old car.

My brother and I look very different.
I don't look like *my brother.*

My sister and I are very different.

I have *brown* eyes.
He has *blue* eyes.

I have *short, curly* hair.
He has *long, straight* hair.

I'm *tall* and *thin.*
He's *short* and *heavy.*

NEW VOCABULARY

after	get together	never
all the time	go out	news
always	grandchildren	newspaper reporter
baby	Hello.	often
both	him	rarely
boyfriend	Hollywood	say
bring	how often	scientist
candy	journalist	see
close (adj)	laboratory	sometimes
college	long	speak to
conversation	look like	straight
curly	lucky	them
escalator	magazine	travel
experiment	make	unfortunately
eye	month	us
famous	movie star	world

LANGUAGE NOTES

1. **Pronunciation**

   The <u>s</u> ending of the 3rd person singular in the simple present tense has three pronunciations:

   a. When a verb ends in a voiceless consonant sound, the ending is pronounced [s]:

   > [p] hel<u>ps</u>
   > [t] si<u>ts</u>
   > [k] thin<u>ks</u>

   b. When a verb ends in a voiced consonant or vowel sound, the ending is pronounced [z]:

   > [d] rea<u>ds</u>   [l] cal<u>ls</u>
   > [v] lo<u>ves</u>   [o] g<u>oes</u>
   > [n] liste<u>ns</u>

   c. When a verb ends in [s], [z], [š], [ž], [č], or [ǰ], the ending is pronounced [ɪz], which forms an additional syllable on the end of the word. For example:

   > [s] dan<u>ces</u>
   > [č] wat<u>ches</u>
   > [š] wa<u>shes</u>

2. **Spelling Rules**

   a. When a verb ends in the letters <u>s</u>, <u>sh</u>, <u>ch</u>, or <u>x</u>, add <u>es</u>. For example:

   > watch–watch<u>es</u>
   > wash–wash<u>es</u>
   > miss–miss<u>es</u>

   b. When a verb ends in a *y* that is preceded by a consonant, the *y* changes to <u>i</u> and <u>es</u> is added. For example:

   > stud<u>y</u>–stud<u>ies</u>

   c. The verb *go* is spelled *goes* in the 3rd person singular. The verb *do* is spelled *does* in the 3rd person singular.

Text Page 90: *How Often?*

FOCUS

- Introduction of object pronouns
- Review of possessive adjectives: *my, his, her, our, your, their*
- Introduction of time expressions with *every*

GETTING READY

Introduce the object pronouns.

1. Read the words in the grammar box and have students repeat after you chorally and individually.

2. Draw a face on the board and say: "This is George."

   Then say these sentences and have students repeat:

   > (Point to yourself.) "George likes *me.*"
   > (Point to a female student.) "George likes *her.*"
   > (Point to a male student.) "George likes *him.*"
   > (Gesture to everyone.) "George likes *us.*"
   > (Point to one student and say to *that* student) "George likes *you.*"
   > (Point to 2 students.) "George likes *them.*"

INTRODUCING THE MODEL

1. Have students look at the model illustration.
2. Set the scene: "Two friends are talking."
3. Present the model.
4. Full-Class Choral Repetition.
5. Ask students if they have any questions; check understanding of new vocabulary: *how often? boyfriend.*
6. Group Choral Repetition.
7. Choral Conversation.
8. Call on one or two pairs of students to present the dialog.

   (For additional practice, do Choral Conversation in small groups or by rows.)

SIDE BY SIDE EXERCISES

Examples

1. A. How often do you speak to your daughter?
   B. I speak to her every day.

2. A. How often do you write to your son at college?
   B. I write to him every week.

1. **Exercise 1:** Introduce the new expression *speak to.* Call on two students to present the dialog. Then do Choral Repetition and Choral Conversation Practice.
2. **Exercise 2:** Introduce the new word *college.* Same as above.

3. **Exercises 3–10:**

> **New vocabulary:** 2. *college* 3. *year* 4. *month* 5. *grandchildren*
> 7. *say, hello.* 8. *all the time*

Either Full-Class Practice or Pair Practice.

WORKBOOK

Pages 75–76 (Exercise A)

EXPANSION ACTIVITY

Students' Daily Activities

Have students talk about themselves and what they do every day (week, night, weekend, etc.).

1. Write these verbs on the board:

watch	read	drink	wash
sleep late	listen to	brush	call
study	eat	clean	speak
play			write

You may also want to include a list of adverbial phrases: *every* (*day, night, week, weekend, month, year, Monday, Tuesday*), and so forth.

2. Have students ask each other questions with *How often* and the list of verbs. Students should answer the questions as truthfully as possible.

Text Page 91: *She Usually Studies in the Library*

FOCUS

> • Simple present tense: contrast of *s* and *non-s* endings
> (See **Chapter Overview** for pronunciation of these endings.)
> • Adverbs of frequency
> (Percentage figures in the box at the top right of the student text page refer to amounts of time.)

GETTING READY

1. Form sentences using the *s* and *non-s* endings for each verb in the grammar boxes. For example, have students listen and repeat:

   "I eat – He eats."
   "I write – He writes."

2. Listening Exercise. Write on the board:

   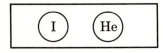

   a. Have students listen as you read these *s* and *non-s* verbs: *speaks, clean, watches, reads, eat.*
   b. For each verb, have students say "I" if they don't hear a final *s* sound; have students say "He" if they hear a final *s* sound.

3. Introduce the adverbs *always, usually, sometimes, rarely, never.*

   a. Have students read these words in the box at the top of the page.
   b. Say each word and have students repeat chorally and individually.
   c. Make a sentence with each word to show the meaning. Describe yourself. For example, describe your clothing habits:

      "I *always* wear shoes."
      "I *usually* wear a watch."
      "I *sometimes* wear gloves."
      "I *rarely* wear a hat."
      "I *never* wear a tie."

   d. For each adverb, call on a student to make a sentence describing himself or herself.

INTRODUCING THE MODEL

1. Have students look at the model illustration.
2. Set the scene: "Two students are talking about their friend."
3. Present the model.
4. Full-Class Choral Repetition.
5. Have students open their books and look at the model. Ask if there are any questions; check understanding of vocabulary.
6. Group Choral Repetition.
7. Choral Conversation.
8. Call on one or two students to present the model.
   (For additional practice, do Choral Repetition in small groups or by rows.)

SIDE BY SIDE EXERCISES

Examples

> 1. A. Does Sally usually eat lunch in the cafeteria?
>   B. No. She rarely eats lunch in the cafeteria. She usually eats lunch outside.
>
> 2. A. Does Andrew always watch the news after dinner?
>   B. No. He never watches the news after dinner. He always watches game shows after dinner.

1. **Exercise 1:** Introduce the new word *outside*. Call on two students to present the dialog. Then do Choral Repetition and Choral Conversation.

2. **Exercise 2:** Introduce the new word *news*. Same as above.

3. **Exercises 3–6:**

> **New vocabulary:**   3. *magazine*   5. *bring, candy*

Culture Note

> *The National Inquirer* (Exercise 3) is a weekly newspaper that contains sensational news stories and gossip about famous personalities. *Time* Magazine is a weekly news magazine with world news, national U.S. news, sports, movies, science, and other topical concerns. Both of these publications are very popular in the United States.

Either Full-Class Practice or Pair Practice.

WORKBOOK

Pages 76–78 (Exercises B, C, D, E, F)

Exercise Notes

> Workbook p. 76: In Exercise B, encourage students to look up new words in the dictionary when answering questions 10–14.
>
> Workbook p. 77: Students practice adverbs of frequency.

EXPANSION ACTIVITIES

1. Correct the Statement

Ask Student A to make a statement about Student B using *always, usually, sometimes, rarely* or *never*. For example:

> "Sam always cooks dinner."
> "Sally never studies English."

Student B must respond "That's true," or "That's not true."
If Student B responds "That's not true," then he or she must correct the statement. For example:

> "Sally never studies English."
> "That's not true. She always studies English."

If students need ideas, write key words on the board. For example:

wears _____	works _____
eats _____	watches TV _____
reads _____	dances _____
studies _____	drinks _____
sings _____	plays _____

2. *It's the Truth*

a. Write the following cues on the board:

always	
usually	
sometimes	
rarely	
never	

movies	TV	my parents
beach	visit	on Sunday
eat	bored	breakfast
homework	on Saturday	clean

b. Have students make true statements about themselves, using an adverb of frequency and one of the cues. For example:

"I always do my homework after dinner."
"I never watch cartoons on TV."
"My parents are rarely angry at me."

Text Page 92: *We Have Noisy Neighbors*

FOCUS

The irregular verb *have*

GETTING READY

Introduce the forms of the verb *have*. Read the forms in the box at the top of the page and have students repeat chorally and individually. For example:

"I have brown eyes."
"You have brown eyes."
"He has brown eyes."

Have students use other eye colors, depending on the color of their eyes and their friends' eyes: brown, blue, green.

INTRODUCING THE MODEL

1. Have students look at the model illustration.
2. Set the scene: "Friends are talking."
3. Present the model.
4. Full-Class Choral Repetition.
5. Have students open their books and look at the dialog. Ask students if they have any questions.
6. Group Choral Repetition.
7. Choral Conversation.
8. Call on one or two pairs of students to present the dialog.
   (For additional practice, do Choral Conversation in small groups or by rows.)

SIDE BY SIDE EXERCISES

Examples

1. A. Do you have a cat?
   B. No. I have a dog.
2. A. Do Mr. and Mrs. Hill have a new car?
   B. No. They have an old car.

1. **Exercise 1:** Call on two students to present the dialog. Then do Choral Repetition and Choral Conversation Practice.
2. **Exercise 2:** Same as above.
3. **Exercises 3–6:**

New vocabulary: 3. *escalator* 5. *straight, curly* 6. *baby, eye*

EXPANSION ACTIVITY

Class Interviews

1. Have students write a true statement about themselves using *have*. For example:

   "I have a new computer."
   "I have a large dog."
   "My house has a big yard."

2. Collect the statements and write them on the board or on a handout for the class.

3. Have students interview others in the class to find out "who has what." For example:

   A. Do you have a new computer?
   B. No, I don't.

   A. Does your house have a big yard?
   B. Yes, it does.

4. When students have completed their interviews, call on people to tell what they have learned about others in the class. For example:

   "Bob has a new computer."
   "Barbara's house has a big yard."

Text Page 93

ON YOUR OWN: *Very Different*

FOCUS

> • Review of *have*
> • Simple present tense: Contrast of *s* and *non-s* endings

INTRODUCING THE MODEL

There are 2 model conversations. Introduce and practice each model before going on to the next. For each model:

1. Have students look at the model illustration.
2. Set the scene:

   1st model: "A man is comparing himself to his brother."
   2nd model: "A woman is comparing herself to her sister."

3. Have students read silently, or follow along silently as the model is read aloud by you, by one or more students, or on the tape.
4. Ask students if they have any questions; check understanding of new vocabulary:

   1st model: *both, long, look like*
   2nd model: *journalist, go out*

Culture Note

> The suburbs are residential areas (either towns or small cities) that are located near large cities. In the United States, people who work in the city often live in the suburbs and commute to work.

ON YOUR OWN ACTIVITY

Model 1

In this exercise students say or write sentences in which they compare themselves to two people: someone they look like and someone they don't look like. Students can compare themselves to family members, friends, other students in class, or famous people.

1. Give some examples. Make sentences about yourself or read these:

   A. Who do you look like?
   B. I look like my father.
       We both have brown eyes and black hair.
       We're both tall and thin.

   A. Who *don't* you look like?
   B. I don't look like my mother.
       I have brown eyes and she has gray eyes.
       I'm tall and she's short.

2. Have students write similar sentences for homework and then present them in class the next day.

Model 2

In this exercise, students again compare themselves to someone else. Write on the board:

	You	Another Person
a. occupation?		
b. city?		
c. house? apartment?		
d. single? married? divorced?		
e. play a sport?		
f. play an instrument?		
g. on the weekend?		

The letter cues *a* through *g* on the board are suggested topics for writing these sentences. Introduce the new words *occupation, divorced.*

1. For homework, have students choose a person to compare themselves with, and then write at least five sentences. They can use all or some of the suggested topics.
2. Have students present their comparisons in the next class.

WORKBOOK

Pages 80–81

Exercise Note

Workbook p. 80: Exercise H is a dictation that reviews the vocabulary and structures taught in the chapter. Read the dictation or play the tape several times so that students can listen, write, and make any corrections.

EXPANSION ACTIVITIES

1. Carol and Jane

Practice the verb *have* and new vocabulary by telling this story.

a. Draw two people on the board:

Carol   Jane

Say: "Carol and Jane are sisters.
       Carol has short, curly brown hair.
       She has brown eyes.

       Jane has long, straight brown hair.
       She has brown eyes."

b. Point to Carol and ask students: "Tell me about Carol." Students answer using the picture as a cue.

c. Next, point to Jane and ask students: "Tell me about Jane."

d. Ask students: "Does Jane look like her sister?" "Does Carol look like her sister?" Students answer "Yes" or "No" and explain why. For example:

> "Carol has short hair, and Jane has long hair."
> "They both have brown eyes and brown hair."

2. **Practice with Pictures**

Bring magazine pictures of people to class. Have students describe the people in the pictures.

3. **Guessing Game**

Take turns describing someone in class. Others have to guess the student you are describing.
For example:

A. She has long, curly black hair. She has brown eyes.
B. It's (name)!

4. **True or False?**

Talk about the two brothers or the two sisters on text page 93.

a. Give the brothers and sisters names. Write them on the board or have the students write the names in their books. For example: *John* and *Bob, Jane* and *Sally.*

b. Make true and false statements about the brothers and sisters. Have students respond "That's true" or "That's not true." If students respond "That's not true," they must correct the statement. For example:

Teacher	Students
"Jane lives in Chicago."	"That's true."
"She's a journalist."	"That's not true. She's a teacher."
"Sally has a large house."	"That's not true. She has a large apartment."
"She plays tennis."	"That's true."
"John has brown hair."	"That's true."
"John is short and fat."	"That's not true. He's tall and thin."

c. Have students make true and false statments. Have other students answer as before.

READING: *Close Friends*

FOCUS

- Object pronouns
- Simple present tense
- Adverbs of frequency

NEW VOCABULARY

close	Hollywood	movie star	see
conversation	laboratory	newspaper reporter	think
experiment	lucky	often	travel
famous	make	scientist	unfortunately
get together			world

PREVIEWING THE STORY (optional)

Have students talk about the story title and/or illustrations. Introduce new vocabulary.

READING THE STORY

1. Have students read silently, or follow along silently as the story is read aloud by you, by one or more students, or on the tape.
2. Ask students if they have any questions; check understanding of vocabulary.
3. Check students' comprehension, using some or all of the following questions:

   a. Why are they so lucky?
   b. What does Greta do?
   c. When do they see her?
   d. What does she tell them about?
   e. What does Dan do?
   f. When do they see him?
   g. What does he tell them about?
   h. What do Bob and Carol do?
   i. When do they see them?
   j. What do they tell them about?
   k. Why don't they see Greta, Dan, Bob, and Carol very often?

CHECK-UP

What's the Word?

1. He	6. his	11. she	16. them
2. his	7. him	12. her	17. they
3. him	8. He	13. her	18. them
4. him	9. She	14. her	19. They
5. he	10. Her	15. Their	20. their

Listening

Have students complete the exercises as you play the tape or read the following:

Who and what are they talking about?

1. A. How often do you see her?
   B. I see her every day. (a)

2. A. How often do you wash them?
   B. I wash them every year. (b)

3. A. Do you write to him very often?
   B. Yes. I write to him every week. (a)

4. A. Is it broken?
   B. Yes. He's fixing it now. (a)

5. A. I see them all the time.
   B. That's nice. (b)

6. A. I rarely visit him.
   B. Oh, really? (a)

IN YOUR OWN WORDS

1. Make sure students understand the instructions.
2. Have students do the activity as written homework, using a dictionary for any new words they wish to use.
3. Have students present and discuss what they have written, in pairs or as a class.

Page 75   A.   WHAT ARE THEY SAYING?

1. you   2. him
3. it   4. them
5. her   6. me
7. us   8. them
9. it   10. them

Page 76   C.   WRITE AND SAY IT

1. feeds   7. goes
2. helps   8. dances
3. fixes   9. studies
4. talks   10. sits
5. brushes   watches
6. washes

Page 78   E.   WHAT'S THE WORD?

1. her   2. them
3. ~~it~~ him   4. him
5. them   6. it

Page 78   F.   LISTEN

Listen to each sentence. Put a check next to the appropriate picture.

1. I usually listen to her.
2. I never read it.
3. I help him when I'm at school.
4. I always sit with them.
5. I play with him every day.
6. I don't like them.

Answers

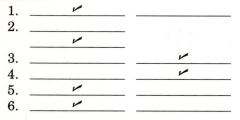

Page 79   G.   WHAT ARE THEY SAYING?

1. Does   2. don't
   have   have
   doesn't have   have
   has
3. has   4. have
   have
5. does   6. Do, have
   have   don't have
   has   have
7. Does
   have
   has

Page 80   H.   LISTEN: *My Grandmother*

Listen to the story. Write the missing words.

My grandmother has brown eyes and gray curly hair. She's short and heavy. She lives with us, and I'm very glad. Here's why I think she's wonderful.

When we go to parties, my grandmother always dances with me. When I talk to her, she always listens to me, and when my friends talk to her, she listens to them.

When I have difficult homework, my grandmother usually helps me. When I'm hungry, she always feeds me. When we eat together, she always talks to me, and when I'm upset she always sits with me.

My grandmother is rarely upset. When our clothes are dirty, she washes them. When the sink is broken, she fixes it. When my little sisters are noisy, she plays with them.

My grandmother is really wonderful.

Answers

1. has   13. feeds
2. hair   14. me
3. lives   15. eat
4. us   16. always
5. think   17. talks
6. go   18. sits
7. dances   19. me
8. talk   20. washes
9. listens   21. fixes
10. her   22. plays
11. them   23. them
12. helps

Page 80 I. YES OR NO

1. Yes, she does.
2. No, she doesn't.
3. No, she isn't.
4. Yes, she is.
5. Yes, she does.
6. No, she doesn't.
7. No, she isn't.
8. Yes, she does.
9. No, she isn't.
10. Yes, she is.

Page 81 K. WHAT'S THE WORD?

1. to
2. with
3. with
4. to
5. in
6. about
7. on
8. to
9. at
10. in
11. to
12. for
13. at
14. of
15. on, in
16. to, on

GRAMMAR

Simple Present Tense

I always **cry** when I'm sad.
I never **wash** the dishes in the bathtub.

Present Continuous Tense

I'm crying because I'm sad.
I'm washing the dishes in the bathtub today.

Adjectives

I'm	angry.	hot.	sick.
	cold.	hungry.	thirsty.
	embarrassed.	nervous.	tired.
	happy.	sad.	

FUNCTIONS

Asking for and Reporting Information

Why *are you crying?*
 I'm crying because *I'm sad.*

What *are you doing?*
 I'm *washing the dishes in the bathtub.*

Do you usually *wash the dishes in the bathtub?*

My *sink* is broken.

Describing Feelings-Emotions

I'm *angry/cold/embarrassed/happy/hot/
 hungry/nervous/sad/sick/thirsty/tired.*

When I'm *nervous* I *bite my nails.*

Expressing Surprise-Disbelief

That's strange!

Sympathizing

I'm sorry to hear that.

NEW VOCABULARY

angry
answer (v)
back and forth
bad
bathtub
bite (v)
blush
bus
business
by
candlelight
cold
computer
computer programmer
custodian
deliver
direct (v)
dish
doctor
drive
early
embarrassed
employee

energetic
flu
happy
hard (adv)
hitchhike
hot
hungry
insurance company
job
lamp
letter
mail
mail carrier
nails
nervous
nobody
office
operate
out
perspire
police officer
receptionist
ride (v)

rush
sad
school bus
secretary
shiver
shout
sick
staff
take *the bus*
thirsty
tired
traffic
truck
type
unusual
yawn

as a result
have a bad day
it's snowing very hard
on strike
That's strange!

Text Page 98: *I Always Cry When I'm Sad*

FOCUS

- Contrast of the simple present and present continuous tenses: *I'm smiling. / I always smile.*
- *Why* questions with the present continuous tense
- Adjectives describing emotional and physical states

GETTING READY

1. Introduce these new words. Use your own visuals, *Side by Side* Picture Cards 75–85, or the illustrations on text page 99:

nervous	sick	thirsty
sad	cold	angry
happy	hot	embarrassed
tired	hungry	

   a. For each word, point to the visual and say the word one or more times. Act out the meaning whenever possible.

   b. Have students repeat chorally and individually.

   c. After introducing all the words, point to each visual and have students tell you the word.

2. Review and contrast present continuous and simple present tense forms.

   a. Write on the board:

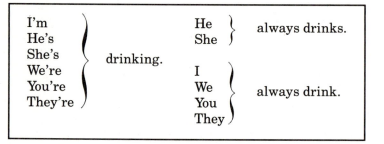

   b. Make sentences using these forms. Have students repeat chorally. For example:

   "He's drinking."   "He always drinks."

   c. Do the same with the verbs *go* and *study*.

INTRODUCING THE MODEL

1. Have students look at the illustration.
2. Set the scene: "Two people are talking."
3. Present the model.
4. Full-Class Choral Repetition.
5. Ask students if they have any questions; check understanding of vocabulary.
6. Group Choral Repetition.
7. Choral Conversation.

8. Call on one or two pairs of students to present the dialog.
   (For additional practice, do Choral Conversation in small groups or by rows.)
9. Practice the model with other pronouns. Substitute *she*, *he*, and *they*. Put on the board:

she   he   they

For each pronoun, have students listen, repeat, and practice as usual.

Examples

she	Why is she crying? She's crying because she's sad. She always cries when she's sad.
he	Why is he crying? He's crying because he's sad. He always cries when he's sad.
they	Why are they crying? They're crying because they're sad. They always cry when they're sad.

SIDE BY SIDE EXERCISES

Examples

1. A. Why are you smiling?
   B. I'm smiling because I'm happy.
      I always smile when I'm happy.

2. A. Why is he shouting?
   B. He's shouting because he's angry.
      He always shouts when he's angry.

In the following exercises, use the illustrations in the text or *Side by Side* Picture Cards 86–93 to introduce the new vocabulary.

1. **Exercise 1:** Introduce the new word *smile*. Call on two students to present the dialog. Then do Choral Repetition and Choral Conversation Practice.
2. **Exercise 2:** Introduce the new word *shout*. Same as above.
3. **Exercises 3–10:**

> **New vocabulary:**   3. *bite nails*   6. *doctor*   7. *shiver*   8. *perspire*
>   9. *yawn*   10. *blush*

Either Full-Class Practice or Pair Practice.

WORKBOOK

Pages 82–85

Exercise Note

Workbook p. 84: Students practice the contrast of the simple present and present continuous tenses.

EXPANSION ACTIVITY

Act It Out!

1. Make word cards for the following actions:

cry	eat	bite nails	perspire
smile	yawn	drink	blush

2. Have students take a word card *without showing it to anyone.*
3. Have each student act out the action on his or her word card.
4. Then call on pairs of students to create conversations like the ones on text page 98.

ON YOUR OWN: *What Do You Do When You're Nervous?*

FOCUS

> Students describe how they usually react to emotional states. For example:
>
> *When I'm nervous I bite my nails.*
> *When I'm thirsty I drink tea.*

GETTING READY

1. Present the following model:

> A. What do you do when you're nervous?
> B. When I'm nervous I *walk back and forth.*

2. Full-Class Choral Repetition.
3. Group Choral Repetition.
4. Choral Conversation.
5. Call on one or two pairs of students to practice the dialog.

   Culture Note

   In these exercises, students tell how they personally react to different emotional and physical states. You may want to discuss cultural differences in these reactions. For example, a common reaction to angry feelings in one culture may be shouting; in another it may be silence. You may also want to discuss differences in male and female expression of emotion. For example, in one culture, men and women may often cry when they are sad; in another culture, men may not usually cry.

6. Substitute the word *perspire* for *back and forth* and practice as above.
7. Next substitute *bite my nails* and practice as above.
8. Then ask students: "What do *you* do when you're nervous?" Have students answer using any vocabulary they wish.

ON YOUR OWN ACTIVITY

1. For homework, have students write exercises 2–11, using exercise 1 as a guide. Encourage students to use dictionaries to find new words they need to describe themselves.
2. The next day in class, call on pairs of students to ask and answer:

> A. What do you do when you're _____?
> B. When I'm _____ I _____.

Students shouldn't refer to their written homework when practicing.

Examples

> 2. A. What do you do when you're sad?
>   B. When I'm sad I cry.
>   (or "When I'm sad I go to my room.")
>
> 3. A. What do you do when you're happy?
>   B. When I'm happy I smile.
>   (or "When I'm happy I sing Irish songs.")

EXPANSION ACTIVITIES

1. Review Vocabulary with Visuals

Use your own visuals or *Side by Side* Picture Cards 75–93 to review the vocabulary on text pages 98 and 99.

a. Point to a visual; ask a *Yes/No* question.

b. Have students answer "Yes" or "No." If the answer is "No," have them give the correct information.

c. Examples:

| "Is he happy?" | "Is he smiling?" | "Is she smiling?" | "Is she happy?" |
| "Yes." | "Yes." | "No. She's crying." | "No. She's sad." |

2. Sentence Game

Write answers for exercises 1–11 on cards. You can use your students' homework answers or write new ones. Cut each card in half. For example:

> When I'm happy   I tell jokes.

Mix up all these cards and have students put them back together to make meaningful sentences. Have students try new combinations to see how many sentences are possible.

3. Talking about Yourself and Others

a. Have students review the answers to questions on page 99. Students should listen to each others' answers carefully. You may want to make a list of responses on the board. For example:

> | cry | sleep | walk back and forth |
> | shout | watch TV | go to bed early |

b. Then have students ask the question: "Do you _____ when you're _____?" They may choose any emotion they like and then choose one of the actions written on the board. For example: "Do you shout when you're angry?"

c. Have students answer others' questions. Encourage them to give truthful answers: "No. I don't _____ when I'm _____." or "Yes. I _____ when I'm _____." Encourage students to expand their answers. For example:

> "No. I don't shout when I'm angry. I listen to music.
>   But (name of student) shouts when he/she's angry."

Text Pages 100–101: *I'm Washing the Dishes in the Bathtub*

FOCUS

> Contrast of the simple present and present continuous tenses:
>
> *I NEVER wash the dishes in the bathtub, but I'm washing the dishes in the bathtub TODAY.*

INTRODUCING THE MODEL

1. Have students look at the model illustration.
2. Set the scene: "Two friends are talking. One is surprised because the other is doing something very strange."
3. Present the model.
4. Full-Class Choral Repetition.
5. Ask students if they have any questions; check understanding of new vocabulary: *dish, bathtub, That's strange!*
6. Group Choral Repetition.
7. Choral Conversation.
8. Call on one or two pairs of students to present the dialog.

   (For additional practice, do Choral Conversation in small groups or by rows.)

SIDE BY SIDE EXERCISES

Examples

---

1. A. What are you doing?!
   B. I'm sleeping on the floor.
   A. That's strange! Do you USUALLY sleep on the floor?
   B. No. I NEVER sleep on the floor, but I'm sleeping on the floor TODAY.
   A. Why are you doing THAT?!
   B. Because my BED is broken.
   A. I'm sorry to hear that.

2. A. What are you doing?!
   B. I'm cooking on the radiator.
   A. That's strange! Do you USUALLY cook on the radiator?
   B. No! I NEVER cook on the radiator, but I'm cooking on the radiator TODAY.
   A. Why are you doing THAT?
   B. Because my STOVE is broken.
   A. I'm sorry to hear that.

---

1. **Exercise 1:** Introduce the new word *floor.* Call on two students to present the dialog.
2. **Exercise 2:** Introduce the new word *radiator.* Same as above.

3. **Exercises 3–5:**

> **New vocabulary:**   3. *candlelight, lamp*   5. *hitchhike*

Either Full-Class Practice or Pair Practice.

4. **Exercise 6:**   Have students use the model as a guide to create their own conversations using vocabulary of their choice. Encourage students to use dictionaries to find new words they want to use. This exercise can be done orally in class or for written homework. If you assign it for homework, you should do one example in class to make sure students understand what's expected. Have students present their conversations in class the next day. (They can bring in *props* if they wish.)

WORKBOOK

Pages 86–89

Exercise Note

Workbook p. 86:   Students practice the present continuous and simple present tenses. Note that the pairs of sentences always use the same verb. You can also do this exercise orally. For each exercise, call on a pair of students, one to read the sentence on the left, the other to read the sentence on the right.

EXPANSION ACTIVITY

Practice sh *and* s *sounds*

1. Have students practice saying these words with *sh* sounds. Write some or all of them on the board; have students repeat after you.

shout	blush	station
shiver	wash	Swedish
shirt	dishes	fiction
short	international	
sure	Russian	

2. Have students practice saying these words with *s* sounds. Write some or all of them on the board; have students repeat after you.

sing	baseball	what's
sad	office	sports
listen	Miss	study
hospital	fix	sleeps

Text Page 102

READING: *A Bad Day at the Office*

FOCUS

> Contrast: Simple present and present continuous tenses

NEW VOCABULARY

answer	flu	on strike
as a result	insurance company	operate
computer	job	out
computer programmer	letter	receptionist
custodian	nobody	secretary
employee	office	staff
energetic		type

PREVIEWING THE STORY (optional)

Have students talk about the story title and/or illustration. Introduce new vocabulary.

READING THE STORY

1. Have students read silently, or follow along silently as the story is read aloud by you, by one or more students, or on the tape.
2. Ask students if they have any questions; check understanding of vocabulary.

   Culture Note

   Strikes are common in the United States. Employees may go on strike if they are unable to reach agreement with their company regarding pay raises, benefits, working conditions, and other issues.

3. Check students' comprehension, using some or all of the following questions:

   a. What does Mr. Blaine do?
   b. What kind of staff does he have?
   c. Where are Mr. Blaine's employees today?
   d. Who is there?
   e. Why is Mr. Blaine answering the telephone?
   f. Why is Mr. Blaine typing letters?
   g. Why is Mr. Blaine operating the computer?
   h. Why is Mr. Blaine fixing the radiator?

CHECK-UP

True or False?

1. False
2. False
3. True
4. False
5. False

Listening

Have students complete the exercises as you play the tape or read the following:

Listen and choose the best answer.

1. What are you doing? (b)
2. What does the secretary do? (a)
3. What is the receptionist doing? (b)
4. Is he angry? (b)
5. What do you do when you're sick? (a)

READING: *Early Monday Morning in Centerville*

FOCUS

> Contrast: Simple present and present continuous tenses

NEW VOCABULARY

business	drive	mail	ride	traffic
deliver	early	mail carrier	rush	truck
direct (v)	hard (adv)	police officer	take the bus	unusual

PREVIEWING THE STORY (optional)

Have students talk about the story title and/or illustration. Introduce new vocabulary.

READING THE STORY

1. Have students read silently, or follow along silently as the story is read aloud by you, by one or more students, or on the tape.

2. Ask students if they have any questions; check understanding of vocabulary.

3. Check students' comprehension, using some or all of the following questions:

    a. Is early Sunday morning usually a very busy time in Centerville?
    b. What do men and women usually do?
    c. How do they get there?
    d. What do children usually do?
    e. How do they get there?
    f. Is the city usually busy?
    g. What do trucks do?
    h. What do mail carriers do?
    i. What do police officers do?
    j. Is Monday morning usually quiet in Centerville?

CHECK-UP

The Snowstorm

1.	driving	6.	take	11.	delivering food
2.	taking	7.	taking	12.	deliver mail
3.	going	8.	ride	13.	delivering mail
4.	walk	9.	riding	14.	direct traffic
5.	walking	10.	deliver food	15.	directing traffic

WORKBOOK

Check-Up Test: Page 90

WORKBOOK ANSWER KEY AND LISTENING SCRIPTS

Page 82   A.   WHAT'S THE WORD?

1.	hot	2.	tired
3.	angry	4.	embarrassed
5.	happy	6.	thirsty
7.	sad	8.	nervous
9.	hungry	10.	sick

Page 83   B.   TELL ME WHY

1. She's smiling because she's
   smiles when she's happy
2. I'm yawning because I'm
   yawn when I'm tired
3. They're shouting because they're
   shout when they're angry
4. We're shivering because we're
   shiver because we're cold
5. He's perspiring because he's
   perspires when he's hot
6. They're crying because they're
   cry when they're sad
7. He's going to a restaurant because he's
   goes to a restaurant when he's hungry
8. He's biting his nails because he's
   bites his nails when he's nervous

Page 86   E.   THAT'S STRANGE!

1.	cooks	9.	watch
2.	study	10.	are reading
3.	clean	11.	helps
4.	plays	12.	are playing
5.	is sleeping	13.	shout
6.	are dancing	14.	drinking
7.	is washing, washes	15.	listens
8.	is smiling		

Page 87   F.   WHAT'S THE QUESTION?

1. Why are you crying?
2. Where do they play tennis?
3. When does she go to the library?
4. Why are they singing?
5. Where is she going?
6. Where does he wash his clothes?

7. What kind of coffee do you like?
8. How many grandchildren does she have?
9. Where is he eating today?
10. How many sweaters are you wearing?
11. What's she doing?
12. What do they play on Tuesday?
13. What kind of shows does he watch?
14. Why are you cooking a big dinner?

Page 88   G.   LISTEN

As you listen to each story, read the following sentences and check *yes* or *no.* You will hear each story twice.

JANE AND BETTY

Jane and Betty are looking for a restaurant. They're very hungry. They usually eat dinner at home, but their mother isn't cooking today.

JACK

Jack never does his homework. His teacher is usually upset. Jack rarely helps his parents. He never washes the dishes, and he rarely washes the clothes. His parents are usually angry at him.

TOM

Tom is usually very happy. He loves his friends and his family, and he usually smiles at them. But today Tom isn't smiling. He's shouting at his little sister because she isn't studying.

VACATION

When my family and I are on vacation, I always have a wonderful time. I usually go to the beach, but when it's cold, I read books and listen to music. Today is a beautiful vacation day, and I'm playing tennis with my sister in the park.

Answers
1. no
2. no
3. yes

4. no
5. yes
6. no

7. yes
8. no
9. no
10. yes
11. no
12. yes

Page 88 H. LOUD AND CLEAR

1. Steven, studying, Spanish
2. Stanley, smiling, likes, suit
3. Alice, nervous, talks, boss
4. sunny, Stuart, school, bicycle
5. Sam, sleeping, sister, singing, song
6. Wilson, hospital, Mrs., sorry, sick
7. Boris, next, bus, school
8. science, asks, question, students, listen

CHECK-UP TEST: *CHAPTERS 11–12*

Page 90 A.

1. her
2. them
3. it
4. him
5. us

Page 90 B.

1. shouting
2. go
3. dancing
4. fixes
5. washes

Page 90 C.

1. do
2. is
3. Does
4. Are
5. do

Page 90 D.

1. When does she go to the supermarket?
2. Why is he yawning?
3. Where are they sleeping?
4. How many children does she have?
5. What are you drinking?

Page 90 E.

Listen to each question. Put a circle around the correct answer.

Ex. What are Fred and Jane doing today?

1. What do you usually do when you go to parties?
2. Where are you going today?
3. What does Robert usually do when he's nervous?
4. What kind of food does Mrs. Jones usually cook?
5. Is Henry fixing the car?

Answers
1. b
2. a
3. b
4. b
5. a

GRAMMAR

Can

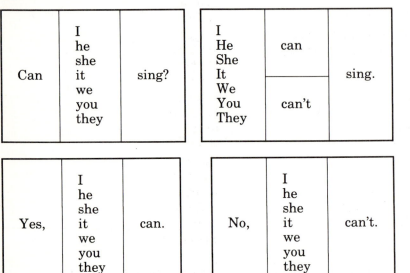

Can	I he she it we you they	sing?

I He She It We You They	can can't	sing.

Yes,	I he she it we you they	can.

No,	I he she it we you they	can't.

Have to

I We You They	have to	work.
He She It	has to	

FUNCTIONS

Inquiring about Ability

Can you *speak Hungarian?*
Can *Michael go to Herbert's party?*

What can you do?

Expressing Ability

I can *speak Rumanian.*

Of course *he* can.

Expressing Inability

No, I can't.

Asking for and Reporting Information

He *fixes cars* every day.
He's a *mechanic.*

What's your name?
  Roy Smith.

Tell me, *Roy,* _____?

Inquiring about Want-Desire

What kind of job are you looking for?
  I'm looking for a job as a
    superintendent.

Expressing Obligation

I have to *do my laundry.*
He has to *go to the doctor.*

Extending an Invitation

Can you *go to a movie* with me on *Friday?*

Declining an Invitation

I'm sorry.   I can't.

Greeting People

Nice to meet you.

NEW VOCABULARY

act
actor
actress
also
annoyed
another
apple pie
application
application fee
application form
apply
ask for
attach
bake
baker
baseball game
believe
black and white
bowling
can
can't
checkers
chef
chess
crowded
dancer
depressed
do *my* laundry
driver's license

duplicate
employment service
eye examination
file (v)
fill out
finally
find
first
go bowling/dancing/jogging/
    sailing/shopping/skating/skiing
has to
have to
hope
ink
jogging
left turn
line
loan (n)
lock
make a *right* turn
marriage license
mechanic
motor
Motor Vehicles Department
park (v)
passport
pay (v)
pick up

print (v)
reception room
repair
right turn
road test
Rumanian
sailing
script
singer
skate (v)
ski (v)
start
submit
take *a test*
teach
then
thing
truck driver
U-turn
violinist
wait
written test

believe it or not
have a party
in person
Nice to meet you.
no wonder

Text Page 106: *Can You?*

FOCUS

> Introduction of *can* and *can't*

GETTING READY

1. Introduce *can* and *can't*. Have students look at the right hand box at the top of the page, or write on the board:

    > Can you _____?   Yes, I can.
    >   No, I can't.

    a. Have students repeat "Yes, I can," chorally and individually.
    b. Have several students answer "Yes, I can," as you ask about their ability to speak their native language:

    > "Can you speak _____?"
    > "Yes, I can."

    c. Call on a few pairs of students to ask and answer the same question.
    d. Have students repeat "No, I can't," chorally and individually.
    e. Have several students answer "No, I can't," as you ask about a language they don't know:

    > "Can you speak _____?"
    > "No, I can't."

    f. Call on a few pairs of students to ask the same or a similar question and answer "No, I can't."

2. Make sentences using the forms in the box at the top of the page; have students repeat chorally and individually. For example:

    > "I can sing."   "I can't sing."
    > "He can sing."   "He can't sing."

INTRODUCING THE MODEL

1. Have students look at the model illustration.
2. Set the scene: "Two diplomats are talking in front of the United Nations Building in New York City."
3. Present the model.
4. Full-Class Choral Repetition.
5. Ask students if they have any questions; check understanding of new vocabulary: *can, can't, Rumanian.*

    ### Language Note

    When *can* is used with another verb (as in *I can skate),* it is unstressed and pronounced [kun]. In other cases, *can* is pronounced [kæn]: *(Yes, I can.)*

6. Group Choral Repetition.
7. Choral Conversation.
8. Call on one or two pairs of students to present the dialog.

(For additional practice, do Choral Conversation in small groups or by rows.)

SIDE BY SIDE EXERCISES

Examples

1. A. Can Mary ski?
   B. No, she can't. But she can swim.

2. A. Can Sam cook Chinese food?
   B. No, he can't. But he can cook French food.

3. A. Can they play the violin?
   B. No, they can't. But they can play the piano.

1. **Exercise 1:** Introduce the new word *ski*. Call on two students to present the dialog. Then do Choral Repetition and Choral Conversation Practice.
2. **Exercise 2:** Same as above.
3. **Exercises 3–8:**

   New vocabulary: 5. *chess, checkers*   8. *skate*

   Culture Note

   Chess and *checkers* (Exercise 5): These are popular board games in the United States.

   Either Full-Class Practice or Pair Practice.
4. **Exercise 9:** Here students talk about themselves. Have pairs of students ask and answer, using any vocabulary they wish.

WORKBOOK

Pages 91–92 (Exercises A, B)

EXPANSION ACTIVITIES

1. Students Talk about Themselves

   a. Put some or all of these words on the board or on word cards. You can also use visuals for these activities:

play *(football)*	ski
play the *(piano)*	cook
speak *(French)*	sing
fix *(cars)*	swim

b. Point to each activity and call on pairs of students to ask about and describe their *own* abilities. For example:

"Can you ski?"   "Can you speak French?"   "Can you dance?"
"No, I can't."   "Yes, I can."   "No, I can't. But I can sing."

c. You can practice *he* or *she* by talking about the student who has just answered.

"Can he/she _____?"

2. Talking about Sports Celebrities

Bring in magazine or newspaper photographs of famous local, national or international sports personalities. Have students talk about each one, using *can* and an appropriate verb. Introduce any new vocabulary students will need in order to tell about the people in the pictures. For example:

(a picture of)	Student
a basketball player	He can play basketball.
an ice skater	She can skate.
a soccer player	He can play soccer.
a golfer	She can play golf.
a swimmer	She can swim.
a long-distance runner	He can run.

Text Page 107: *Of Course They Can*

FOCUS

> • Professions and related activities:
>   *He's a mechanic. He fixes cars every day.*
>   *She's a truck driver. She drives a truck every day.*
> • Emphatic short answers with *can:*
>   *Of course he can.*

GETTING READY

1. Practice *Of Course* _____ *can,* using *I, he, she, you, they.*

   a. Ask questions about students' ability to speak their native language(s). Encourage students to answer emphatically:

      "OF COURSE _____ CAN!"

   b. Ask: "Can I speak _____?"
      "Can *(name of a male student)* speak _____?"
      "Can *(name of a female student)* speak _____?"
      "Can *(names of students)* speak _____?"
      "Can we speak _____?"

INTRODUCING THE MODEL

1. Have students look at the model illustration.
2. Set the scene: "Two people are talking about Jack."
3. Present the model.
4. Full-Class Choral Repetition.
5. Ask students if they have any questions; check understanding of new vocabulary: *mechanic.*
6. Group Choral Repetition.
7. Choral Conversation.
8. Call on one or two pairs of students to present the dialog.

   (For additional practice, do Choral Conversation in small groups or by rows.)

SIDE BY SIDE EXERCISES

Examples

> 1. A. Can Arthur play the violin?
>   B. Of course he can. He plays the violin every day. He's a violinist.
> 3. A. Can Fred and Ginger dance?
>   B. Of course they can. They dance every day. They're dancers.

Use the illustrations in the text or *Side by Side* Picture Cards 94–104 to introduce the new vocabulary.

1. **Exercise 1:** Introduce the new word *violinist.* Call on two students to present the dialog. Then do Choral Repetition and Choral Conversation Practice.

2. **Exercise 2:** Introduce the new word *singer.* Same as above.

3. **Exercises 3–9:**

> **New vocabulary:**   3. *dancer*   4. *chef*   5. *bake, baker, apple pies*   6. *act, actor*
> 7. *actress*   8. *teach*   9. *drive, truck, truck driver*

Either Full-Class Practice or Pair Practice.

WORKBOOK

Pages 92–94 (Exercises C, D, E, F, G)

Exercise Notes

Workbook p. 93:   For additional practice with Exercise F, you can have students read the story aloud, and then ask and answer questions with *can.* For example: "Can Bob speak Russian?" "No, he can't." "Can Sally speak Spanish?" "We don't know."

Workbook p. 94:   Students practice the contrast of the full-form pronunciation of *can* in yes/no statements and short answers and its reduced pronunciation in statements.

EXPANSION ACTIVITIES

1. Practice Professions with Visuals

a. Review the professions on text page 107 using your own visuals or *Side by Side* Picture Cards 94–104. For example:

> Point to a visual and ask: "What does he/she do?"
> Have students answer: "He's/She's a *(teacher)*."

b. Teach additional names of professions according to your students' interests. Use your own visuals or *Side by Side* Picture Cards 105–120:

doctor	secretary
nurse	factory worker
dentist	businessman/businesswoman
carpenter	salesman/saleswoman
plumber	computer programmer
scientist	mail carrier
police officer	painter

Point to each visual and say: "He's/She's a _____."
Have students repeat chorally and individually.
Point to each visual; have students ask and answer:

> "What does he/she do?"
> "He's/She's a _____."

2. Role Play Professions

Use visuals or word cards of professions to assign imaginary professions to students in the class. Have students create conversations based on the models on text pages 106 and 107.

a. Students can talk about themselves and their imaginary professions.

> A.   Can you fix cars?
> B.   Of course I can. I fix cars every day. I'm a mechanic. Can YOU fix cars?
> A.   No, I can't. But I can cook. I cook every day. I'm a cook.

b. Students can talk about other people in the class and their imaginary professions:

A. Can *(Henry)* drive a truck?
B. Of course he can. He drives a truck every day. He's a truck driver.

A. Can *(Jane)* bake apple pies?
B. No, she can't. But she can dance. She dances every day. She's a dancer.

3. Guessing Game

Give one student a card with a profession on it. Have other students ask Yes/No questions with *Do* in order to guess the profession. For example, students can ask:

"Do you cook every day?"
"Do you drive a truck every day?"

4. Listening Practice: Who Am I?

Make statements about the people on text page 107. Have students respond by telling who you're talking about. For example:

Teacher:	I like math.	Teacher:	I like songs.
Student:	Eleanor.	Student:	Anita.
Teacher:	I work in the kitchen.	Teacher:	I have a restaurant.
Student:	Lois.	Student:	Stanley.
Teacher:	We like the theater.	Teacher:	We like music.
Student:	Elizabeth, Katherine, Richard.	Student:	Fred and Ginger.
Teacher:	I like Beethoven.		
Student:	Arthur.		

5. Visuals: What Can These People Do?

Collect magazine or newspaper photographs that show people practicing various professions. Teach additional names of professions, and teach the actions that accompany these professions. For example:

police officer — direct (traffic)
hairdresser — fix, cut (hair)
architect — design, draw (buildings)
secretary — type, answer (the telephone)

Have students talk about the photographs. (Some photographs could be of famous people.)
For example:

He's a politician. He works in (name of capital city).
He can help the people. / He can make laws.

She's an electrician. She works with electricity.
She can fix lamps and televisions.

They're computer programmers. They work with computers.
They can program computers.

She's a dancer. She works in a night club.
She can dance.

He's a salesperson. He works in a big department store.
He can sell many things.

READING: *The Ace Employment Service*

FOCUS

Can

NEW VOCABULARY

employment service	lock
file (v)	motor
find	reception room
hope	repair

PREVIEWING THE STORY (optional)

Have students talk about the story title and/or illustration. Introduce new vocabulary.

READING THE STORY

1. Have students read silently, or follow along silently as the story is read aloud by you, by one or more students, or on the tape.
2. Ask students if they have any questions; check understanding of vocabulary.

   Culture Note

   An employment service, or employment agency, finds jobs for people by matching their skills with the lists of available jobs they have on file.

3. Check students' comprehension, using some or all of the following questions:

   a. Where are Roy, Susan, Lana, and and Tina sitting?
   b. Why?
   c. What kind of job is Roy looking for?
   d. What can he do?
   e. What kind of job is Susan looking for?
   f. What can she do?
   g. What kinds of jobs are Lana and Tina looking for?
   h. What can they do?

CHECK-UP

Q & A

1. Call on a pair of students to present the model.
2. Have students work in pairs to create new dialogs.
3. Call on pairs to present their new dialogs to the class.

Listening

Have students complete the exercises as you play the tape or read the following:

```
Listen and circle.

  1.  I can speak English.  (a)
  2.  He can't swim.  (b)
  3.  They can't ski.  (b)
  4.  She can play the piano.  (a)
  5.  We can dance.  (a)
  6.  I can't type.  (b)
```

```
Choose what each person can do.

  1.  I can sing. I can't dance.  (a)
  2.  He can't file. He can type.  (b)
  3.  She can't fix motors. She can repair locks.  (b)
  4.  He can cook. He can't bake.  (a)
  5.  I can drive a truck. I can't drive a bus.  (a)
  6.  She can't teach history. She can teach science.  (b)
```

Text Page 110: *They Can't Go to Herbert's Party*

FOCUS

> Introduction of *have to* to express obligation:
> *I have to work.*
> *He has to go to the doctor.*

GETTING READY

1. Write *have to* and *has to* on the board. Introduce *have to* by describing typical obligations. For example:

   "You *have to* go to school on Monday, but you *don't have to* go to school on Sunday."
   "In this class you *have to* speak English."
   "You *have to* eat every day."

2. Form sentences using the words in the grammar box. Have students repeat chorally after you. For example:

   "I have to work."
   "We have to work."
   "She has to work."

INTRODUCING THE MODEL

1. Have students look at the model illustration.
2. Set the scene: "Herbert is depressed. He's having a party today, but his friends can't go to his party. They're all busy."
3. Present the model.
4. Full-Class Choral Repetition.
5. Ask students if they have any questions; check understanding of new vocabulary: *depressed, have a party, has to.*

   ### Language Note

   In informal speech, *have to* is usually pronounced [hafta]: (*I **have to** go.*); *has to* is usually pronounced [hasta]: (*He **has to** go.*).

6. Group Choral Repetition.
7. Choral Conversation.
8. Call on one or two pairs of students to present the dialog.

   (For additional practice, do Choral Conversation in small groups or by rows.)

SIDE BY SIDE EXERCISES

Examples

> 1. A. Can Peggy go to Herbert's party?
>   B. No, she can't. She has to fix her car.

> 2. A. Can George and Martha go to Herbert's party?
>   B. No, they can't. They have to go to the supermarket.

1. **Exercise 1:** Call on two students to present the dialog. Then do Choral Repetition and Choral Conversation Practice.
2. **Exercise 2:** Same as above.
3. **Exercises 3–7:**

   Either Full-Class Practice or Pair Practice.
4. **Exercise 8:** Here students pretend they are Herbert's friends and tell why they can't go to his party.

WORKBOOK

Pages 95–96

Exercise Note

> Workbook p. 96: In Exercise I, encourage students to use dictionaries when writing about themselves.

EXPANSION ACTIVITIES

1. *Role Play: Having a Party*
   a. Have each student write a simple schedule showing *Monday* through *Friday* and one thing he or she has to do on each day. Students can use the vocabulary on text page 110 or any vocabulary they wish. For example:

      > Monday   — wash my car
      > Tuesday   — go to the dentist
      > Wednesday — fix my TV
      > Thursday   — study English
      > Friday   — go to the bank

   b. Call on pairs of students to create conversations, using the following framework:

      > A. What do you have to do on _____?
      > B. On _____ I have to _____.

   c. Pretend you are having a party. Create conversations with your students where you *invite* them and they either accept or decline, depending upon their *schedules* from above. For example:

      > You: I'm having a party on Monday. (Gesture to a student)
      >   Can you go to my party?
      > Student: No, I can't. I have to go to the doctor.
      >
      > You: (pointing to Student B) Can you go to my party?
      > Student: No, I can't. I have to wash my car.

      Keep changing the day of your party to expand the practice.

2. *Listening Practice: Who Am I?*

Make statements about the people on text page 110. Have students respond by telling who you're talking about. For example:

Teacher:	She has a toothache.	Teacher:	They're studying.
Student:	Nancy.	Student:	Carl and Tim.
Teacher:	She has dirty laundry.	Teacher:	She's in the garage.
Student:	Linda.	Student:	Peggy.
Teacher:	He needs money.	Teacher:	He's outside.
Student:	Ted.	Student:	Ted.
Teacher:	They need food.	Teacher:	He's sick.
Student:	George and Martha.	Student:	Michael.
Teacher:	His living room is dirty.	Teacher:	It's his birthday.
Student:	Henry.	Student:	Herbert.

READING: *Applying for a Driver's License*

FOCUS

> Have to

NEW VOCABULARY

also	black and white	left turn	right turn
annoyed	crowded	line	road test
another	driver's license	long	script
application	duplicate	make a turn	start
application fee	eye examination	Motor Vehicles	submit
application form	fill out	Department	take a test
apply	finally	no wonder	then
ask for	first	park (v)	thing
attach	ink	pay	U-turn
believe	in person	pick up	wait
believe it or not		print	written test

PREVIEWING THE STORY (optional)

Have students talk about the story title and/or illustrations. Introduce new vocabulary.

READING THE STORY

1. Have students read silently, or follow along silently as the story is read aloud by you, by one or more students, or on the tape.
2. Ask students if they have any questions; check understanding of vocabulary.

   Culture Note

   The Motor Vehicles Department gives driving tests to people. If they pass, the Motor Vehicles Department gives them licenses.

3. Check students' comprehension, using some or all of the following questions:

   a. Why is Henry annoyed?
   b. What does he have to do first?
   c. Can he ask for the form by telephone?
   d. Can he ask for it by mail?
   e. Where does he have to go?
   f. How many copies of the form does he have to fill out?
   g. Can he use a pencil?
   h. Can he use blue ink?
   i. Can he write in script?
   j. What does he have to attach to the application form?
   k. Can they be old?
   l. Can they be large?
   m. Can they be black and white?
   n. Then how many long lines does he have to wait in? Why?
   o. What does he have to do during the road test?

CHECK-UP

Answer These Questions

1. No, he can't.
2. He has to go to the Motor Vehicles Department.
3. He has to attach two photographs.
4. No, he can't.
5. He has to start the car, make a right turn, a left turn, and a U-turn, and he has to park his car on a crowded city street.

Fix This Sign

1. Pick up an application form.
2. Fill out the form in duplicate.
3. Pay the application fee.
4. Have an eye examination.
5. Take a written test.
6. Take a road test.

IN YOUR OWN WORDS

1. Make sure students understand the instructions.
2. Have students do the activity as written homework, using a dictionary for any new words they wish to use.
3. Have students present and discuss what they have written, in pairs or as a class.

Text Page 113

ON YOUR OWN: *I'm Sorry. I Can't.*

FOCUS

Using *can* and *have to* to extend and decline an invitation

INTRODUCING THE MODEL

There are 2 model conversations. Introduce and practice each one separately. For each model:

1. Have students look at the model illustration.
2. Set the scene: "Two friends are talking."
3. Present the model.
4. Full-Class Choral Repetition.
5. Ask students if they have any questions; check understanding of new vocabulary: *do my laundry, go skating*.
6. Group Choral Repetition.
7. Choral Conversation.
8. Call on one or two pairs of students to present the dialog.

SIDE BY SIDE EXERCISES

Examples

1. A. Mary. Can you go sailing with me on Tuesday?
   B. I'm sorry. I can't. I have to visit a friend in the hospital.

2. A. Jack. Can you have dinner with me on Saturday?
   B. I'm sorry. I can't. I have to study.

1. Have students look at the two columns at the bottom of the page. The expressions on the left are activities someone might do with a friend. The expressions on the right are reasons someone might use to decline an invitation.
2. Go over the vocabulary. Use your own visuals or *Side by Side* Picture Cards 121–134.

go to a movie, baseball game, have lunch, go swimming, go dancing, go skating, go skiing, go shopping, go bowling, go sailing, go jogging, visit, work

Culture Note

   Jogging, or running at a slow pace for exercise, is very popular in the United States. Many people jog early in the morning, before going to work or school, or late in the day.

3. Have students think of other reasons for declining an invitation. Add them to the list.

4. Have students create dialogs based on the model. Either Full-Class Practice or Pair Practice.

5. **Writing Practice**

   For homework, have students write out 5 conversations based on the model. Encourage students to use dictionaries to find new words. Have students present their conversations in class the next day without referring to their written homework.

WORKBOOK

Pages 97–98

   Exercise Note

   Workbook p. 98:   Students practice *can't* and *have to*.

WORKBOOK ANSWER KEY AND LISTENING SCRIPTS

Page 91 A. CAN OR CAN'T

1. can't play
   can play the
   guitar
2. can ski
   can't skate
3. can't play
   can play checkers
4. can dance
   can't sing
5. can't play
   can play the piano
6. can't cook
   can cook Greek
   food
7. can swim
   can't ski
8. can speak
   can't speak
   Spanish

Page 92 C. PUZZLE

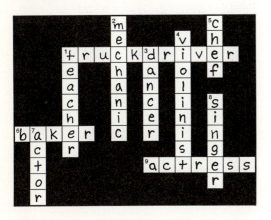

Page 92 D. LISTEN

Listen to each sentence. Put a circle around the word you hear.

1. My grandmother can speak Russian.
2. My sister can't sing.
3. My sister can't bake.
4. John and his brother can play checkers.
5. I can't drive a car.
6. My father can't play football.
7. Tommy can play the violin.
8. I can't drive a bus.
9. Can you cook Mexican food?
10. Mr. and Mrs. Johnson can ski.
11. They can't read Greek newspapers.
12. They can play soccer.

Answers

1.	can	5.	can't	9.	can
2.	can't	6.	can't	10.	can
3.	can't	7.	can	11.	can't
4.	can	8.	can't	12.	can

Page 93 E. WHAT'S THE QUESTION?

1. Can she bake?
2. Can he play baseball?
3. Can they play the violin?
4. Can you drive?
5. Can they skate?
6. Can he swim?

Page 93 F. THE NELSON FAMILY

1. is
2. ugly
3. sad
4. is
5. teacher
6. speaks
7. speak
8. plays
9. hot
10. every
11. play
12. can
13. reads
14. plays
15. can
16. songs
17. plays
18. can
19. play

Page 95 H. WHAT ARE THEY SAYING?

1. have to
2. has to
3. have to
4. Do, have to
   don't
5. Do, have to
   do
6. doesn't have to

Page 96 I. A BUSY WEEK

1. He has to go to the supermarket.
2. She has to fix the car.
3. She has to wash the clothes.
4. They have to paint the bedroom.
5. They have to go to the dentist.
6. He has to clean the yard.

1. can't go skiing
   has to study
2. can't play tennis
   have to work
3. can't go swimming
   has to do the
     laundry
4. can't go sailing
   have to wash the
     kitchen floor
5. can't go jogging
   has to go to the
     dentist
6. can't go dancing
   has to teach
7. can't play cards
   have to fix the TV
8. can't go to the zoo
   has to go to the doctor

TEACHER'S NOTES

GRAMMAR

Future: Going to

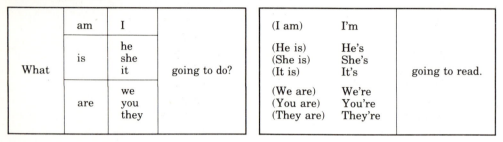

What	am	I	going to do?
	is	he she it	
	are	we you they	

(I am)	I'm	going to read.
(He is)	He's	
(She is)	She's	
(It is)	It's	
(We are)	We're	
(You are)	You're	
(They are)	They're	

Time Expressions

I'm going to wash my clothes	today.	tomorrow.	right now.
	this morning.	tomorrow morning.	right away.
	this afternoon.	tomorrow afternoon.	immediately.
	this evening.	tomorrow evening.	at once.
	tonight.	tomorrow night.	

I'm going to fix my car	this next	week.	Sunday.	January.	July.
		month.	Monday.	February.	August.
		year.	Tuesday.	March.	September.
			Wednesday.	April.	October.
		spring.	Thursday.	May.	November.
		summer.	Friday.	June.	December.
		fall (autumn).	Saturday.		
		winter.			

It's	11:00 (eleven o'clock).
	11:15 (eleven fifteen / a quarter after eleven.)
	11:30 (eleven thirty / half past eleven.)
	11:45 (eleven forty-five / a quarter to twelve.)
	noon.
	midnight.

Want to

| I We You They | want to | study. |
| He She It | wants to | |

FUNCTIONS

Inquiring about Intention

What are you going to do tomorrow?
When are you going to *wash your clothes?*

Expressing Intention

I'm going to *paint my kitchen.*
I'm going to *wash them this week.*

Expressing Want-Desire

I want to *go swimming.*
I really want to *go swimming.*

Asking for and Reporting Information

What's the forecast?
What's the weather today?
What's the weather forecast for tomorrow?
    The radio says it's going to *rain.*
    According to the newspaper, it's going to *be sunny.*

What time is it?
    It's *7:30.*

What time does the *movie* begin?
    It begins at *8:00.*

Tell me, _____ ?

NEW VOCABULARY

a quarter after
a quarter to
according to
afternoon
at once
autumn
become
begin
Boston
buy
California
celebrate
certainly
clear
cold (n)
concerned
concert
cut
entire
evening
fall (n)
finish
fire (n)
fire (v)
foggy
forecast
fortune
fortune teller
future
get
get a haircut
get married
get up
give
going to
half past
happen
have a picnic
high school
holiday

hurry
hurt
immediately
iron (v)
late (for)
leave
meet
midnight
money
move
movies
New Year's Eve
next
next month
next week
next year
noon
o'clock
pack
parent
plane
play (n)
plumber
put on
really
right away
right now
salary
save
shave
spring
suitcase
summer
take a bath
take a shower
take a trip
take a vacation
television
this afternoon
this evening

this month
this morning
this week
tomorrow
tomorrow afternoon
tomorrow evening
tomorrow morning
tomorrow night
tonight
train (n)
try
used car
want (to)
what time
win
winter

January
February
March
April
May
June
July
August
September
October
November
December

be in a car accident
fall in love
Happy New Year!
I don't know.
just in case
look forward to
Oh no!
Really?
the radio says
What time is it?

Text Page 116: *What Are They Going to Do Tomorrow?*

FOCUS

Introduction of the future
tense with *going to:* $\left.\begin{array}{l} am \\ is \\ are \end{array}\right\}$ + *going to* + *verb*

What's Fred going to do tomorrow?
He's going to fix his car.

GETTING READY

1. Introduce the word *tomorrow*; use a calendar to indicate *tomorrow*.
2. Introduce *going to*. For example:

    "Every day I read the newspaper.
      Tomorrow I'm *going to read* the newspaper."

    "I'm wearing my glasses.
      I always wear my glasses.
      Tomorrow I'm *going to wear* my glasses."

3. Form sentences with *going to* and the words in the boxes at the top of text page 116. Have students repeat chorally. (When you read from the box on the left, form contractions.) For example:

    I'm *going to* read.
    He's *going to* read.

INTRODUCING THE MODEL

1. Have students look at the model illustration.
2. Set the scene: "Two people are talking about Fred."
3. Present the model.
4. Full-Class Choral Repetition.
5. Ask students if they have any questions; check understanding of new vocabulary: *tomorrow, going to.*

    Language Note

    In informal speech, many speakers pronounce *going to* as *gonna*. Tell your students they will frequently hear this pronunciation.

6. Group Choral Repetition.
7. Choral Conversation.
8. Call on one or two pairs of students to present the dialog. (For additional practice, do Choral Conversation in small groups or by rows.)

SIDE BY SIDE EXERCISES

Examples

> 1. A. What's Mary going to do tomorrow?
>   B. She's going to clean her apartment (clean her house/living room).
>
> 2. A. What are Carol and Dan going to do tomorrow?
>   B. They're going to wash their clothes (do their laundry).
>
> *Answer Key:*
> 3. I'm going to paint my kitchen.
> 4. He's going to play baseball.
> 5. We're going to play cards.
> 6. He's going to listen to music.

1. **Exercise 1:** Call on two students to present the dialog. Then do Choral Repetition and Choral Conversation Practice.

2. **Exercise 2:** Same as above.

3. **Exercises 3–6:** Either Full-Class Practice or Pair Practice.

WORKBOOK

Pages 99–100

Exercise Note

Workbook p. 100: Students practice the pronunciation of *going to* as *gonna.*

EXPANSION ACTIVITIES

1. *Students Talk about Themselves*

Ask students and have students ask each other:

> "What are you going to do tomorrow?"
> "What are you going to do this weekend?"
> "What are you going to do on your vacation?"

2. *Word Associations*

Make a list of verbs that students have already studied or use the following list. Have students listen carefully as you give them a verb in the future. Have them repeat the verb and complete the sentence with any appropriate ending. For example:

Teacher	Student
I'm going to play . . .	I'm going to play cards/baseball/music.
He's going to read . . .	He's going to read a book/the newspaper.
We're going to listen to . . .	We're going to listen to the radio/music.
He's going to do . . .	He's going to do his homework/the laundry.
They're going to vacuum . . .	They're going to vacuum their living room/their apartment.
I'm going to fix . . .	I'm going to fix my car/my bicycle.

Text Page 117: *They're Going to the Beach*

FOCUS

> • Going to go = going to
> • Future time expressions

GETTING READY

1. Model the following conversations and have students repeat after you:

   A. What's John going to do tomorrow?
   B. He's going to go to a concert. (or) He's going to a concert.

   A. What's Maria going to do tomorrow?
   B. She's going to go swimming. (or) She's going swimming.

   A. What are Bob and Bill going to do tomorrow?
   B. They're going to go to the bank. (or) They're going to the bank.

2. Write on the board and point out *going to go = going to:*

   > He's going to go to a concert tomorrow. = He's going to a concert tomorrow.

3. Write cues on word cards and have students answer questions in the future: For example:

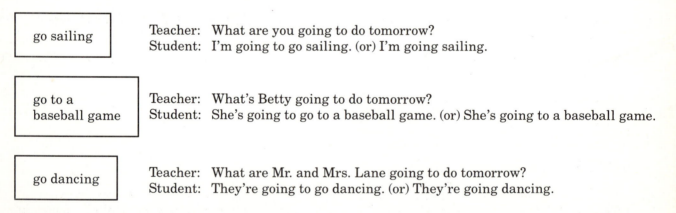

   | go sailing |

   Teacher: What are you going to do tomorrow?
   Student: I'm going to go sailing. (or) I'm going sailing.

   | go to a baseball game |

   Teacher: What's Betty going to do tomorrow?
   Student: She's going to go to a baseball game. (or) She's going to a baseball game.

   | go dancing |

   Teacher: What are Mr. and Mrs. Lane going to do tomorrow?
   Student: They're going to go dancing. (or) They're going dancing.

4. Introduce future time expressions for *today* and *tomorrow*. Read the examples in the boxes at the top of text page 117. Have students repeat chorally.

INTRODUCING THE MODEL

1. Have students look at the model illustration.
2. Set the scene: "Two people are talking about Mr. and Mrs. Brown."
3. Present the model.
4. Full-Class Choral Repetition.
5. Ask students if they have any questions; check understanding of vocabulary.
6. Group Choral Repetition.

7. Choral Conversation.

8. Call on one or two pairs of students to present the dialog.

   (For additional practice, do Choral Conversation in small groups or by rows.)

9. Practice future time expressions for *today* and *tomorrow*. Substitute the words in the box at the top of text page 117 for the expression in the model. For example:

   > A. What are Mr. and Mrs. Brown going to do this morning?
   > B. They're going (to go) to the beach.
   >
   > A. What are Mr. and Mrs. Brown going to do tomorrow afternoon?
   > B. They're going (to go) to the beach.

   Do Choral Repetition, Choral Conversation, and call on pairs of students.

SIDE BY SIDE EXERCISES

Examples

> 1. A. What's Jane going to do tomorrow evening?
>   B. She's going (to go) to a concert.
>
> 2. A. What are Ken and Barbara going to do tonight?
>   B. They're going (to go) to a movie.
>
> *Answer Key:*
> 3. I'm going (to go) to a baseball game.
> 4. We're going (to go) skiing.
> 5. He's going (to go) to the library.

1. **Exercise 1:** Call on two students to present the dialog. Then do Choral Repetition and Choral Conversation Practice.

2. **Exercise 2:** Same as above.

3. **Exercises 3–5:**

   > **New vocabulary:**   1. *concert*   2. *movies*

   Either Full-Class Practice or Pair Practice.

4. **Exercise 6:** Have students use the model as a guide to create their own conversations, using vocabulary of their choice. Encourage students to use dictionaries to find new words they want to use. This exercise can be done orally in class or for written homework. If you assign it for homework, you should do one example in class to make sure students understand what's expected. Have students present their conversations in class the next day.

EXPANSION ACTIVITIES

1. **George's Vacation**

   a. Put the following on the board:

S	M	T	W	T	F	S
go sailing	*go swimming*	*go to the beach*	*go to a restaurant*	*go to a concert*		

   b. Tell a story about George.

   > "George is going on vacation.
   > On Sunday George is going sailing.
   > On Monday he's going swimming."
   > (Continue for Tuesday, Wednesday, Thursday.)

   c. Ask students *What* and *When* questions about George's plans. Students can answer by looking at the schedule on the board. For example:

   > A. What's George going to do on Monday?
   > B. On Monday he's going to go swimming. (or) He's going swimming.

   > A. When is George going to a concert?
   > B. He's going to go to a concert on Thursday. (or) He's going to a concert on Thursday.

   d. Call on pairs of students to ask and answer questions about George's vacation schedule. Leave Friday and Saturday *open*. Have students decide what George is going to do.

2. **Students' Plans**

   Have students make up their own schedules similar to the one in Expansion Activity 1, above. In pairs, have students ask one another what their plans are. Encourage them to use all the future time expressions practiced in this lesson. For example:

   > A. What are you going to do tomorrow night?
   > B. I'm going to a movie. What are YOU going to do tomorrow night?
   > A. I'm going to stay home and watch TV.

FOCUS

> Practice *going to* with time expressions

GETTING READY

1. Introduce these new words:

The months of the year		The seasons
January	*July*	*spring*
February	*August*	*summer*
March	*September*	*fall (autumn)*
April	*October*	*winter*
May	*November*	
June	*December*	

    a. Practice the months by asking students about their birthdays or other important holidays. For example:

    > "When is your birthday?"
    > "It's in (March)."

    b. Practice the seasons by asking about the typical weather. For example:

    A. How's the weather in the $\begin{Bmatrix} \text{spring} \\ \text{summer} \\ \text{fall} \\ \text{winter} \end{Bmatrix}$?

    B. It's usually $\begin{Bmatrix} \text{warm} \\ \text{hot} \\ \text{cool} \\ \text{cold} \\ \text{sunny} \\ \text{cloudy} \end{Bmatrix}$.

2. Review object pronouns.

    a. Have students listen as you say each of the sentences below.
    b. Call on students to substitute the object pronoun and say the sentence.

Teacher	Student
Ex. I'm going to wash *my car.*	I'm going to wash *it.*
1. I'm going to wash *my windows.*	I'm going to wash *them.*
2. I'm going to clean *my apartment.*	I'm going to clean *it.*
3. I'm going to visit *my friends.*	I'm going to visit *them.*
4. I'm going to visit *Mary.*	I'm going to visit *her.*
5. I'm going to visit *John.*	I'm going to visit *him.*
6. I'm going to visit *Mr. and Mrs. Jones.*	I'm going to visit *them.*

INTRODUCING THE MODEL

There are 2 model conversations. Introduce and practice each separately. For each model:

1. Have students look at the model illustration.
2. Set the scene:

    1st model: "Two roommates are talking."
    2nd model: "A wife and husband are talking. The wife is very upset."

3. Present the model.
4. Full-Class Choral Repetition.
5. Ask students if they have any questions; check understanding of new vocabulary:

    1st model: *this week*
    2nd model: *plumber, right now*

6. Group Choral Repetition.
7. Choral Conversation.
8. Call on one or two pairs of students to present the dialog.

    (For additional practice, do Choral Conversation in small groups or by rows.)

9. Introduce the time expressions under the 1st model. Have pairs of students practice the model again, substituting some of these time expressions. For example:

    A.   When are you going to wash your clothes?
    B.   I'm going to wash them next month.

10. Introduce the time expressions under the 2nd model. Have pairs of students practice the model again, substituting these time expressions.

SIDE BY SIDE EXERCISES

In these exercises, students answer the questions using any of the time expressions on text page 118.

Examples

---

1. A.   When are you going to wash your car?
    B.   I'm going to wash it next week.

2. A.   When are you going to call your grandmother?
    B.   I'm going to call her this Sunday.

---

1. **Exercise 1:**   Call on two students to present the dialog. Then do Choral Repetition and Choral Conversation Practice.
2. **Exercise 2:**   Same as above.
3. **Exercises 3–8:**

    New vocabulary: 4. *cut*   5. *plant flowers*   8. *iron*

    Either Full-Class Practice or Pair Practice.

4. **Exercise 9:**   Students talk about themselves. Have pairs of students create dialogs using any of the time expressions on text page 118.

WORKBOOK

Pages 101–102 (Exercises D, E)

EXPANSION ACTIVITIES

1. *Practice* Going to *with Word Cards or Visuals*

   Make word cards for a variety of activities. You can also use your own visuals or *Side by Side* Picture Cards. Suggested activities:

go to Paris	write to _____
do _____ homework	call _____
go to the dentist	visit _____
go to the beach	go to the supermarket
plant flowers	go to a movie
do your laundry	play _____
cut your hair	

   a. Have each student draw a card or visual and ask another student:

      A. When are you going to *(go to Paris)*?

   b. The other student can answer using any time expression. For example:

      B. I'm going to *(go to Paris)* $\begin{cases} \text{tonight} \\ \text{tomorrow} \\ \text{this Sunday} \\ \text{next month} \\ \text{next year} \\ \text{on Monday} \end{cases}$

   c. Practice *he* and *she:*

      Give cards or visuals to pairs of students. Have them create conversations about other students in the class. For example:

      A. When is Hector going to go to Paris?
      B. He's going to go to Paris next month.

2. *Scrambled Sentences: The Smiths Are Going on Vacation*

   Here is the Smith family's vacation schedule.

   > On Sunday the Smiths are going to Acapulco, Mexico.
   > On Monday they're going to go swimming.
   > On Tuesday they're going to eat in a Mexican restaurant, and they're going to go to a concert.
   > On Wednesday they're going to visit friends in a nearby city.
   > On Thursday they're going to write letters to their friends.
   > On Friday they're going to go shopping, and they're going to go dancing at a night club.
   > On Saturday they're going to have a party.

   a. Write each sentence on a strip of paper; then cut the words apart. Mix up the words in each sentence and clip them together.

   b. Divide the class into small groups of 2 to 5 students. Give each group one or two sentences to unscramble.

   c. When everyone has put the words in correct order, have one student from each group write the sentence(s) on the board (in order of the days of the week). Now you have the Smiths' schedule on the board.

   d. Call on several pairs of students to ask and answer questions about the Smiths. For example:

      "When are they going to have a party?"
      "What are they going to do on Monday?"

3. Vocabulary Review: Finish the Sentence

Review vocabulary by saying a verb and having students repeat the verb and adding an appropriate ending to a sentence. For example:

Teacher	Student
He's going to wash . . .	He's going to wash his car/He's going to wash his hair/He's going to wash his pants.
They're going to call . . .	They're going to call their grandchildren/They're going to call their friends.
We're going to visit . . .	We're going to visit our family/We're going to visit you.
I'm going to fix . . .	I'm going to fix my car/I'm going to fix my bicycle.
You're going to plant . . .	You're going to plant flowers/You're going to plant a tree.
He's going to iron . . .	He's going to iron his pants/He's going to iron his shirt.

Text Page 120

READING: *Happy New Year!*

FOCUS

Future: Going to

NEW VOCABULARY

begin	finish	move
Boston	get	New Year's Eve
buy	Happy New Year!	save
California	high school	take a vacation
celebrate	holiday	thirty-first
entire	looking forward to	used car
	money	

PREVIEWING THE STORY (optional)

Have students talk about the story title and/or illustration. Introduce new vocabulary.

READING THE STORY

1. Have students read silently, or follow along silently as the story is read aloud by you, by one or more students, or on the tape.
2. Ask students if they have any questions; check understanding of vocabulary.
3. Check students' comprehension, using some or all of the following questions:

   a. What day is it?
   b. Why are the Simpsons happy this New Year's Eve?
   c. What are Bob and Sally going to do next year?
   d. What's Lucy going to do?
   e. What's Tom going to do?

CHECK-UP

Complete the Conversation

1. what are you going to
2. I'm going to
3. What's he going to
4. He's going to
5. What are they going to
6. They're going to

Listening

Have students complete the exercises as you play the tape or read the following:

> Listen and choose the words you hear.
>
> 1. A. When are you going to visit me?
>   B. Next month. (a)
>
> 2. A. When are you going to begin your vacation?
>   B. This Sunday. (a)
>
> 3. A. When is your son going to call my daughter?
>   B. This afternoon. (b)
>
> 4. A. When are your neighbors going to move?
>   B. Next November. (a)
>
> 5. A. When is she going to get her driver's license?
>   B. Next week. (b)
>
> 6. A. When are you going to do your laundry?
>   B. This evening. (a)
>
> 7. A. When are we going to go to the concert?
>   B. This Thursday. (b)
>
> 8. A. When is your daughter going to finish college?
>   B. Next winter. (a)
>
> 9. A. When are you going to buy a car?
>   B. Tomorrow. (a)
>
> 10. A. When is the landlord going to fix the window?
>   B. At once. (b)

Text Page 121: *What's the Forecast?*

FOCUS

Introduction of *want to* + *verb*

GETTING READY

1. Introduce *want to* by telling about something you want to do. For example:

   "I want to watch TV tonight, but I can't.
   I have to work."

2. Introduce *wants to* by telling what someone else wants to do.

   "Joe wants to buy a car, but he can't. He doesn't have $8,000."

3. Form sentences with the words in the box at the top of the page. Have students repeat chorally and individually. For example:

   "I want to study."
   "We want to study."

INTRODUCING THE MODEL

1. Have students look at the model illustration.
2. Set the scene: "Two friends are talking."
3. Present the model.
4. Full-Class Choral Repetition.
5. Ask students if they have any questions; check understanding of new vocabulary: *I don't know, want to, really, forecast, the radio says, according to.*

   ### Culture Note

   Weather forecasts are a regular part of TV and radio news programs in the United States. Daily newspapers also publish weather forecasts.

   ### Language Notes

   In informal speech, many speakers pronounce *want to* as *wanna* and *wants to* as *wansta*. Tell your students they may hear these pronunciations.

   Note *going to* + verb: *going to rain, going to snow;* with adjectives: *going to be sunny, going to be cloudy,* etc.

6. Group Choral Repetition.
7. Choral Conversation.
8. Call on one or two pairs of students to present the dialog.

   (For additional practice, do Choral Conversation in small groups or by rows.)

SIDE BY SIDE EXERCISES

Examples

---

1. A. What are you going to do tomorrow?
    B. I don't know. I want to have a picnic, but I think the weather is going to be bad.
    A. Really? What's the forecast?
    B. The radio says it's going to rain.
    A. That's strange! According to the newspaper, it's going to be nice.
    B. I hope you're right. I REALLY want to have a picnic.

2. A. What are you going to do tomorrow?
    B. I don't know. I want to go skiing, but I think the weather is going to be bad.
    A. Really? What's the forecast?
    B. The radio says it's going to be warm.
    A. That's strange! According to the newspaper, it's going to snow.
    B. I hope you're right. I REALLY want to go skiing.

---

1. **Exercise 1:** Introduce the new expression *have a picnic*. Call on two students to present the dialog. Then do Choral Repetition and Choral Conversation Practice.

2. **Exercise 2:** Same as above.

3. **Exercises 3–6:**

New vocabulary: 5. *foggy, clear*

Either Full-Class Practice or Pair Practice.

WORKBOOK

Pages 102–106 (Exercises F, G, H, I, J, K, L)

Exercise Notes

Workbook p. 105: In Exercise K, encourage students to use dictionaries when writing about themselves.

Workbook p. 106: Students practice the pronunciation of *want to* as *wanna* and *wants to* as *wansta*.

EXPANSION ACTIVITIES

1. Students Talk about Themselves

a. For homework, have each student make a list of several things he or she wants to do next year. Encourage students to use dictionaries to find new words to express their real-life goals.

b. In the next class, have students present their ideas conversationally. Call on pairs of students to ask and answer:

   A. What do you want to do next year?
   B. Next year I want to *(learn German, visit my aunt in Mexico, and buy a bicycle)*.

c. Practice "He/She wants to _____."

    After a few students have presented their ideas, talk about them:

      A. What does (Bob) want to do next year?

      B. He wants to _____.

2. *Discuss the Weather*

See the suggestions at the bottom of text page 121. Ask students questions about the weather today and tomorrow. For homework, you can have students listen to the local forecast and present the forecast in English during the next class. Have students point to a map showing the region in your country as they tell the forecast.

Text Pages 122–123: *What Time Is It?*

FOCUS

> • Time expressions:
>   *It's 7:30.*
>   *It begins at 8:00.*
>
> • Present continuous tense:
>   *I'm shaving!*
>
> • Review of *going to, have to, want to:*
>   *We're going to be late.*
>   *We have to leave* RIGHT NOW!
>   *I don't want to be late for the movie.*

GETTING READY

Practice time expressions using a large clock or clock face with movable hands to display the time.

1. Review the numbers 1–12.
2. Introduce the time expressions for each hour, as you point to the hands of the clock.

   "It's one o'clock."
   "It's two o'clock."
   "It's three o'clock."

   .
   .
   .

   "It's twelve o'clock."
   "It's (twelve o'clock) noon."
   "It's (twelve o'clock) midnight."

   a. Say each new expression one or more times.
   b. Have students repeat chorally and individually.
   c. Practice conversationally. Ask students "What time is it?" as you point to the clock.

3. Review numbers 1–60.
4. Using the same approach as above, introduce time expressions for the quarter and half hours.

It's one fifteen.	It's one thirty.	It's one forty-five.
It's two fifteen.	It's two thirty.	It's two forty-five.

5. Review time expressions:

   a. Set the clock hands at various times, such as 11:00, 1:15, 3:30, 8:45, and ask "What time is it?"
   b. Give the clock to a student and call out a time; have the student set the clock.

6. Introduce and practice these alternative expressions in the same way:

   11:15 – "It's a quarter after eleven."
   11:30 – "It's half past eleven."
   11:45 – "It's a quarter to twelve."

INTRODUCING THE MODEL

1. Have students look at the model illustration.

2. Set the scene: "A husband and wife are talking. They're going to a movie, and she's upset because he isn't ready.

3. Present the model.

4. Full-Class Choral Repetition.

5. Ask students if they have any questions; check understanding of new vocabulary: *at (8:00), late (for), leave, shave, Please try to hurry!, Oh no!*

6. Group Choral Repetition.

7. Choral Conversation.

8. Call on one or two pairs of students to present the dialog.

   (For additional practice, do Choral Conversation in small groups or by rows.)

SIDE BY SIDE EXERCISES

Examples

1. A. What time does the football game begin?
   B. It begins at 2:00.
   A. At 2:00?! Oh no! We're going to be late!
   B. Why? What time is it?
   A. It's 1:30! We have to leave RIGHT NOW!
   B. I can't leave now. I'm taking a bath!
   A. Please try to hurry! I don't want to be late for the football game.

2. A. What time does the plane leave?
   B. It leaves at 4:15.
   A. At 4:15?! Oh no! We're going to be late!
   B. Why? What time is it?
   A. It's 3:45! We have to leave RIGHT NOW!
   B. I can't leave now. I'm putting on my clothes!
   A. Please try to hurry! I don't want to be late for the plane.

1. **Exercise 1:** Introduce the new vocabulary *football game, take a bath.* Call on two students to present the dialog. Then do Choral Repetition and Choral Conversation Practice.

2. **Exercise 2:** Introduce the new vocabulary *plane, put on.* Same as above.

3. **Exercises 3–6:**

   New vocabulary: 3. *get up*   4. *pack, suitcase*   5. *train, take a shower*
   6. *play (n)*

   Either Full-Class Practice or Pair Practice.

4. **Exercise 7:** Have students use the model as a guide to create their own conversations, using vocabulary of their choice. Encourage students to use dictionaries to find new words they want to use. This exercise can be done orally in class or for written homework. If you assign it for homework, you should do one example in class to make sure students understand what's expected. Have students present their conversations in class the next day.

WORKBOOK

Pages 107–109

Exercise Note

Workbook p. 109:   Students practice time expressions for days of the week, months, and seasons.

EXPANSION ACTIVITIES

1. **Role Play: I Think We're Going to Be Late!**

   Have students role play new situations, using the same conversational framework at the top of text page 123.

   a.   Make up situation cues like the ones below and write them on cards.

   b.   Give cards to pairs of students and allow some time for preparation.

   c.   Have students present their conversations to the class (with books closed).

   d.   Sample situation cues:

   | a parent and child |
   | a baseball game |
   | 2:00/1:30 |
   | parent/taking/bath |

   | husband and wife |
   | a party |
   | 8:00/7:45 |
   | one is talking to the boss on the phone |

   | 2 roommates |
   | a movie |
   | 4:15/3:45 |
   | one roommate/doing/homework |

2. **Talk about Daily Schedules**

   Put your own morning schedule on the board or have one student in the class volunteer to tell what he or she does every morning before going to work or school.

   a.   Put times and key words on the board (or use stick figure drawings). For example:

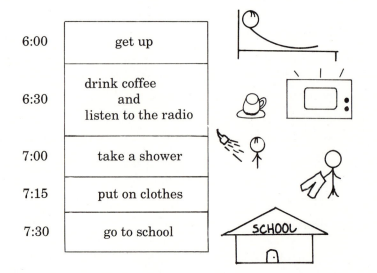

6:00	get up
6:30	drink coffee and listen to the radio
7:00	take a shower
7:15	put on clothes
7:30	go to school

b. Talk about *every day*.

Ask questions about the schedule; then call on pairs of students to ask and answer. For example:

A. What time does Mary get up every day?
B. She gets up at 6:00.

c. Talk about *tomorrow*.

Again, you ask a few questions; then call on pairs of students to ask and answer. For example:

A. What's Mary going to do at 7:30 tomorrow?
B. She's going to go to school.

d. Talk about other students' daily schedules by asking or having students ask each other questions such as:

What time do you usually get up in the morning?
What do you usually do in the morning?
What time do you usually leave your apartment?
What time do you usually have lunch?

3. *What's Playing at the Movies?*

Make copies of the movie schedule from the newspaper and hand them out to the class. Ask:

What's playing at the _____*(name of theater)*_____?
What time does it begin?

4. *Schedules*

Bring copies of bus, plane, or train schedules to class. Ask:

What time does the train for _____ leave?
What time does the bus for _____ leave?
What time does the flight to _____ leave?
What time does flight _____ leave?

READING: *The Fortune Teller*

FOCUS

Future: Going to

NEW VOCABULARY

be in a car	fall in love	get a haircut	move
accident	fire (n)	give	parent
become	fire (v)	happen	salary
certainly	fortune	hurt	take a trip
cold (n)	fortune teller	just in case	television
concerned	future	meet	win

PREVIEWING THE STORY (optional)

Have students talk about the story title and/or illustrations. Introduce new vocabulary.

READING THE STORY

1. Have students read silently, or follow along silently as the story is read aloud by you, by one or more students, or on the tape.
2. Ask students if they have any questions; check understanding of vocabulary.
3. Check students' comprehension, using some or all of the following questions:

   a. Who is Walter visiting?
   b. What's he concerned about?
   c. What's Madame Sophia telling him?
   d. According to Madame Sophia, what's going to happen in January? in February? in March? in April? in May? in June? in July? in August? in September? in October? in November? in December?
   e. Does Walter believe any of this?
   f. What's he going to do, just in case?

CHECK-UP

Q & A

1. Call on a pair of students to present the models.
2. Have students work in pairs to create new dialogs.
3. Call on pairs to present their new dialogs to the class.

WORKBOOK

Check-Up Test: Pages 110–111

Page 99   A.   WHAT ARE THEY GOING TO DO?

1. She's going to study English.
2. They're going to play tennis.
3. She's going to wash her car.
4. We're going to do our exercises.
5. He's going to read the newspaper.
6. They're going to paint their bathroom.
7. What's, going to do She's going to watch TV.
8. What are, going to do I'm going to listen to music.

Page 100.   B.   AN INTERNATIONAL MOVIE ACTOR

1. He's going to Rome next January.
2. He's going to go to concerts.
3. They're going (to go) to Geneva next February.
4. They're going to go skiing.
5. He's going to work in London.
6. They're going to go shopping in expensive stores, and his son is going to go to the London zoo.
7. They're going (to go) to Honolulu next June.
8. They're going to go swimming and sailing.
9. He's going (to go) to Tokyo next September.
10. He's going to act in a Japanese movie.
11. He's going to Japanese restaurants and baseball games with his friend.

Page 102   E.   WHAT'S THE QUESTION?

1. What are you going to do this afternoon?
2. When is he going to cut his hair?
3. Where are they going to go next summer?
4. When is she going to plant flowers?
5. Why is he going to visit his grandmother?
6. What are they going to do this morning?
7. When are you going to call the plumber?
8. Where is he going to eat tonight?

Page 102   F.   LISTEN

Listen to the following weather forecasts. Put a circle around the correct answer. You will hear each forecast twice.

TODAY'S WEATHER FORECAST
This is Tom Jones with today's weather forecast. This afternoon it's going to be warm and sunny with temperatures from 70° to 75°. This evening it's going to be cool and very cloudy, but it isn't going to rain.

THE WEEKEND'S FORECAST
This is Nancy Peters with your weekend weather forecast. Tonight it's going to be foggy and cool with 50° temperatures, but on Saturday it's going to be clear and sunny. On Sunday wear your heavy clothes. It's going to be very cold.

MONDAY'S WEATHER FORECAST
This is Dan Richards with Monday's weather forecast. Monday morning it's going to be cool and cloudy, but wear your snow boots when you go to work because in the afternoon and evening it's going to snow. Tuesday's skiing is going to be wonderful. It's going to be sunny and cold.

Answers
1. warm, sunny
2. cool, cloudy
3. cool, foggy
4. sunny, clear
5. cold
6. cool, cloudy
7. snow
8. cold, sunny

Page 103   G.   BAD WEATHER

1. They want to go skating.
   It's going to be warm.
2. He wants to go to a baseball game.
   It's going to be cold.
3. They want to have a picnic.
   It's going to be cloudy.
4. She wants to wash the car.
   It's going to rain.
5. They want to go to the park.
   It's going to be cloudy.
6. He wants to paint the house.
   It's going to snow.

Page 104   H.   YES AND NO

1. He doesn't want to play checkers.
2. She doesn't want to go
3. I don't want to visit
4. They don't want to eat
5. We don't want to study
6. They don't want to drink
7. He doesn't want to dance

Page 104   I.   YES AND NO

1. He isn't going to call
2. I'm not going to fix
3. We aren't going to go
4. They aren't going to live
5. He isn't going to listen
6. It isn't going to be
7. She isn't going to cook

Page 105   J.   FUTURE HOPES

1. What does, want to
   She wants to be
2. What does, want to
   She wants to teach
3. Where does, want to
   She wants to work
4. What does, want to
   He wants to be
5. What does, want to
   He wants to
6. Where does, want to
   He wants to work

Page 107   M.   WHAT TIME IS IT?

1. 2. 3. 4.

5. 6. 7. 8.

9. 10. 11. 12.

Page 107   N.   LISTEN

Listen and write the time you hear.

1. nine thirty
2. five o'clock
3. six fifteen
4. three forty-five
5. eight fifteen
6. half past two
7. seven fifteen
8. eleven forty-five
9. twelve o'clock
10. half past one
11. a quarter after three
12. four forty-five

Answers

1.	9:30	5.	8:15	9.	12:00
2.	5:00	6.	2:30	10.	1:30
3.	6:15	7.	7:15	11.	3:15
4.	3:45	8.	11:45	12.	4:45

Page 108   O.   PAUL SMITH'S DAY

1. He gets up at 8:00.
2. He eats breakfast.
3. He leaves the house at 8:45.
4. School begins at 9:00.
5. He eats lunch at 12:00.
6. His mathematics class begins at 12:30.
7. He studies science.
8. He goes home.

CHECK-UP TEST: *CHAPTERS 13–14*

Page 110   A.

1. want to play tennis
   they can't, have to work
2. want to play baseball
   I can't, have to fix the car
3. wants to watch TV
   she can't, has to go to the doctor

Page 110   B.

1.	are	4.	do
2.	Do	5.	are
3.	does	6.	is

Page 110   C.

1. He doesn't want to study
2. We aren't going to get up
3. They can't play
4. I'm not going to wash
5. He can't speak
6. She doesn't have to cook

Page 111   D.

is going to eat
going to wash, he's going (to go)
he's going to read
he's going to call

Page 111   E.

1. What's he going to do tomorrow?
2. Where are they going to work next summer?
3. What's she going to study next year?
4. When are you going to visit your uncle?

Page 111   F.

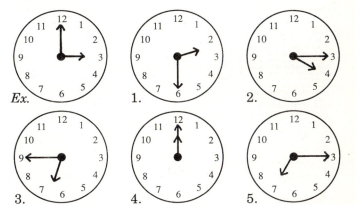

Page 111   G.

Listen to the story. Fill in the correct times.

Every day at school I study English, mathematics, French, science, and music. English class begins at 8:15. I go to mathematics at 10:30. I'm always happy at 11:45 because we have lunch. We go to French class at 12:15. We have science at 1:30, and we go to music at 2:45.

Answers

8:15	12:15
10:30	1:30
11:45	2:45

GRAMMAR

Past Tense

I He She It We You They	worked yesterday.

[t]	I work**ed**. I danc**ed**.
[d]	I clean**ed** my apartment. I play**ed** cards.
[ɪd]	I rest**ed**. I shout**ed**.

Irregular Verbs

eat	–	ate
drink	–	drank
sing	–	sang
sit	–	sat

FUNCTIONS

Asking for and Reporting Information

How do you feel today?
How are you?
  I feel great/fine/okay.
  So-so.
  Not so good.
  I feel terrible.
  I don't feel very well today.

What's the matter?
What seems to be the problem?
  I have a *headache*.
  I have a terrible *headache*.

What did you do yesterday?
  I *worked*.

How *did he get a backache*?

Do you have any idea why?

Responding to Information

I'm glad to hear that.
I'm sorry to hear that.

Greeting People

Hello, Doctor _____? This is _____.
  Hello, _____.

Checking Understanding

A backache?

Indicating Understanding

I see.

Inquiring about Want-Desire

Do you want to *make an appointment*?

Inquiring about Ability

When can you *see me*?

Suggesting

How about *tomorrow at 2 o'clock*?
  That's fine.

Expressing Gratitude

Thank you very much.

NEW VOCABULARY

again	glad	spaghetti
all afternoon	go home	steps
all day	great	stereo (n)
all evening	guest	stomachache
all morning	Hawaii	terrible
all night	headache	thank you
arrive	how about	toothache
ask for	inside	turn on
backache	invite	wait
cheese	last night	yesterday
cracker	love (v)	
dessert	make an appointment	Do you have any idea why?
did	meal	How about . . . ?
dust (v)	pie	How are you?
earache	prepare (for)	I'm glad to hear that.
enjoy	rest (v)	I'm sorry to hear that.
feel	seconds	inside and out
fence	serve	Not so good.
fine	show (v)	Thank you very much.
front steps	sore throat	What seems to be the problem?
furniture	So-so.	What's the matter?

LANGUAGE NOTES

1. **Pronunciation of the *ed* ending**

   The *ed* ending of regular verbs in the past tense is pronounced as follows:

   a. When a verb ends in a voiceless consonant sound other than [t], the ending is pronounced [t].

[k]	worked	[č]	watched
[s]	danced	[š]	washed

   b. When a verb ends in a voiced consonant sound or a vowel sound, the ending is pronounced [d]:

[v]	shaved	[i]	studied
[l]	smiled	[e]	played
[n]	cleaned		

   c. When a verb ends in a [t] or a [d] sound, the ending is pronounced [ɪd] and forms an additional syllable:

[t]	shouted	waited
	painted	planted

2. **Spelling Rules**

   a. When a verb ends in a *y* that is preceded by a consonant, the *y* changes to *i* when *ed* is added. For example: study—stud*ied*.

   b. When a verb ends in *e,* add only *d.* For example: smile—smil*ed*.

Text Page 128: *How Do You Feel Today?*

FOCUS

- Talking about how one feels
- Describing common physical ailments

INTRODUCING THE 1st MODEL

People are telling how they feel, using expressions which range from very positive *(I feel great)* to very negative *(I feel terrible)*. (Note that their facial expressions reflect how they feel.)

There are 6 model conversations. Introduce and practice each before going on to the next.

A. How do you feel today?	A. How do you feel today?
B. I feel great!	B. So-so.
A. I'm glad to hear that.	A. I'm sorry to hear that.
A. How do you feel today?	A. How do you feel today?
B. I feel fine.	B. Not so good.
A. I'm glad to hear that.	A. I'm sorry to hear that.
A. How do you feel today?	A. How do you feel today?
B. I feel okay.	B. I feel terrible.
A. I'm glad to hear that.	A. I'm sorry to hear that.

1. Have students look at the illustration at the top of the page.
2. Set the scene: "People are talking about how they feel."
3. Present the model.
4. Full-Class Choral Repetition.
5. Ask students if they have any questions; check understanding of new vocabulary: *How do you feel? great, fine, okay, So-so, not so good, terrible, I'm glad to hear that, I'm sorry to hear that.*
6. Group Choral Repetition.
7. Choral Conversation.
8. Call on one or two pairs of students to present the dialog.

   (For additional practice, do Choral Conversation in small groups or by rows.)

INTRODUCING THE MODEL

1. Have students look at the model illustration.
2. Set the scene: "Two people are talking."
3. Present the model.
4. Full-Class Choral Repetition.
5. Ask students if they have any questions; check understanding of new vocabulary: *What's the matter? headache.*
6. Group Choral Repetition.

7. Choral Conversation.

8. Call on one or two pairs of students to present the dialog.

   (For additional practice, do Choral Conversation in small groups or by rows.)

SIDE BY SIDE EXERCISES

Examples

1. A. What's the matter? B. I have a stomachache.	2. A. What's the matter? B. I have a toothache.	3. A. What's the matter? B. I have a backache.

Use the illustrations in the text, *Side by Side* Picture Cards 140–146, or your own visuals to introduce the new vocabulary for *ailments.*

1. **Exercise 1:** Introduce the word *stomachache.* Call on two students to present the dialog. Then do Choral Repetition and Choral Conversation Practice.

2. **Exercise 2:** Introduce the word *toothache.* Same as above.

3. **Exercises 3–6:**

   New vocabulary: 3. *backache*   4. *earache*   5. *sore throat*   6. *cold*

   Either Full-Class Practice or Pair Practice.

Ask Another Student in Your Class

In this exercise students choose one of the two conversations to talk about how they feel today. Have pairs of students create conversations using the vocabulary they have learned on this page. This can be either Full-Class Practice or Pair Practice.

WORKBOOK

Pages 112–113

   Exercise Note

   Workbook p. 113:   Students practice ailments and word stress to indicate contrast.

EXPANSION ACTIVITY

Picture Story: My Friends Are Sick

Practice talking about how people feel by telling this story and having students ask and answer questions about it.

1. Draw 7 stick figures on the board and write names under them. (To help students remember the vocabulary, the first letter of each name is also the first letter of the ailment that person has.)

Sally   Stanley   Harry   Tommy   Edward   Carol   Barbara

2. Tell this story, pointing to each person as you tell about him or her: "All my friends are sick today. They all feel TERRIBLE! What's the matter with them?"

Sally has a *sore throat.*   *Tommy* has a *toothache.*   *Carol* has a *cold.*
Stanley has a *stomachache.*   *Edward* has an *earache.*   *Barbara* has a *backache.*
Harry has a *headache.*

3. Create conversations about the story. First you ask the questions; then have students ask and answer. For example:

A. How does Sally feel today?
B. She feels terrible!
A. What's the matter?
B. She has a sore throat.
A. I'm sorry to hear that.

Text Page 129: *What Did You Do Yesterday?*

FOCUS

> • Past tense of regular verbs
> • Pronunciations of *ed* ending: [t], [d], or [ɪd]

GETTING READY

1. Introduce the new word *yesterday.*
2. Introduce the past tense:

    a. Read the pairs of sentences in the box at the top of the page.

    b. Have students repeat each sentence chorally and individually.

    c. Practice the 3 pronunciations of the *ed* ending (see **Chapter Overview,** Pronunciation).

    > 1) From the smaller box near the top of the page, read the simple forms and the past tense forms of the verbs *work, play,* and *rest.*
    >
    > 2) Have students repeat each form chorally and individually.
    >
    > 3) Point out the pronunciation cues for the final sounds: [t], [d], [ɪd].
    >
    > 4) Say the simple form and have a student tell you the past tense form.

WHAT DID YOU DO YESTERDAY?

In these exercises students use the past tense verbs to answer the question *What did you do yesterday?* The exercises are presented in 3 groups: verbs with final [t], [d], and [ɪd] sounds.

INTRODUCING THE MODEL

> A. What did you do yesterday?
> B. I worked.

1. Have students look at the illustration for Exercise 1.
2. Set the scene: "People are talking about yesterday."
3. Present the model.
4. Full-Class Choral Repetition.
5. Ask students if they have any questions.
6. Group Choral Repetition.
7. Choral Conversation.
8. Call on one or two pairs of students to present the dialog.
    (For additional practice, do Choral Conversation in small groups or by rows.)

SIDE BY SIDE EXERCISES

In these exercises students can add objects to the verbs when appropriate.

Examples

---

2. A. What did you do yesterday?
   B. I cooked breakfast (lunch/dinner).

3. A. What did you do yesterday?
   B. I talked on the telephone.

4. A. What did you do yesterday?
   B. I fixed my car.

5. A. What did you do yesterday?
   B. I brushed my teeth.

---

1. **Exercise 2:** Call on two students to present the dialog. Then do Choral Repetition and Choral Conversation Practice.

2. **Exercise 3:** Introduce the expression *talk on the telephone.* Same as above.

3. **Exercises 4–20:**

New vocabulary: 19. *wait for*

Either Full-Class Practice or Pair Practice.

WORKBOOK

Pages 114–115

Exercise Note

Workbook p. 114: Students practice writing and saying the past tense with *I.* Call on several students for each question to have them practice pronouncing the past tense with [t], [d], and [ɪd]. Note Exercise 5: study→studied.

EXPANSION ACTIVITIES

1. Practice with Visuals

Use your own visuals for the verbs on text page 129 or *Side by Side* Picture Cards 147–167. Give these visuals to students.

a. Ask students holding visuals: "What did you do yesterday?" Have students answer, using the past tense of the verb shown in the visual.

b. Call on pairs of students holding visuals. Have them ask and answer the question "What did you do yesterday?"

2. Pronunciation Practice: Pete, Ted, and David Stories

Tell the following stories to provide additional practice with the final [t] [d] and [ɪd] pronunciations of regular past tense verbs.

a. *A Story about Pete* – [*t*]

   1) Write on the board:

   > Pete: cook<u>ed</u>   fix<u>ed</u>   talk<u>ed</u>   wash<u>ed</u>

   2) Say: "This is my friend Pete. Yesterday Pete cooked breakfast,he fixed his bicycle, he talked to his sister on the telephone, and he washed his car."

   3) Have students tell you what *Pete* did. For example:

   > A. What did Pete do yesterday?
   > B. He cooked breakfast.

   4) Have students pretend to be *Pete*. Have them tell you everything they did:

   > A. Pete, what did you do yesterday?
   > B. I cooked breakfast, I fixed my bicycle, I talked to my sister on the telephone, and I washed my car.

b. *A Story about Ted* – [*d*]

   1) Write on the board:

   > Ted: clean<u>ed</u>   listen<u>ed</u>   play<u>ed</u>   stud<u>ied</u>

   2) Say: "This is my cousin, Ted. Yesterday, Ted cleaned his apartment, he listened to the radio, he played cards, and he studied English."

   3) Have students practice talking about *Ted* the same way they did for *Pete*.

c. *A Story about David* – [ɪd]

   1) Write on the board:

   > David: plant<u>ed</u>   paint<u>ed</u>   rest<u>ed</u>   wait<u>ed</u>

   2) Say: "This is my neighbor, David. Yesterday David planted flowers, he painted his living room, and then he rested and waited for a long distance phone call."

   3) Have students practice talking about *David* the same way they did for *Pete* and *Ted*.

Text Pages 130–131:   *What's the Matter?*

FOCUS

- Practice using the past tense for all persons
- Introduction to irregular verbs:

eat–ate	*drink–drank*
sing–sang	*sit–sat*

GETTING READY

1. Read all the forms in the right-hand box at the top of the page. Have students repeat chorally. For example:

   "I worked yesterday."
   "We worked yesterday."
   "You worked yesterday."

2. Substitute a few other verbs and practice with all the pronouns.

INTRODUCING THE MODEL

1. Have students look at the model illustration.
2. Set the scene: "Two people are talking about David."
3. Present the model.
4. Full-Class Choral Repetition.
5. Ask students if they have any questions; check understanding of new vocabulary: *all day, How did he get it?*
6. Group Choral Repetition.
7. Choral Conversation.
8. Call on one or two pairs of students to present the dialog.

   (For additional practice, do Choral Conversation in small groups or by rows.)
9. Introduce the expressions *all morning, all afternoon, all evening, all night.* Have pairs of students practice the model again, using these expressions in place of *all day.*

SIDE BY SIDE EXERCISES

Examples

1. A. How does Jane feel?
   B. Not so good.
   A. What's the matter?
   B. She has a sore throat.
   A. Why?
   B. Because she talked on the telephone all day (morning/afternoon/evening/night).

2. A. How does George feel?
   B. Not so good.
   A. What's the matter?
   B. He has an earache.
   A. Why?
   B. Because he listened to the radio all day (morning/afternoon/evening/night).

Key Words for the Exercises:

3. headache—studied
4. backache—danced
5. sore throat—shouted
6. cold—waited in the rain

7. backache—planted flowers
8. headache—her baby cried
9. earache—his dog barked

1. **Exercise 1:** Call on two students to present the dialog. Then do Choral Repetition and Choral Conversation Practice.

2. **Exercise 2:** Same as above.

3. **Exercises 3–9:**

   Either Full-Class Practice or Pair Practice.

4. Introduce the irregular verbs at the top of text page 131. Read the forms and have students repeat chorally and individually.

5. **Exercise 10:** Introduce the new word *candy*. Call on two students to present the dialog. Then do Choral Repetition and Choral Conversation Practice.

6. **Exercise 11:** Same as above.

7. **Exercises 12–15:**

New vocabulary:	12. *soda*	14. *cookies*

   Either Full-Class Practice or Pair Practice.

WORKBOOK

Pages 116–119

Exercise Note

Workbook p. 118: Students practice the three pronunciations of the past tense ending. In the final exercise, students practice with any vocabulary they wish.

EXPANSION ACTIVITIES

1. **Role Play: How Do You Feel?**

   Have students write and act out original dialogs based on the conversations on text pages 130–131. The dialogs should begin: "How do you feel?"

2. **Students' Stories: Review of Irregular Past Tense Verbs**

   a. Write these verbs on the board:

sat	ate	drank	sang

   or use *Side by Side* Picture Cards 168–171.

   b. Have each student write a story, using all four verbs, about what he or she did yesterday. Examples:

   > "Yesterday I sat in a restaurant all day. I ate cookies, I drank wine, and I sang Spanish songs."
   > "Yesterday I sat in my apartment all morning. I ate candy, I drank soda, and I sang."

   Have students tell their stories to the class.

3. *Practice with Verbs*

a. Write the following conversational framework on the board:

> A. Do you _____ very often?
> B. Yes. I _____ yesterday, and I'm going to _____ tomorrow.

b. Model the following conversation and have students repeat:

>   A. Do you plant flowers very often?
>   B. Yes. I planted flowers yesterday, and I'm going to plant flowers tomorrow.

c. Call on pairs of students to create conversations based on the model. As cues for their conversations, put the following on word cards:

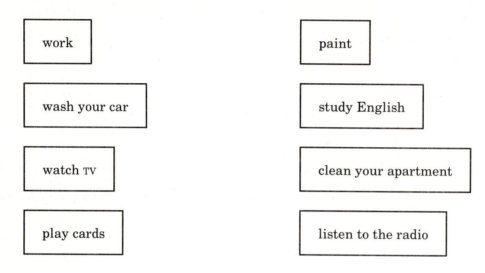

work	paint
wash your car	study English
watch TV	clean your apartment
play cards	listen to the radio

Text Page 131

ON YOUR OWN: *Do You Want to Make an Appointment?*

FOCUS

- Making an appointment with the doctor
- Review of ailments
- Review of the past tense

ON YOUR OWN ACTIVITY

Students use the *skeletal model* to create their own conversations, using any vocabulary they wish.

1. Introduce the new words and expressions:

Hello	Do you have any idea why?	How about . . . ?
How are you?	make an appointment	That's fine.
What seems to be the problem?	When can you see me?	Thank you very much.

2. Have students write their conversations for homework and then present them in class the next day.

Example

A. Hello, Doctor Smith? This is Mr. Jones.
B. Hello, Mr. Jones. How are you?
A. I don't feel very well today.
B. I'm sorry to hear that. What seems to be the problem?
A. I have a TERRIBLE stomachache.
B. Do you have any idea why?
A. Well, Doctor . . . I ate candy all day yesterday.
B. I see. Do you want to make an appointment?
A. Yes, please. When can you see me?
B. How about tomorrow at two o'clock?
A. That's fine. Thank you very much.

EXPANSION ACTIVITY

Practice with Visuals: Contrast of the Simple Present Tense and Past Tense

1. Put this conversational model on the board:

A. What did _____ do yesterday?
B. _____ all day.
A. Does _____ usually _____ all day?
B. No. But _____ all day yesterday!

2. Use your own visuals or *Side by Side* Picture Cards of everyday and leisure activities to provide cues for pairs of students to create conversations based on the model. For example:

(visual: a man sitting in the park)

A. What did Bill do yesterday?
B. He sat in the park all day.
A. Does he usually sit in the park all day?
B. No. But he sat in the park all day yesterday!

READING: *The Wilsons' Party*

FOCUS

Past tense: Regular and irregular verbs

NEW VOCABULARY

arrive	fence	inside and out	seconds
ask (for)	front steps	invite	serve
cheese	furniture	last night	show (v)
cracker	go home	love (v)	slides
dessert	guest	meal	spaghetti
dust (v)	Hawaii	pie	steps
enjoy	inside	prepare (for)	stereo
			turn on

PREVIEWING THE STORY (optional)

Have students talk about the story title and/or illustrations. Introduce new vocabulary.

READING THE STORY

1. Have students read silently, or follow along silently as the story is read aloud by you, by one or more students, or on the tape.
2. Ask students if they have any questions; check understanding of vocabulary.
3. Check students' comprehension, using some or all of the following questions:

   a. What did Margaret Wilson do in the morning?
   b. What did Bob do?
   c. What did Mrs. Wilson do?
   d. What did Mr. Wilson do?
   e. What did Margaret do in the afternoon?
   f. What did Bob do?
   g. What did Mr. and Mrs. Wilson do?
   h. What did the guests do after they arrived at the Wilsons' party?
   i. What did they talk about?
   j. What did the Wilsons do at 9:00?
   k. Tell about the meal.
   l. What did everybody do after dinner?
   m. What did Bob do?
   n. What did Margaret do?
   o. What did Mr. and Mrs. Wilson do?
   p. What did everybody do after that?

CHECK-UP

Answer These Questions

> 1. They arrived at about 7:30.
> 2. They sat in the living room.
> 3. They ate cheese and crackers and drank wine.
> 4. They served dinner at 9:00.
> 5. She sang.

Listening

Have students complete the exercises as you play the tape or read the following:

> Listen and choose the word you hear.
>
> 1. I studied at the library all day. (b)
> 2. We work at the restaurant all day. (a)
> 3. They stayed home all afternoon. (b)
> 4. I plant flowers in my garden in the spring. (a)
> 5. They invited their friends to their parties. (b)
> 6. Mr. and Mrs. Franklin drink lemonade all summer. (a)
> 7. Tim and Bill sat in their living room all morning. (b)
> 8. They finish their work at four o'clock. (a)
> 9. Mr. Wilson cooked dinner for his family. (b)
> 10. The people at the party ate cheese and crackers. (b)
> 11. She watched TV in the living room. (b)
> 12. He cleaned the basement every day. (b)

IN YOUR OWN WORDS

1. Make sure students understand the instructions.
2. Have students do the activity as written homework, using a dictionary for any new words they wish to use.
3. Have students present and discuss what they have written, in pairs or as a class.

WORKBOOK ANSWER KEY AND LISTENING SCRIPTS

Page 112 A. ALL MY FRIENDS ARE SICK

1. He has a toothache.
2. She has a stomachache.
3. What's the matter with
   He has a headache.
4. What's the matter with
   She has a sore throat.
5. What's the matter with
   He has an earache.
6. What's the matter with
   She has a cold.
7. I have a backache.

Page 112 B. LISTEN

Listen to the story. Write the correct number next to each picture.

Helen is home today with her family because her sisters and brothers are all sick. What's the matter with them?

1. Her brother David has a very bad headache. He feels terrible.
2. Her sister Patty isn't at school because she has a toothache.
3. Edward has a sore throat.
4. Alice is very upset because she has a backache.
5. What's the matter with Jack? He doesn't know, but he feels terrible.

Helen's family is sick today, but not Helen.

6. Helen feels fine.

Answers

6	5	2
3	1	4

Page 114 D. WHAT DID YOU DO YESTERDAY?

1. I played
2. I worked.
3. I painted
4. I watched
5. I studied
6. I cleaned
7. I planted
8. I cooked
9. I skated
10. I fixed
11. I visited
12. I listened
    washed

Page 115 E. LISTEN

Listen to each sentence. Put a circle around the correct word.

1. I study.
2. I studied.
3. I worked.
4. I work.
5. I wait for the train.
6. I waited for the bus.
7. I bake.
8. I cooked breakfast.
9. I played cards.
10. I play the piano.
11. I fixed the car.
12. I visited my friends.
13. I skate.
14. I rest.
15. I rested.

Answers

1. every day
2. yesterday
3. yesterday
4. every day
5. every day
6. yesterday
7. every day
8. yesterday
9. yesterday
10. every day
11. yesterday
12. yesterday
13. every day
14. every day
15. yesterday

Page 116   F.   JOHN'S DAY AT HOME

1. He cooked dinner.
2. He baked an apple pie.
3. He planted flowers.
4. He washed the car.
5. He painted the bedroom.
6. He fixed the TV.
7. He rested.

Page 116   G.   WHAT DID EVERYBODY DO?

1. He worked
2. They played baseball
3. He baked (cookies)
4. They danced
5. She waited for the bus
6. We painted the bathroom
7. What did, do
   She studied English
8. What did
   do
   They skated

Page 119   I.   BILL'S WEDDING

1. played
2. sang
3. ate
4. danced
5. sat
6. talked
7. sat
8. cried
9. ate
10. drank
11. talked

Page 119   J.   THE DAY AFTER BILL'S WEDDING

1. Because he danced with all his cousins and his aunts last night.
2. Because she ate cookies and candy all night.
3. Because she sat on the sofa and talked about her children all night.
4. Because you talked with everybody at the wedding.

TEACHER'S NOTES

GRAMMAR

Past Tense:
Yes/No Questions

Did	I he she it we you they	work?

Short Answers

Yes,	I he she it we you they	did.

No,	I he she it we you they	didn't.

Past Tense:
WH-Questions

What did	I he she it we you they	do?

Irregular Verbs

buy	– bought
do	– did
forget	– forgot
get	– got
go	– went
have	– had
meet	– met
read	– read
steal	– stole
take	– took
write	– wrote

Time Expressions

Did you study English	yesterday? yesterday morning? yesterday afternoon? yesterday evening? last night?

FUNCTIONS

Asking for and Reporting Information

Did you *go to the bank this afternoon?*
  Yes, I did.
  No, I didn't.

Did you *have a good day today?*
  No, I didn't. *I had a* TERRIBLE *day.*

What happened?

Why did you *have a bad headache?*
  Because *my boss shouted at me.*

What did you do *last night?*
What time did you *get up?*
How did you *get to class today?*

I had a *stomachache this morning.*
I met *an old friend on the way to class.*

Expressing Obligation

I had to *go to the post office before class.*

Forgetting

I forgot *my English book.*

Apologizing

I'm sorry *I'm late.*

Greeting People

Hi, *Mary!*

NEW VOCABULARY

banana
before
brush (v)
cup
didn't
even though
excuse (n)
factory
get angry
girlfriend
go back home
however
minute

miss (v)
morning exercises
on the way
on time
pleasant
quick
record (n)
repair shop
steal
subway
supervisor
take the subway

thief
tomato
yesterday afternoon
yesterday evening
yesterday morning

an hour early
have a good day
half a mile
rush out of the house
Well, . . .
What happened?

Text Page 136: *I Brushed My Teeth*

FOCUS

> • Yes/No questions with regular verbs in the past tense;
>   short answers:
>   *Did you study English?*
>   *No, I didn't.*
>
> • Time expressions:
>   *today/this morning/this afternoon/this evening/tonight*
>   *yesterday/yesterday morning/yesterday afternoon/yesterday evening/last night*

GETTING READY

1. Read the sample sentences in the boxes at the top of the page. Have students repeat each one chorally.
2. Write the framework below on the board and practice it using each of the persons (I, he, she, we, you, they):

> _____ cooked.   Yes, _____ did.
> Did _____ cook?   No, _____ didn't.

   a. Read each sentence using a pronoun. For example:

      "He cooked."
      "Did he cook?"
      "Yes, he did."
      "No, he didn't."

   b. Have students repeat each line chorally.

INTRODUCING THE MODEL

1. Have students look at the model illustration.
2. Set the scene: "A mother is talking to her son."
3. Present the model.
4. Full-Class Choral Repetition.
5. Ask students if they have any questions; check understanding of new vocabulary: *brush*.
6. Group Choral Repetition.
7. Choral Conversation.
8. Call on one or two pairs of students to present the dialog.
   (For additional practice, do Choral Conversation in small groups or by rows.)
9. Introduce the time expressions under the model. Have pairs of students practice the model again using these time expressions in place of *this morning*.

SIDE BY SIDE EXERCISES

Examples

> 1. A. Did he study English last night?
>   B. No, he didn't. He studied Spanish.
>
> 2. A. Did she wash her windows this morning?
>   B. No, she didn't. She washed her car.

1. **Exercise 1:** Call on two students to present the dialog. Then do Choral Repetition and Choral Conversation Practice.

2. **Exercise 2:** Same as above.

3. **Exercises 3–6:**

> **New vocabulary:**   5. *record*

Either Full-Class or Pair Practice.

WORKBOOK

Pages 120–121

EXPANSION ACTIVITIES

1. ***Students Talk about Themselves:*** ***Practice with*** **Yes, I did. No, I didn't.**

   a. Use your own visuals, *Side by Side* Picture Cards, or write these activities on the board:

   > study _____   call _____   work
   > wash _____   plant _____   dance
   > play _____   paint _____   ski
   > listen to _____   brush _____   skate

   b. Have students ask each other *Yes/No* questions about yesterday using the verbs shown on the visuals or on the board. Call on pairs of students. For example:

   > A. Did you play cards yesterday?   A. Did you study English yesterday?
   > B. No, I didn't.   B. Yes, I did.

2. ***Practice with Negative Sentences:*** ***Steve and Bill Story***

   a. Say: "I have two friends, Steve and Bill. They're very different. I'm going to tell YOU about Steve, and you're going to tell ME about Bill."

   b. Give an example: Write the two sentences below on the board and read them:

   > Steve worked yesterday.
   > Bill didn't work yesterday.

c. Have students listen as you read each statement about *Steve.* Then ask a student, "What about *Bill?*" Have students change the verb to the negative form and make a statement about *Bill.*

1. Steve *shaved* yesterday morning.
   (Bill *didn't shave* yesterday morning.)
2. Steve *cleaned* his apartment.
   (Bill *didn't clean* his apartment.)
3. Steve *called* his mother yesterday.
   (Bill *didn't call* his mother yesterday.)
4. Steve *painted* his garage yesterday.
   (Bill *didn't paint* his garage yesterday.)
5. Steve *cooked* dinner last night.
   (Bill *didn't cook* dinner last night.)
6. Steve *danced* at a night club all night.
   (Bill *didn't dance* at a night club all night.)

d. Ask the class: "What did Bill do yesterday?" Have students make up answers, using any vocabulary they wish.

3. *Dictation*

Dictate these sentences to the class. Tell students to listen carefully to the endings of words before they write them.

1. He worked.
2. Did they work?
3. She didn't work.
4. Did they study?
5. She studied.
6. I didn't study.

Text Page 137: *We Went to the Supermarket*

FOCUS

- Irregular verbs in the past tense:

go–went	*buy–bought*
take–took	*write–wrote*
get–got	*read–read*
have–had	*do–did*

- Yes/No questions with irregular verbs in the past tense:

  Did you go to the bank?
  No, we didn't.

- Time expressions

GETTING READY

1. Introduce the past tense of *go: went.*
2. Read the sample sentences in the boxes at the top of the page. Have students repeat chorally.

INTRODUCING THE MODEL

1. Have students look at the model illustration.
2. Set the scene: "Friends are talking."
3. Present the model.
4. Full-Class Choral Repetition.
5. Ask students if they have any questions; check understanding of new vocabulary: *went.*
6. Group Choral Repetition.
7. Choral Conversation.
8. Call on one or two pairs of students to present the dialog.

   (For additional practice, do Choral Conversation in small groups or by rows.)
9. Practice the model with other pronouns. Put on the board:

Sally   Bob   Mr. and Mrs. Jones

Call on pairs of students to practice the model again using these names. For example:

   A. Did Sally go to the bank this afternoon?
   B. No, she didn't. She went to the supermarket.

SIDE BY SIDE EXERCISES

Examples

---

1. A. Did you go skating yesterday?
   B. No, I didn't. I went skiing.

2. A. Did you take the subway this morning?
   B. No, I didn't. I took the bus.

---

1. **Exercise 1:** Call on two students to present the dialog. Then do Choral Repetition and Choral Conversation Practice.

2. **Exercise 2:** Introduce the new vocabulary *take the subway, take the bus.* Same as above.

3. **Exercises 3–8:**

New vocabulary: 5. *banana, tomato* 6. *girlfriend*

Language Note

Exercise 7: The present and past tense forms of the verb *read* are spelled the same, but are pronounced differently: present tense [rid]
past tense [red]

Either Full-Class Practice or Pair Practice.

WORKBOOK

Pages 122–124 (Exercises D, E, F)

Exercise Note

Workbook p. 123: Have students complete the exercises with words that rhyme. Probable answers: *They painted the door. He called his brother. We bought tomatoes. He got up at eleven.*

EXPANSION ACTIVITIES

1. *Review Irregular Past Tense Forms*

   Say the simple form of the following verbs and have students tell you the past tense forms.

a. eat–ate	d. sit–sat	g. get–got	j. write–wrote
b. drink–drank	e. go–went	h. have–had	k. read–read
c. sing–sang	f. take–took	i. buy–bought	l. do–did

2. *Practice with Irregular Verbs: Steve and Bill Story*

   a. Say: "I'm going to talk about my friends Steve and Bill. I'm going to tell YOU about Bill, and you're going to tell ME about Steve."

   b. Give an example. Write these sentences on the board and read them:

Bill didn't get up at 7:00 this morning.
Steve got up at 7:00.

---

c. Have students listen as you read each statement about *Bill*. Then ask a student, "What about *Steve*?" Have students change the verb from the negative to affirmative and make the statement about *Steve*.

1. Bill *didn't take* a shower yesterday.
    (Steve *took* a shower yesterday.)
2. Bill *didn't have* breakfast yesterday.
    (Steve *had* breakfast yesterday.)
3. Bill *didn't eat* lunch at a restaurant.
    (Steve *ate* lunch at a restaurant.)
4. Bill *didn't write* to his brother last night.
    (Steve *wrote* to his brother last night.)
5. Bill *didn't read* a story at night.
    (Steve *read* a story at night.)
6. Bill *didn't do* his exercises yesterday.
    (Steve *did* his exercises yesterday.)
7. Bill *didn't have* a good day.
    (Steve *had* a good day.)

Homework first !

3. **Chain Game: *Practice with Irregular Verbs***

Practice the irregular verbs on text page 137 by playing the following game with your students:

a. Start the chain game by saying:

A. { I went skiing yesterday.
    { Did *you* go skiing yesterday?

b. The student you ask must answer "No, I didn't," make a new statement using the verb *go,* and ask another student, who then continues the *chain.* For example:

B. { No, I didn't. I went skating.
    { Did *you* go skating?
C. { No, I didn't. I went bowling.
    { Did *you* go bowling?
              etc.

The chain can continue as long as students can think of new vocabulary.

Other examples:

A. I got up at 7:00 this morning.
    Did *you* get up at 7:00?
B. No, I didn't. I got up at 7:30 this morning.
    Did *you* get up at 7:30 this morning?
C. No, I didn't. I got up at 8:00 this morning.
    Did *you* get up at 8:00 this morning?
              •
              •
              •

A. I had a headache yesterday.
    Did *you* have a headache?
B. No, I didn't. I had a stomachache.
    Did *you* have a stomachache?
              •
              •
              •

swim

run

sing

Text Pages 138–139: *Mary's Terrible Day*

FOCUS

- Practice with regular and irregular verbs in the past tense
- *Why* questions

INTRODUCING THE MODEL

1. Have students look at the model illustrations in the text.
2. Set the scene: "This is a story about Mary."
3. Present the model.
4. Full-Class Choral Repetition.
5. Ask students if they have any questions; check understanding of new vocabulary: *miss the bus, arrive late for work.*
6. Call on one or two students to present the model.

   (For additional practice, do Choral Repetition in small groups or by rows.)

SIDE BY SIDE EXERCISES

Mary is talking to a friend about the chain of unfortunate events in her day. In this conversation Mary answers her friend's questions and, in so doing, she retells the story at the top of the page in reverse order.

Answer Key

> A. Hi, Mary! Did you have a good day today?
> B. No, I didn't. I had a TERRIBLE day.
> A. What happened?
> B. I had a bad headache all afternoon.
> A. Why did you have a bad headache?
> B. Because my boss shouted at me.
> A. Why did your boss shout at you?
> B. Because I arrived late for work.
> A. Why did you arrive late for work?
> B. Because I had to walk to the office.
> A. Why did you have to walk to the office?
> B. Because I missed the bus.
> A. Why did you miss the bus?
> B. Because I got up late.
> A. Why did you get up late?
> B. Because I went to a party last night.

1. Set the scene: "Mary is talking to her friend."
2. With books closed, have students listen as you present the first 8 lines of the dialog.
3. Full-Class Choral Repetition.
4. Have students open their books and look at the dialog. Ask if there are any questions and check understanding of new vocabulary: *What happened?*

5. Group Choral Repetition.

6. Choral Conversation.

7. Call on one or two pairs of students to present the dialog.

   (For additional practice, do Choral Conversation in small groups or by rows.)

8. Call on one or two pairs of students to complete each of the remaining 4 question-answer sets in the dialog. Do Choral Repetition and Choral Conversation Practice after each.

9. *Pair Practice:*   Have all the students practice the dialog in pairs. Then have pairs present the dialog to the class.

HOW ABOUT YOU?

Have students answer the questions, in pairs or as a class.

WORKBOOK

Page 124 (Exercise G)

EXPANSION ACTIVITY

More Practice with Mary's Day

Have students use the key words below as cues for the activities that follow.

Key words (write on the board):

1. go/party	5. arrive late/work
2. get up late	6. boss/shout
3. miss/bus	7. have/bad headache
4. walk/office	

1. Call on students to retell some or all of the story about Mary.

2. Have students role play the conversation at the bottom of the page. Call on students: one pretends to be *Mary* and another *Mary's friend.*

3. Practice with *she:*   Have students create conversations about Mary. They can begin:

   A.   What happened to Mary?
   B.   She had a bad headache all afternoon.
   A.   Why did she have a bad headache?

4. Practice with *he:*   Change *Mary* to *Marvin.* Have pairs of students create conversations about *Marvin.* They can begin:

   A.   What happened to Marvin?
   B.   He had a bad headache all afternoon.

Text Pages 139–140: *Excuses/I'm Sorry I'm Late*

FOCUS

- Making excuses
- Further practice with verbs in the past tense

EXCUSES

This exercise is preparation for the following **On Your Own** exercise.

1. Read each excuse, using one of the suggestions in parentheses to fill in the blank; have students repeat. Introduce the new words: *before class, forget–forgot, go back home, meet–met, on the way, thief, steal–stole.*
2. Call on students to say each excuse using different vocabulary. For example:

   > I missed the bus.
   > I missed the train.
   > I missed the subway.

3. Have students think of additional excuses they might use for being late to class.
4. Discuss the attitude toward time in your culture. When is it important to be on time? When is it acceptable to be late? How late can you be?

   ### Culture Note

   The expression *on time* represents an important concept in U.S. culture. In the United States, people are generally expected to arrive *on time* (at the invited or appointed time). When people are not on time, they commonly offer an excuse, giving the reason why they are late.

ON YOUR OWN: *I'm Sorry I'm Late*

INTRODUCING THE MODEL

1. Have students look at the model illustration.
2. Set the scene: "A teacher and a student are talking. The teacher is upset because the student is late for class."
3. Present the model.
4. Full-Class Choral Repetition.
5. Ask students if they have any questions; check understanding of new vocabulary: *well, excuse.*
6. Group Choral Repetition.
7. Choral Conversation.
8. Call on one or two pairs of students to present the dialog.

   (For additional practice, do Choral Conversation in small groups or by rows.)

9. For homework, have students write their own conversations based on the model. Students can use any excuses they wish. Have students role play their conversations in the next class. The students playing the part of the teacher should sit at your desk while the one who is late comes in the door.

WORKBOOK

Pages 125–126

Exercise Note

Workbook p. 126:   These poems are a review of the past tense.

EXPANSION ACTIVITY

Picture Story: Past Tense

Make up a story about the events in someone's day yesterday.

1. Put times and key words (or stick figures) on the board. For example:

7:00
(get up)

8:15
(walk to work)

12:45
(meet a friend
and have lunch)

5:00
(go home)

6:30
(eat dinner)

8:00
(read the
newspaper)

10:00
(go to bed)

2. Tell about that person's day. For example:

> "Jim got up at 7:00 yesterday.
> At 8:15 he walked to work.
> He met a friend at 12:45 and they had lunch.
> He went home at 5:00.
> At 6:30 he ate dinner.
> At 8:00 he read the newspaper.
> He went to bed at 10:00."

3. Ask *What* and *When* questions about *Jim;* then call on pairs of students to ask and answer questions. For example:

> "What time did Jim get up yesterday?"
> "When did he meet a friend?"

READING: *Late for Work*

FOCUS

> Past tense

NEW VOCABULARY

an hour early	half a mile	on time
cup	however	quick
even though	minute	repair shop
factory	morning	rush out of the house
got (get) angry	exercises	supervisor

PREVIEWING THE STORY (optional)

Have students talk about the story title and/or illustration. Introduce new vocabulary.

READING THE STORY

1. Have students read silently, or follow along silently as the story is read aloud by you, by one or more students, or on the tape.
2. Ask students if they have any questions; check understanding of vocabulary.
3. Check students' comprehension, using some or all of the following questions:

   a. Did Victor get up at 7 A.M. this morning?
   b. When did he get up?
   c. Did he do his morning exercises for twenty minutes?
   d. How long did he do them?
   e. Did he take a long shower?
   f. What did he do?
   g. Did he have a big breakfast?
   h. What did he have?
   i. Did he leave for work at 8 o'clock?
   j. When did he leave for work?
   k. Did Victor drive to work this morning?
   l. Why not?
   m. What did he have to take?
   n. How far did he walk from his house to the center of town?
   o. How long did he wait for the bus?
   p. How far did he walk after he got off the bus?
   q. Did Victor get to work on time?
   r. How late did he get there?
   s. What did his supervisor do?

CHECK-UP

Listening

Have students complete the exercises as you play the tape or read the following:

> Listen and write the missing words.
>
> Shirley enjoyed her day off yesterday. She got up late, went jogging in the park, took a long shower, and ate a big breakfast. In the afternoon, she went to the movies with her sister, and in the evening, she had dinner with her parents. After dinner they sat in the living room and talked. Shirley had a very pleasant day off yesterday.

1. got up
2. went
3. took
4. ate
5. went
6. had
7. sat
8. talked
9. had

HOW ABOUT YOU?

Have students answer the questions, in pairs or as a class.

WORKBOOK ANSWER KEY AND LISTENING SCRIPTS

Page 120 A. CORRECT THE SENTENCE

1. She didn't fix the TV.
   She fixed the car.
2. They didn't paint their bedroom.
   They painted their kitchen.
3. He didn't wash the clothes.
   He washed the windows.
4. They didn't play chess.
   They played cards.
5. He didn't talk to his uncle.
   He talked to his aunt.
6. She didn't wait for the train.
   She waited for the bus.
7. She didn't study mathematics.
   She studied English.
8. He didn't call the doctor.
   He called the plumber.

Page 121 B. LISTEN: *Sally and Her Brother*

Listen to the story. Write the missing words.

Sally is very tired today. She worked all day yesterday, and her family didn't help her. Yesterday morning she fixed the car. Yesterday afternoon she painted the bathroom. Yesterday evening she cleaned the basement. She didn't rest all day.

Sally's brother isn't very tired today. Yesterday he didn't work. He didn't fix the car. He didn't paint the bathroom, and he didn't clean the basement. What did he do? He talked on the telephone all morning. He listened to music all afternoon, and he rested in front of the TV all evening.

Answers
1. worked
2. help
3. fixed
4. painted
5. cleaned
6. rest
7. work
8. fix
9. paint
10. clean
11. talked
12. listened
13. rested

Page 121 C. WRITE ABOUT SALLY AND HER BROTHER

1. Yes, she did.
2. No, he didn't.
3. Yes, she did.
4. Yes, he did.
5. No, she didn't.
6. Did Sally fix
7. Did Sally paint
8. Did her brother listen
9. Did her brother clean
10. Did Sally rest
11. Did Sally clean

Page 122 D. YESTERDAY

1. didn't take, took
2. didn't buy, bought
3. didn't go, went
4. didn't write, wrote
5. didn't get up, got up
6. didn't have, had
7. didn't read, read
8. didn't do, did
9. didn't eat, ate
10. didn't drink, drank
11. didn't sit, sat
12. didn't sing, sang
13. didn't take, took
14. didn't go, went
15. didn't buy, bought
16. didn't have, had

Page 124 F. WHAT'S THE QUESTION?

1. Did you go
2. Did he buy
3. Did they write
4. Did she have
5. Did you get up
6. Did you read
7. Did you go
8. Did they have

9. Did you eat
10. Did he buy
11. Did they drink
12. Did she sing
13. Did she go
14. Did you sit

Page 124   G.   LISTEN

Listen to each question. Put a circle around the correct answer.

1. When did Betty go to the bank?
2. What does Fred study at school?
3. When did Peter do his homework?
4. What did you buy at the store?
5. What kind of music do you listen to?
6. Who did he visit in Paris?
7. When does Nancy write to her grandmother?
8. Where did Alice and Jane play basketball?
9. When do Mr. and Mrs. Johnson go dancing?
10. When did Billy clean his room?

Answers

1.	b	6.	b
2.	a	7.	a
3.	b	8.	b
4.	b	9.	a
5.	a	10.	b

Page 125   H.   BUT THEY DIDN'T

1. did, go, He went
2. did, drink, He drank
3. did, study, He studied

4. did, go, She went
5. did, forget, She forgot
6. did, call, She called

7. did, go, They went
8. did, eat, They ate
9. did, listen, They listened

10. did, go, She went
11. did, meet, She met
12. did, They talked

GRAMMAR

To Be: Past Tense

I He She It	was	happy.
We You They	were	

I He She It	wasn't	tired.
We You They	weren't	

Was	I he she it	late?
Were	we you they	

Yes,	I he she it	was.
	we you they	were.

No,	I he she it	wasn't.
	we you they	weren't.

FUNCTIONS

Asking for and Reporting Information

How about you?

Were you *at the ballgame last night?*
 No, I wasn't. I was *at the movies.*

Did you *sleep well last night?*
 Yes, I did.
 No, I didn't.

Where were you born?
Where did you grow up?
Where did you go to school?
What did you study?
When did you move?
Where?
What did you look like?
What did you do *with your friends?*
How old were you when *you began to talk?*

Were you *tall?*
Did you have *curly hair?*

Inquiring about Likes/Dislikes

Did you like *school?*

Who was your favorite *teacher?*
What was your favorite *subject?*

Describing

We were always *sad.*
Now we're *happy.*

NEW VOCABULARY

assembly line
back home
ballgame
born
bread
cereal
comfortable
cute
dimple
dog food
dull
enormous
floor wax
freckles
full
game

grow up
healthy
hero
hobby
how old
ice cream
milk
miss
paint (n)
Peru
shampoo
shiny
skim milk
soap
spare time
still

subject
tiny
toothpaste
uncomfortable
United States
village
vitamins
was
wasn't
were
weren't
window cleaner
word

go on a date
six years old

Text Page 144: *PRESTO Commercials*

FOCUS

Introduction of the past tense forms of the verb *to be:* *was/were*

GETTING READY

Introduce *was* and *were*. Form sentences using the words in the box at the top of the page. Say each sentence and have students repeat chorally and individually.

INTRODUCING THE MODEL

1. Have students look at the model illustration.
2. Set the scene: "This is a TV commercial for PRESTO Vitamins."
3. Present the model.
4. Full-Class Choral Repetition.
5. Ask students if they have any questions; check understanding of new vocabulary: *vitamins, How about you?*

    ### Culture Note

    The following exercises are versions of TV commercials for household products. These types of commercials are common on U.S. television. They often include claims that using the advertised product will improve the viewer's appearance, health, or happiness.

6. Call on one or two students to present the commercial.

    (For additional practice, do Choral Repetition in small groups or by rows.)

SIDE BY SIDE EXERCISES

Examples

---

1. Before our family bought PRESTO Ice Cream, we were always sad.
        I was sad.
        My wife/husband was sad.
        My children were sad, too.
    Now we're happy because WE bought PRESTO Ice Cream.
    How about you?

2. Before our family bought PRESTO Bread, we were always hungry.
        I was hungry.
        My wife/husband was hungry.
        My children were hungry, too.
    Now we're full because WE bought PRESTO Bread. How about you?

---

1. **Exercise 1:** Introduce the new word *ice cream.* Call on one or two students to present the commercial. Then do Choral Repetition and Choral Conversation Practice.

2. **Exercise 2:** Introduce the new words *bread, full.* Same as above.

3. **Exercises 3–5:**

New vocabulary   3. *soap, dirty, clean*   4. *cereal, healthy*   5. *skim milk*

Either Full-Class Practice or Pair Practice.

4. **Exercise 6:** Have students use the model as a guide to create a new commercial for another PRESTO product, using vocabulary of their choice. Encourage students to use dictionaries to find new words they want to use. This exercise can be done orally in class or for written homework. If you assign it for homework, you should do one example in class to make sure students understand what's expected. Have students act out their commercials in class the next day.

WORKBOOK

Page 127

EXPANSION ACTIVITIES

1. Practice **Was** *and* **Were** *with Visuals*

a. Begin by telling this story:

"Yesterday I really wanted to see you. I called you on the phone, but you weren't there. I went to your house, but you weren't there. *Where were you?*"

b. Use *Side by Side* Picture Cards, your own visuals, or word cards for places around town. Hold up different visuals as you ask students the questions below. Students answer according to the visuals. For example:

"Where were you?"	*"Where was (male's name)?"*
"I was at the bank."	"He was in the park."
"I was at the movies."	"He was at Stanley's International Restaurant."
"Where were you and (any name)?"	*"Where was (female's name)?"*
"We were at the supermarket."	"She was at the police station."
"We were at a concert."	"She was at the zoo."

2. Talk about the Weather

Ask students questions about the weather yesterday, last week, and last month. For example:

A. How was the weather last week?
B. It was cloudy and cold.

Text Page 145: *Before I Bought PRESTO Shampoo . . .*

FOCUS

> Contrast of present tense and past tense forms of the verb *to be:*
>   *am/is/are   was/were*

INTRODUCING THE MODEL

1. Have students look at the model illustration.
2. Set the scene: "A woman is talking about PRESTO Shampoo."
3. Present the model.
4. Full-Class Choral Repetition.
5. Ask students if they have any questions; check understanding of new vocabulary: *shampoo.*
6. Call on one or two students to present the commercial.

   (For additional practice, do Choral Repetition in small groups or by rows.)

SIDE BY SIDE EXERCISES

Examples

> 1. Before we bought PRESTO Toothpaste, our teeth were yellow.
>   Now they're white.
>
> 2. Before we bought PRESTO Paint, our house was ugly.
>   Now it's beautiful.

1. **Exercise 1:** Introduce the new word *toothpaste.* Call on a student to tell about PRESTO Toothpaste. Then do Choral Repetition.
2. **Exercise 2:** Introduce the new word *paint.* Call on a student to tell about PRESTO Paint. Then do Choral Repetition.
3. **Exercises 3–6:**

> **New vocabulary:**   3. *furniture, comfortable, uncomfortable*   4. *dog food, tiny, enormous*
>   5. *window cleaner*   6. *floor wax, dull, shiny*

   Introduce the new vocabulary one exercise at a time. Call on one or two students to do each exercise. (For more practice, do Choral Repetition.)

4. **Exercise 7:** Have students use the model as a guide to write a new commercial for another PRESTO product, using vocabulary of their choice. Encourage students to use dictionaries to find new words they want to use. This exercise can be done orally in class or for written homework. If you assign it for homework, you should do one example in class to make sure students understand what's expected. Have students present their commercials in class the next day. Encourage students to bring in products from home to use as *props.*

EXPANSION ACTIVITY

Before/Now Commercials with Real Objects

1. Bring real objects to class and provide key words on the board, such as:

   > a PRESTO watch (late/on time)
   > a pair of PRESTO shoes (uncomfortable/comfortable) (tired/energetic)
   > a PRESTO exercise book (thin/heavy)
   > a PRESTO coat (cold/warm)
   > a PRESTO fan (hot/cool)

2. Give the *products* to students and allow a short time for preparation. Encourage students to expand their commercials and say as much as possible about the *products*.

Text Page 146:   *Were You at the Ballgame Last Night?*

FOCUS

> Negative forms of the verb *to be:* *wasn't, weren't*

GETTING READY

Introduce *wasn't* and *weren't*. Form sentences with the words in the grammar box at the top of page 146. Say each sentence and have students repeat chorally and individually. For example:

> "I wasn't at home."
> "He wasn't tired."
> "They weren't hungry."

INTRODUCING THE MODEL

1. Have students look at the model illustration.
2. Set the scene: "Two friends are talking."
3. Present the model.
4. Full-Class Choral Repetition.
5. Ask students if they have any questions; check understanding of new vocabulary: *ballgame.*
6. Group Choral Repetition.
7. Choral Conversation.
8. Call on one or two pairs of students to present the dialog.
   (For additional practice, do Choral Conversation in small groups or by rows.)

SIDE BY SIDE EXERCISES

Examples

> 1. A. Was it hot yesterday?
>   B. No, it wasn't. It was cold.
>
> 2. A. Were they at home this morning?
>   B. No, they weren't. They were in school.
>
> *Answers to Exercises 3–8:*
> 3. No, she wasn't. She was happy.
> 4. No, he wasn't. He was a chef.
> 5. No, we weren't. We were at the beach.
> 6. No, you weren't. You were a noisy baby.
> 7. No, he wasn't. He was late.
> 8. No, she wasn't. She was on time.

1. **Exercise 1:** Call on two students to present the dialog. Then do Choral Repetition and Choral Conversation Practice.
2. **Exercise 2:** Same as above.
3. **Exercises 3–8:** Either Full-Class Practice or Pair Practice.

EXPANSION ACTIVITY

Chain Game: Practice **Was/Were, Wasn't/Weren't**

Use chain games to practice the verb *to be* in the past tense with a variety of vocabulary words.

1. Write on the board:

> I was _____ yesterday.

2. Start the game by saying:

> "I was at the beach yesterday.
>   Were YOU at the beach yesterday?"

3. The student you ask must answer, "No, _____," make a new statement, and ask another student:

> "No, I wasn't. I was at the ballgame.
>   Were YOU at the ballgame?"

4. Each student thereafter must do the same; the game can continue as long as students can think of new vocabulary to use.

   Another example:

> My grandparents were _____.

Start the game by saying:

> "My grandparents were teachers.
>   Were YOUR grandparents teachers?"

Text Page 147: *Did You Sleep Well Last Night?*

FOCUS

> Contrast of the simple past tense and past of *to be*

INTRODUCING THE MODEL

There are 2 model conversations. Introduce and practice each model before going on to the next. For each model:

1. Have students look at the model illustration.
2. Set the scene: "Two people are talking."
3. Present the model.
4. Full-Class Choral Repetition.
5. Ask students if they have any questions; check understanding of vocabulary.
6. Group Choral Repetition.
7. Choral Conversation.
8. Call on one or two pairs of students to present the dialog.

   (For additional practice, do Choral Conversation in small groups or by rows.)

SIDE BY SIDE EXERCISES

Examples

> 1. A. Did Tom have a big breakfast today?
>   B. Yes, he did. He was hungry.
>
> 2. A. Did Jane have a big breakfast today?
>   B. No, she didn't. She wasn't hungry.

1. **Exercise 1:** Call on two students to present the dialog. Then do Choral Repetition and Choral Conversation Practice.
2. **Exercise 2:** Same as above.
3. **Exercises 3–8:**

   Either Full-Class Practice or Pair Practice.

WORKBOOK

Pages 130–131

Exercise Note

   Workbook p. 131: Students practice *was/wasn't* and *were/weren't*.

EXPANSION ACTIVITY

Students Talk about Themselves

1. Have students ask each other questions about the recent past using a conversational framework and key words on the board.

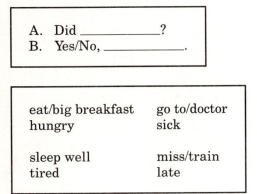

A. Did _____?
B. Yes/No, _____.

eat/big breakfast hungry	go to/doctor sick
sleep well tired	miss/train late

For example:

A. Did you have a big breakfast this morning?
B. Yes, I did. I was hungry.
   or
   No, I didn't. I wasn't hungry.

2. Call on pairs of students to create conversations. Encourage students to expand the conversations, using any additional vocabulary they wish.

For additional conversations, make up more cues. For example:

boss/shout angry	wear/coat cold	go/restaurant hungry
take/bath dirty	have/headache tired	dance all night energetic

Text Page 148

READING: *Maria Gomez*

FOCUS

To be: Past tense

NEW VOCABULARY

assembly line	miss	still
back home	Peru	United States
born	*six* years old	village
grew up (grow up)		word

PREVIEWING THE STORY (optional)

Have students talk about the story title and/or illustration. Introduce new vocabulary.

READING THE STORY

1. Have students read silently, or follow along silently as the story is read aloud by you, by one or more students, or on the tape.
2. Ask students if they have any questions; check understanding of vocabulary.
3. Check students' comprehension, using some or all of the following questions:

   a. Where was Maria Gomez born?
   b. Where did she grow up?
   c. When did she begin school?
   d. Did she go to high school?
   e. Why not?
   f. When did she go to work?
   g. Where did she work?
   h. When did Maria's family move to the United States?
   i. Where did the family move first?
   j. Where did they go after Los Angeles?
   k. Was Maria happy?
   l. Why not?
   m. When did she study English?
   n. Does Maria speak English well now?
   o. What is she studying now?
   p. What does she want to be?
   q. Does she still miss her friends back home?
   r. Is she happy now?
   s. How does she feel about her future?

CHECK-UP

Listening

Have students complete the exercises as you play the tape or read the following:

Listen and choose the best answer based on the story.

1. Maria, where were you born? (a)
2. When did you begin school? (a)
3. Why did you go to work when you were thirteen? (b)
4. How did you feel when you arrived in the United States? (a)
5. What are you studying now? (b)

IN YOUR OWN WORDS

1. Make sure students understand the instructions.
2. Have students do the activity as written homework, using a dictionary for any new words they wish to use.
3. Have students present and discuss what they have written, in pairs or as a class.

ON YOUR OWN: *Do You Remember Your Childhood?*

FOCUS

> • Students talk about their childhoods
> • Review of the past tense

ON YOUR OWN ACTIVITY

1. Go over the questions. Introduce the new vocabulary:

> 1. cute, dimple, freckles   2. game   3. subject   4. spare time, hobby
> 5. hero   6. how old, begin–began, I was _____ years old, first words   9. go on a date

2. For homework, have students write answers to questions 1–9. Also have them think of three additional questions to ask other students (10–12).

3. In the next class, have students ask and answer the questions. (They should not refer to their written homework when practicing.)

   This can be Full-Class Practice or Pair Practice. If Pair Practice, have students report back to the class. For example:

   > "Mary was short.
   >   She had black curly hair."

   > "Bill didn't like school.
   >   He liked sports and TV."

   > "George began to walk when he was one year old.
   >   He started school when he was six years old."

WORKBOOK

Pages 132–134
Check-Up Test: Pages 135–136

> #### *Exercise Note*
>
>   Workbook p. 134:   Students review the past tense of *to be*.

EXPANSION ACTIVITY

How Old Was He/She?

Use a time line like the one below to talk about someone's childhood.

1. Put the time line on the board:

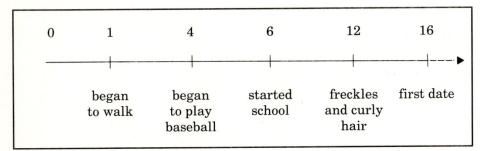

2. Tell about that person. For example:

   "Mary began to walk when she was one year old.
   When she was four years old she began to play baseball.
   She started school when she was six years old.
   When she was twelve years old she had freckles and curly hair.
   She went on her first date when she was sixteen years old."

3. Ask questions. For example:

   "When did Mary begin to walk?"
   "How old was she when she started school?"

4. Call on pairs of students to ask and answer questions.

WORKBOOK ANSWER KEY AND LISTENING SCRIPTS

Page 127 A. A TERRIBLE MORNING

1. was	2. was	3. was
4. was	5. were	6. were
7. was	8. were	
9. were	10. was	11. was

Page 127 B. A BEAUTIFUL MORNING

1. was	2. was	3. was
4. were	5. was	
6. were	7. were	

Page 127 C. LISTEN

Listen to each sentence. Put a circle around the word you hear.

1. Mary is happy today.
2. Mrs. Wilson was very busy today.
3. The children were very noisy this morning.
4. The weather was beautiful today.
5. John is very hungry this morning.
6. We were very tired this evening.
7. Sally's clothes are always dirty.
8. Anita and Carmen are very sick today.
9. My grandmother was very angry.
10. Our homework is very easy today.
11. My sister and I are very upset.
12. Nancy and Rita were at school today.

Answers

1. is	5. is	9. was
2. was	6. were	10. is
3. were	7. are	11. are
4. was	8. are	12. were

Page 128 D. BEFORE AND NOW

1. was	2. was
it's beautiful	I'm heavy
3. was	4. was
it's cold	she's happy
5. were	6. were
were	we're full
they're quiet	

7. was, was	8. were
it's expensive	they're dirty
9. were	
you're, tired	

Page 129 E. A THIEF STOLE A CAR

1. were	2. was
3. was	4. was
5. was	
6. were	
7. Were	
8. wasn't	9. was
10. was	
11. weren't	
12. weren't	
13. was	
14. were	
15. were	
16. were	
17. were	

---

1. Yes, he was.
2. No, it wasn't. (It was brown and curly.)
3. No, he wasn't. (He was young.)
4. Yes, they were.
5. No, he wasn't.
6. No, he wasn't.
7. He was with his friend Tom.
8. They were at the police station.
9. Because a thief stole his friend Tom's car.

Page 130 F. ROBERT'S PARTY

1. Was	2. Did
was, didn't	didn't
didn't	didn't
was	was
3. Were	4. were
weren't	was
didn't	wasn't
was	was

5. did
    was
    wasn't

6. did
    didn't
    didn't
    was

7. Did
    did
    were
    were

1. No, she wasn't.
2. Yes, they were.
3. She was short and heavy. She had straight brown hair and freckles.
4. No, she didn't.
5. She was always embarrassed when she went to parties.

Page 132 H. LISTEN: *Julie and Her Grandparents*

Listen to the conversation. Fill in the missing words.

A. How old were you when you met Grandmother?
B. I was twelve years old, and she was eleven.
A. Where did you meet?
B. We went to school together, and I sat next to your grandmother in science class.
A. Did you help her with her science homework?
B. No, I didn't. She helped me. She was a very good student, but I wasn't.

Answers
old were, met
was twelve, was
did, meet
went, sat next
Did, help
didn't, helped, was, wasn't

1. He was twelve years old.
2. They went to school together.
3. He sat next to Julie's grandmother.
4. No, he didn't.
5. She helped him. She was a very good student, but he wasn't.

Page 132 I. LISTEN: *Miss Gaylord*

Listen to the conversation. Fill in the missing words.

A. Miss Gaylord. What did you look like when you were a child? Were you very beautiful? Did you have many boyfriends?
B. My sisters were pretty, but I was short and heavy. I had straight brown hair and freckles. I didn't like boys, and they didn't like me. When I went to parties, I was always embarrassed.

Answers
did, look, were, Were
Did, have
sisters, was, had
hair, didn't, didn't like
went, parties, was

Page 133 J. LISTEN: *Grandchildren*

Listen to the conversation. Fill in the missing words.

A. How old was Tommy when he began to walk?
B. He was ten months old, and I bought him his first pair of shoes. When he began to talk, his first words were "shoes" and "thank you."
A. Really? Did I tell you about my grandson Jimmy? He was eight months old when he began to walk.
B. Yes, you did, but that's okay. I love to hear about Jimmy. How old is he now?
A. He's twenty years old.

Answers
old was, walk
was ten, bought, of
talk, were, shoes, thank you
Did, eight months
began to walk
did, How, is
twenty years

1. He was ten months old.
2. His first words were "shoes" and "thank you."
3. He was eight months old.
4. He's twenty years old.

CHECK-UP TEST: *CHAPTERS 15–17*

Page 135 A.

1. Was
    wasn't, was
2. were
    were, wasn't
3. were, weren't
    were

Page 135 B.

1. was, I'm heavy
2. were, they're rich
3. were, were, we're tired

Page 135 C.

1. didn't have, had
2. didn't listen, listened
3. didn't visit, visited
4. didn't go, went

Page 136 D.

1. Did she write
2. Did you play
3. Did they have
4. Did she read
5. Did he go

Page 136 E.

got up, brushed
cleaned, didn't eat, drank
walked, bought, waited
took

Page 136 F.

Listen to each sentence. Put a circle around the word you hear.

Ex. Sally was very sad this morning.

1. My mother is very tired today.
2. Was Helen busy this morning?
3. John and Judy are very hungry this afternoon.
4. My aunt and uncle were at a concert.
5. Mr. Jones was late.

Answers
1. is
2. was
3. are
4. were
5. was

BOOK 1 FINAL TEST

A. Fill in the blanks.

his	her	its	my	our	their	your

Ex. I brush ___my___ teeth every day.

1. Mary is very beautiful. _____ hair is brown and curly.
2. Where are John's clothes? _____ clothes are on the floor.
3. Where's Mr. and Mrs. Smith's car? _____ car is in the garage.
4. We don't have a dining room, but _____ kitchen is very large.

B. Fill in the blanks.

her	him	it	me	them	us	you

Ex. Do you like Mary? Of course I like ___her___.

1. When the sink is broken, I always fix _____.
2. When my brother is at home, I always play with _____.
3. When my neighbors are at home, I always visit _____.
4. When my sister and I are hungry, my mother always feeds _____.

C. Fill in the blanks.

How many	What	When	Where	Who	Why

Ex. _____Where_____ do you live? In Rome.

1. _____ does George go to the bank? On Friday.
2. _____ are they smiling? Because they're happy.
3. _____ are you going? To the supermarket.
4. _____ brothers do you have? Three.
5. _____ are you drinking? Coffee.

D. Fill in the blanks.

do	does	is	are

Ex. _____Do_____ you like John?

1. Why _____ you crying?
2. When _____ Barbara usually study English?
3. _____ Mary cooking dinner today?
4. _____ you usually clean the house on Monday?
5. What _____ the children doing?

E. Complete the sentences.

Ex. What's Jane doing? _____She's cleaning_____ her room.   That's strange. She never cleans her room.

1. What are Bob and Judy doing? _____ the newspaper.   That's strange. They never read the newspaper.
2. What's Sally doing? _____ to music.   That's strange. She never listens to music.
3. What are you and your sister doing? _____   That's strange. You never dance.
4. What's Jack doing? _____ the car.   That's strange. He never fixes the car.
5. What are you doing? _____ my uncle.   That's strange. You never call your uncle.

F. Complete the sentences.

YES!   NO!

Ex. I play the piano.   I _____*don't*_____ ____*play*____ the guitar.

Robert __*speaks*__ English.   He doesn't speak French.

1. Helen drinks tea.   She _____ _____ coffee.

2. Johnny _____ the dishes.   He doesn't wash his clothes.

3. Our children eat candy.   They _____ _____ tomatoes.

4. Peter _____ a dog.   He doesn't have a cat.

G. Write the sentences in the plural.

Ex. This is a beautiful beach. _____ *These are beautiful beaches.* _____

1. This watch is gold. _____

2. This dress wasn't expensive. _____

3. Who is that handsome man? _____

4. Why is that child sad? _____

H. Complete the sentences.

Ex. We usually listen to records.   We _____*didn't*_____ _____*listen*_____ to records yesterday.

                                        We _____*listened*_____ to the radio.

1. I usually bake cookies.   I _____ _____ cookies yesterday.

                                        I _____ an apple pie.

2. Martha usually helps her   She _____ _____ her mother yesterday.
    mother.
                                        She _____ her father.

3. We usually have dinner   We _____ _____ dinner at 6:00 yesterday.
    at 6:00.
                                        We _____ dinner at 8:00.

4. George usually goes to   He _____ _____ to the movies yesterday.
    the movies on Saturday.
                                        He _____ to the beach.

I. Complete the sentences.

Every morning I get up at 7:00, I read the newspaper, and I clean my room. At 8:00 I eat breakfast, and at 8:30 I take the bus to work. Now write about yesterday.

Yesterday I _____*got up*_____ at 7:00, I _____ the newspaper, and I _____

my room. At 8:00 I _____ breakfast, and at 8:30 I _____ the bus to work.

J. Give short answers.

Ex. Is Mary tall? No, _____ *she isn't* _____ .

1. Are Henry and Frank studying?   No, _____ .

2. Was Jane at home yesterday?   No, _____ .

3. Can Mr. Wilson play chess?   No, _____ .

4. Were you hungry this morning?   No, _____ .

5. Is there a restaurant in your neighborhood?   No, _____ .

K. Listen to each question. Put a circle around the correct answer.

Ex.
```
a.  She's cooking Italian food.
b.  She cooks French food.
c.  She cooked German food.
```
(b. is circled)

1.
```
a.  They play tennis.
b.  They're playing soccer.
c.  They played baseball.
```

3.
```
a.  He studies.
b.  He's working.
c.  He played all day.
```

5.
```
a.  Every day.
b.  Yesterday.
c.  He feeds the birds.
```

2.
```
a.  She's reading.
b.  She yawns.
c.  She rested.
```

4.
```
a.  Yes, he does.
b.  Yes, he is.
c.  Yes, he was.
```

6.
```
a.  She goes to Paris.
b.  She goes in June.
c.  She went to Rome.
```

BOOK 1 ALTERNATIVE FINAL TEST

Fill in the missing words.

My _____₁ is Linda. I'm _____₂ teacher. I _____₃ in _____₄ apartment _____₅ New York with _____₆ husband George. George _____₇ a chef. He _____₈ Italian food at a very good restaurant. I sometimes help _____₉ in the restaurant when I'm _____₁₀ busy.

My husband and I _____₁₁ working today because we're on vacation. We're going to _____₁₂ swimming this afternoon, and this evening we're _____₁₃ _____₁₄ see a movie. I'm very happy today because I _____₁₅ have _____₁₆ work.

Yesterday afternoon George _____₁₇ I _____₁₈ tennis, and yesterday evening we _____₁₉ to a concert. We _____₂₀ a very good time.

What _____₂₁ we going to do tomorrow? I _____₂₂ know, but I'm sure we're _____₂₃ _____₂₄ _____₂₅ a wonderful time.

Book 1 Final Test Answer Key

A. 1. Her
   2. His
   3. Their
   4. our

B. 1. it
   2. him
   3. them
   4. us

C. 1. When
   2. Why
   3. Where
   4. How many
   5. What

D. 1. are
   2. does
   3. Is
   4. Do
   5. are

E. 1. They're reading
   2. She's listening
   3. We're dancing
   4. He's fixing
   5. I'm calling

F. 1. doesn't drink
   2. washes
   3. don't eat
   4. has

G. 1. These watches are gold.
   2. These dresses weren't expensive.
   3. Who are those handsome men?
   4. Why are those children sad?

H. 1. didn't bake/baked
   2. didn't help/helped
   3. didn't have/had
   4. didn't go/went

I. read, cleaned, ate, took

J. 1. they aren't
   2. she wasn't
   3. he can't
   4. I wasn't
   5. there isn't

Book 1 Alternative Final Test Answer Key

name, a, live, an, in, my, is, cooks, him, not, aren't, go, going to, don't, to, and, played, went, had, are, don't, going to have

Numerical List

1. bedroom
2. bathroom
3. living room
4. dining room
5. kitchen
6. basement
7. yard
8. garage
9. restaurant
10. bank
11. supermarket
12. library
13. park
14. movie theater
15. post office
16. zoo
17. hospital
18. read
19. cook
20. study
21. eat
22. watch TV
23. sleep
24. play the piano
25. play cards
26. play baseball
27. drink
28. dance
29. sing
30. listen to the radio
31. fix _____ car
32. fix _____ sink
33. fix _____ TV
34. feed _____ dog
35. clean _____ yard
36. clean _____ apartment
37. paint
38. do _____ exercises
39. wash _____ car
40. wash _____ clothes
41. brush _____ teeth
42. tall–short
43. young–old
44. heavy–thin
45. new–old
46. pretty–ugly
47. handsome–ugly
48. rich–poor
49. large/big–small/little
50. expensive–cheap
51. sunny
52. cloudy
53. raining
54. snowing
55. hot

56. warm
57. cool
58. cold
59. school
60. church
61. police station
62. fire station
63. train station
64. bus station
65. laundromat
66. gas station
67. drug store
68. cafeteria
69. bakery
70. barber shop
71. beauty parlor
72. clinic
73. department store
74. doctor's office
75. nervous
76. sad
77. happy
78. tired
79. sick
80. cold
81. hot
82. hungry
83. thirsty
84. angry
85. embarrassed
86. cry
87. smile
88. shout
89. smoke
90. shiver
91. perspire
92. yawn
93. blush
94. mechanic
95. violinist
96. singer
97. dancer
98. chef
99. baker
100. actor
101. actress
102. teacher
103. truck driver
104. bus driver
105. doctor
106. nurse
107. dentist
108. carpenter
109. plumber
110. scientist
111. policeman

112. secretary
113. factory worker
114. businessman
115. businesswoman
116. salesman
117. saleswoman
118. computer programmer
119. mailman
120. painter
121. go to a movie
122. go to a baseball game
123. have lunch/dinner
124. go swimming/swim
125. go dancing/dance
126. go skating/skate
127. go skiing/ski
128. go shopping/shop
129. go bowling/bowl
130. go sailing/sail
131. go jogging/jog
132. go to the doctor
133. go to the bank
134. visit a friend in the hospital
135. get up
136. take a bath
137. take a shower
138. put on clothes
139. write
140. headache
141. stomachache
142. toothache
143. backache
144. earache
145. sore throat
146. cold
147. work
148. cook
149. talk on the telephone
150. fix _____ car
151. brush _____ teeth
152. dance
153. smoke
154. watch TV
155. play cards
156. study
157. shave
158. smile
159. clean
160. cry
161. listen to the radio
162. yawn
163. shout
164. paint
165. wait for the bus

166. plant flowers
167. rest
168. eat
169. sing
170. drink
171. sit
172. tomatoes
173. eggs
174. bananas
175. apples
176. cheese
177. milk
178. ice cream
179. bread
180. crackers
181. beans
182. garlic
183. rice
184. flour
185. cookies
186. yogurt
187. soda
188. orange juice
189. jam and jelly
190. beer
191. mayonnaise
192. butter
193. wine
194. melon
195. lettuce
196. pears
197. celery
198. sugar
199. coffee
200. salt and pepper
201. tea
202. onions
203. butcher shop
204. shoe store
205. high school
206. university
207. museum
208. hotel
209. playground
210. parking lot
211. airport
212. candy store
213. newsstand
214. hardware store
215. pet shop
216. motel
217. shopping mall
218. TV station
219. courthouse
220. concert hall

Alphabetical List

actor (100)
actress (101)
airport (211)
angry (84)
apples (175)

backache (143)
baker (99)
bakery (69)
bananas (174)
bank (10)
barber shop (70)
basement (6)
bathroom (2)
beans (181)
beauty parlor (71)
bedroom (1)
beer (190)
big (49)
blush (93)
bowl (129)
bread (179)
brush _____ teeth (41, 151)
bus driver (104)
businesswoman (115)
businessman (114)
bus station (64)
butcher shop (203)
butter (192)

cafeteria (68)
candy store (212)
carpenter (108)
celery (197)
cheap (50)
cheese (176)
chef (98)
church (60)
clean (159)
clean _____ apartment (36)
clean _____ yard (35)
clinic (72)
cloudy (52)
coffee (199)
cold [adjective] (80)
cold [ailment] (146)
cold [weather] (58)
computer programmer (118)
concert hall (220)
cook (19, 148)
cookies (185)
cool (57)
courthouse (219)
crackers (180)
cry (86, 160)

dance (28, 125, 152)
dancer (97)
dentist (107)
department store (73)
dining room (4)

doctor (105)
doctor's office (74)
do _____ exercises (38)
drink (27, 170)
drug store (67)

earache (144)
eat (21, 168)
eggs (173)
embarrassed (85)
expensive (50)

factory worker (113)
feed _____ dog (34)
fire station (62)
fix _____ car (31, 150)
fix _____ sink (32)
fix _____ TV (33)
flour (184)

garage (8)
garlic (182)
gas station (66)
get up (135)
go bowling (129)
go dancing (125)
go jogging (131)
go sailing (130)
go shopping (128)
go skating (126)
go skiing (127)
go swimming (124)
go to a baseball game (122)
go to a movie (121)
go to the bank (133)
go to the doctor (132)

handsome (47)
happy (77)
hardware store (214)
have lunch/dinner (123)
headache (140)
heavy (44)
high school (205)
hospital (17)
hot [adjective] (81)
hot [weather] (55)
hotel (208)
hungry (82)

ice cream (178)

jam and jelly (189)
jog (131)

kitchen (5)

large (49)
laundromat (65)
lettuce (195)
library (12)

listen to the radio (30, 161)
little (49)
living room (3)

mailman (119)
mayonnaise (191)
mechanic (94)
melon (194)
milk (177)
motel (216)
movie theater (14)
museum (207)

nervous (75)
new (45)
newsstand (213)
nurse (106)

old (43, 45)
onions (202)
orange juice (188)

paint (37, 164)
painter (120)
park (13)
parking lot (210)
pears (196)
pepper (200)
perspire (91)
pet shop (215)
plant flowers (166)
play baseball (26)
play cards (25, 155)
playground (209)
play the piano (24)
plumber (109)
policeman (111)
police station (61)
poor (48)
post office (15)
pretty (46)
put on clothes (138)

raining (53)
read (18)
rest (167)
restaurant (9)
rice (183)
rich (48)

sad (76)
sail (130)
salesman (116)
saleswoman (117)
salt (200)
school (59)
scientist (110)
secretary (112)
shave (157)
shiver (90)
shoe store (204)

shop (128)
shopping mall (217)
short (42)
shout (88, 163)
sick (79)
sing (29, 169)
singer (96)
sit (171)
skate (126)
ski (127)
sleep (23)
small (49)
smile (87, 158)
smoke (89, 153)
snowing (54)
soda (187)
sore throat (145)
stomachache (141)
study (20, 156)
sugar (198)
sunny (51)
supermarket (11)
swim (124)

take a bath (136)
take a shower (137)
talk on the telephone (149)
tall (42)
tea (201)
teacher (102)
thin (44)
thirsty (83)
tired (78)
tomatoes (172)
toothache (142)
train station (63)
truck driver (103)
TV station (218)

ugly (46, 47)
university (206)

violinist (95)
visit a friend in the
  hospital (134)

wait for the bus (165)
warm (56)
wash _____ car (39)
wash _____ clothes (40)
watch TV (22, 154)
wine (193)
work (147)
write (139)

yard (7)
yawn (92, 162)
yogurt (186)
young (43)

zoo (16)

Categories

Adjectives

angry (84)
big (49)
cheap (50)
cold (80)
embarassed (85)
expensive (50)
handsome (47)
happy (77)
heavy (44)
hot (81)
hungry (82)
large (49)
little (49)
nervous (75)
new (45)
old (43, 45)
poor (48)
pretty (46)
sad (76)
short (42)
sick (79)
small (49)
tall (42)
thin (44)
thirsty (83)
tired (78)
rich (48)
ugly (46, 47)
young (43)

Ailments

backache (143)
cold (146)
earache (144)
headache (140)
sore throat (145)
stomachache (141)
toothache (142)

Foods

apples (175)
bananas (174)
beans (181)
beer (190)
bread (179)
butter (192)
celery (197)
cheese (176)
coffee (199)
cookies (185)
crackers (180)
eggs (173)
flour (184)
garlic (182)
ice cream (178)
jam and jelly (189)
lettuce (195)
mayonnaise (191)
melon (194)
milk (177)
onions (202)
orange juice (188)
pears (196)
pepper (200)
rice (183)
soda (187)
sugar (198)
tea (201)
tomatoes (172)
wine (193)
yogurt (180)

Community

airport (211)
bakery (69)
bank (10)
barber shop (70)
beauty parlor (71)
bus station (64)
butcher shop (203)
cafeteria (68)
candy store (212)
church (60)
clinic (72)
concert hall (220)
courthouse (219)
department store (73)
doctor's office (74)
drug store (67)
fire station (62)
gas station (66)
hardware store (214)
high school (205)
hospital (17)
hotel (208)
laundromat (65)
library (12)
motel (216)
movie theater (14)
museum (207)
newsstand (213)
park (13)
parking lot (210)
pet shop (215)
playground (209)
police station (61)
post office (15)
restaurant (9)
school (59)
shopping mall (217)
supermarket (11)
train station (63)
TV station (218)
university (206)
zoo (16)

Home

basement (6)
bathroom (2)
bedroom (1)
dining room (4)
garage (8)
kitchen (5)
living room (3)
yard (7)

Professions

actor (100)
actress (101)
baker (99)
bus driver (104)
businessman (114)
businesswoman (115)
carpenter (108)
chef (98)
computer programmer (118)
dancer (97)
dentist (107)
doctor (105)
factory worker (113)
mailman (119)
mechanic (94)
nurse (106)
painter (120)
plumber (109)
policeman (111)
salesman (116)
saleswoman (117)
scientist (110)
secretary (112)
singer (96)
teacher (102)
truck driver (103)
violinist (95)

Verbs

blush (93)
bowl (129)
brush _____ teeth (41, 151)
clean (159)
clean _____ apartment (36)
clean _____ yard (35)
cook (19, 148)
cry (86, 160)
dance (28, 125, 152)
do _____ exercises (38)
drink (27, 170)
eat (21, 168)
feed _____ dog (34)
fix _____ car (31, 150)
fix _____ sink (32)
fix _____ TV (33)
get up (135)
go bowling (129)
go dancing (125)
go jogging (131)
go sailing (130)
go shopping (128)
go skating (126)
go skiing (127)
go swimming (124)
go to a baseball game (122)
go to a movie (121)
go to the bank (133)
go to the doctor (132)
have lunch/dinner (123)
jog (131)
listen to the radio (30, 161)
paint (37, 164)
perspire (91)
plant flowers (166)
play baseball (26)
play cards (25, 155)
play the piano (24)
put on clothes (138)
read (18)
rest (167)
sail (130)
shave (157)
shiver (90)
shop (128)
shout (88, 163)
sing (29, 169)
sit (171)
skate (126)
ski (127)
sleep (23)
smile (87, 158)
smoke (89, 153)
study (20, 156)
swim (124)
take a bath (136)
take a shower (137)
talk on the telephone (149)
visit a friend in the hospital (134)
wait for the bus (165)
wash _____ car (39)
wash _____ clothes (40)
watch TV (22, 154)
work (147)
write (139)
yawn (92, 162)

Weather

cloudy (52)
cold (58)
cool (57)
hot (55)
raining (53)
snowing (54)
sunny (51)
warm (56)